Serial Survivors

Serial Survivors

Women's narratives of surviving rape

Jan Jordan

THE FEDERATION PRESS
2008

Published in Sydney by:
The Federation Press
PO Box 45, Annandale, NSW, 2038
71 John St, Leichhardt, NSW, 2040
Ph (02) 9552 2200 Fax (02) 9552 1681
E-mail: info@federationpress.com.au
Website: http://www.federationpress.com.au

National Library of Australia
Cataloguing-in-Publication entry

Serial Survivors
Author: Jordan, Jan.

Includes index.
Bibliography.
ISBN 978 186287 679 8 (pbk).

Rape – New Zealand – Case studies. Rape victims – New Zealand – Biography.
Rapists – New Zealand – Biography. Serial rape investigation – New Zealand.

363.259532092293

Typeset by The Federation Press, Sydney, NSW.
Printed by Griffin Press, South Australia.

Contents

Acknowledgements

It should come as no surprise that although my name is on the cover, there are many people who have contributed to the writing and publication of this book.

First, I am indebted to the women who agreed to be interviewed, and who so bravely and fully shared their stories. Their strength and resilience encouraged me to persist in making this book happen – without their courage and honesty there would have been no book at all.

I applaud and honour my partner Chris for being such a loyal and committed supporter of this project from its inception, for always believing in me, and for tolerating once again being a 'book widow'. And I extend a big pat to our cat Meer, who spent so many long days patiently sitting on 'her' chair alongside mine at the computer, purring her encouragement.

My thanks to Dave (Chook) Henwood for all his help in facilitating this research, providing contacts, information and resources. I also appreciate the input and assistance of other members of the New Zealand Police.

I am grateful to Justice Anderson for providing access to his sentencing report.

I appreciate the sage advice given at various stages of manuscript development by Professor David Norton, Margie Barr-Brown, and Lizzy Stanley.

My thanks to Harry Ricketts for all he has taught me about the art of writing creative non-fiction and to the members of the writing group his 2004 course spawned, and who have always been so encouraging – Juanita Deely, Patricia Donovan, Trish Harris, Keith Lyons, and Keith Westwater.

I am also grateful for the research assistance so ably and competently provided by Liz Moore, and to the Faculty of Humanities and Social Sciences for the research grant enabling my employment of her services.

This project had its inception some years ago, and I want to acknowledge the positive input received from my good friend and colleague Devon Polaschek, particularly as we spent days together researching police files. I also extend my appreciation to the New Zealand Federation of University Women for providing the grant used for tape transcription, and to the wonderful transcribers: Tracy Anderson, Marianna Churchward, Sandy Taylor and Brenda Watson.

There are many friends who have supported this undertaking in various ways, and in particular I wish to acknowledge Stevan Eldred-Grigg, Liz Kelly, Allison Morris, Jenny Neale, Graeme Tetley, and the members of a Victoria University women's writing group – Deborah Jones, Sara Kindon, Lise Claiborne, and Teresia Teaiwa. I also appreciate my colleagues at the Institute of Criminology and the Crime and Justice Research Centre, Victoria University of Wellington, who have been encouraging and supportive of this venture.

Last, but by no means least, I am indebted to The Federation Press for their willingness to commit to the publication of this book. In particular, I appreciate the initial support shown for this venture by Trisha Vaillappan, and the subsequent advice and sound professional input provided by Ann Cunningham, Clare Hallifax, and Chris Holt.

Together we survived the process of producing this book about an amazing group of women who can inspire us all as 'serial survivors'.

Jan Jordan
Wellington, February 2008

Some quotes and examples form the interview material published here have appeared in previous publications, with permission granted for the following:

Jordan, Jan, *The Word of a Woman? Police, Rape and Belief*, 2004, Palgrave Macmillan.

Jordan, Jan, 'What would MacGyver do? The meaning(s) of resistance and survival', *Violence Against Women*, 11:4 (2005), pp 531-559.

1

The women

Marie was living in a nurses' home when an intruder forced his way into her room and raped her. The offender ran off naked, leaving his clothes and a palm print behind, and other nurses quickly called the police. More than 20 years later she recalled:

> [M]um driving me home and I was looking at all the police cars all around the hospital. I said to mum, 'Oh, I've caused all this!' That's the state I was in. It wasn't til I got home that it hit me.

Kathleen was in her early twenties and living with her partner when, early one morning, he left for work and she went back to sleep. She woke to find someone pressing material down over her face – a man had broken into her home intending to rape her. She was amazed at how her sense of humour prevailed:

> I remember being bound, my hands being tied back, and blindfolded and gagged with the duvet over me, and I was thinking: what would MacGyver do?

Nearly a year later the woman next door, Lorna, was also raped in her home by a stranger and ran to Kathleen's house for help. Lorna said her Christian faith helped her survive, and that she rattled her attacker when, straight after he had raped her, she said she forgave him:

> After that he started flicking through a book which was by my bed, which must have been my bible, and he just softened then ... I was waiting for him to go and I just felt this awesome, awesome peace that I have never felt since, and it was just like God saying, 'I'm here.'

Ann had a stranger break in, sexually assault her, and leave her bound and gagged on the bed. She was terrified he would come back and kill her. She remembered her brother telling her a story about how he freed himself after being trapped in a cave on a diving trip, and used this to calm herself down as she planned her escape. Later she described how the fear stayed with her:

> For years, I'd wake up, I'd have my eyes closed and think, 'Someone's here!' And your heart would be beating so hard that you'd want to vomit and you're too scared to open up your eyes and look.

Isabel was in her early forties when she went to midnight Mass one Christmas Eve. She returned home to find an unknown man waiting inside the house for her. After he had raped her, and she was being interviewed by the police, she wryly commented:

> I kept talking to him and asking if he knew of any more successful ways of persuading women to have sexual intercourse with him.

Raquel was hit hard on the back of the head while getting into her car, after making an ATM cash withdrawal late one night. She quickly decided to act as if she was unconscious in order to avoid further physical injury. Although unable to escape being raped, she felt pleased that she was able to dupe her attacker:

> The fact that I'd fooled him, the fact that he really believed that and that I got the better of him. He didn't like it and that made me feel so good. It's like my little triumph, it's like, 'You didn't have complete control over me.'

When Connie woke to find a man attacking her, she immediately thought of another woman whom she had read about in the newspaper, only a week earlier, who had been raped and killed. Later she found out hers was the same attacker. She believes the spirit of the woman who was murdered helped her survive:

> I didn't know her from a bar of soap, I just felt she must have been watching over me. Because, physically, I know whilst my heart was still inside my body, it was actually over the other side of the king size bed and I was trying to pull it back to survive.... and I think she was there saying, 'You can do it, calm down, you can do it.'

It was a month before her wedding day when Suzanne, sleeping alone in her flat, was thrust into consciousness by an intruder bursting in through the bedroom door. She was scared he would kill her. Later she felt angry when women colleagues offered retrospective advice:

> They were saying, 'You should have done this, why didn't you do that?' But they don't know the situation and I wasn't going to say to them, 'Because I was in bed and he wasn't .... He was expecting me but I wasn't expecting him.'

A man rushed at Frances, trying to throw a scarf over her head, as she was turning up her pathway following an early morning run with friends. A couple of weeks later, while out running again with family members, they came across a distressed woman and discovered that she also had just been attacked – by the same offender. In speaking about the impact, Frances said:

> *The immediate effect was just that feeling of being violated on my own property. It wasn't like I was out in the street somewhere else and I could think, 'It's okay, I'm at home now, I feel safe, I'm safe here.' I've lost that feeling of safety in my own environment.*

Patricia arrived home after her summer holiday, unpacked, visited a girlfriend, drove home and went to sleep. She woke to feel the pressure of a man kneeling astride her on the bed. He tied her arms behind her as he searched for money then, agitated at the noise she was making kicking on the wall of her flat, he ran off:

> *I chased him up the road, and thought, 'What the hell are you going to do if you catch him!' So that is why I came back and rang the police.*

Karen had no idea who the man was who broke into her home and raped her, the night before she was due to move house. Later she was shocked to realise her attacker was mates with one of her closest male friends, and that the two of them had visited her house for coffee previously:

> *I was shattered to find out that it was him. I was absolutely devastated. I couldn't believe that it was someone that had been a guest in my house.*

Shelley was asleep when at 2.30am she woke to the sound of her bedroom door opening. A man shone a torch in her eyes as he lunged towards her. When she struggled, he ordered her to keep quiet or he would harm one of her daughters, describing where she was sleeping down the hallway. Whenever Shelley moved, he told her to remember her daughter. She recalled how she felt on the first 'anniversary':

> *I remember going to bed that night thinking this time exactly one year ago I was piling into bed and my whole life was going to change within two hours.*

Three days before Christmas, 18-year-old Gabriel was getting ready to join her flatmates at a nearby party. As she went to leave the house, she noticed a man in a balaclava standing by the doorway. He bashed her and tied her up with a phone cord before looking round the house for items to steal. When he returned and saw that she had struggled free, he thumped her and tied her wrists and ankles tighter, so that physically she was unable to move:

> I thought, 'What can I do? What can I do to protect myself?' So I closed my eyes really hard and I decided to just fill up the entire room with myself so that as much of that room had me in it, so that there was no room for him in there.

Helen went to enter her flat after having been out with friends and felt someone shove her forcefully through the door. She was too scared to struggle in case he killed her. She was still afraid of her assailant when she went to court to testify but knew she needed to find a way of empowering herself to do so. Helen chose to sprinkle glitter in the witness box to give herself courage. To her this signified:

> This was my room, this was my space.... I am the Goddess of Justice, so that was very much me setting it up for myself.

Jennifer was in her thirties, living with her young daughter while in the process of separating from her husband. She had friends over for a barbecue one Friday night, then watched television before going to bed. She woke to hear the house alarm beeping and, since it had been malfunctioning, got up and went to turn it off. She returned to her bedroom and shut the door, only to see the attacker behind it, waiting for her. Terribly shaken afterwards, she was relieved not to have been raped:

> There was times when I lay there and I thought, 'God, why doesn't he just do it and just get it over with? Maybe I should just lie here.' But there was just something – every time he came towards me to get on the bed, I thought, 'You're not going to do this!'

All of these women were attacked by the same serial rapist. This book tells the stories of their survival.

2

Surviving the attack

Background

In the 1990s fear swept across Auckland, the biggest city in New Zealand, as it became increasingly clear that a growing succession of sexual attacks could be linked to the same offender. Headlines described police 'Hunting an Evil Shadow' [1], screamed of 'Streets of Fear' [2], and profiled the victims of 'The shadow that haunts South Auckland' [3]. Anxiety escalated further as the attacks spread across different sectors of the city, especially when the rapes were no longer confined to lower socio-economic areas. In 1995, following the successful investigation known as Operation Park, Joseph Thompson was arrested [4]. He calmly opened the door to police detectives, inviting them in and announcing he had been waiting for them. He confessed to more rapes than had even been reported, most involving young girls and women from predominantly Māori and Pacific backgrounds. His pleading guilty saved his young victims the ordeal of a court trial, and he was sentenced to preventive detention with a minimum non-parole period of 25 years.

His arrest and imprisonment did not end the attacks and in 1995 the police established Operation Harvey in an attempt to identify the perpetrator of other rapes occurring since 1988, including the rape and murder of Susan Burdett. As a national newspaper observed: 'New Zealand's two most notorious serial rapists were stalking south Auckland streets at the same time, attacking women just hundreds of metres apart.' [5]

Investigators applied the criminal profiling techniques pioneered in the search for Joseph Thompson, and after lengthy file analysis realised that the search for a possible third rapist active in more affluent, central Auckland suburbs, code-named Operation Atlas, was in fact for the same offender. These inquiries were merged, and the hunt was on for the man later identified as Malcolm Rewa (MR). (See Appendix 2 for background details regarding Rewa.)

When he was arrested, MR's demeanour was the complete opposite of Thompson's. MR sought to evade capture, resisted arrest, and initially refused to admit guilt to any offences. When he went to court in 1998, he faced charges involving 27 different women. His initial victim from 1975, Marie, was called to testify, and subsequently she and 14 of the other women he attacked agreed to be interviewed for this book.

How do women survive such attacks? What do they think of in such situations? Where do they turn for help? This chapter addresses these questions.

Ensuring victim compliance

The act of rape involves not only the physical violation of another's body, but an attempt to secure total control and dominance. What many rapists are seeking is a sense of their own power, their ability to subordinate another to their will. Sensing fear in their victims can serve as an aphrodisiac, an indication that their mastery of the situation is being achieved. Most rapists need no other weapon to secure victim compliance. This is often difficult for those outside the situation to understand. In acknowledging the assumptions frequently made by police investigators, Hazelwood and Burgess observed:

> Depending on the passivity and fear of the victim, it is very possible that the offender's mere presence would be enough to control the victim. This is very difficult for a person removed from the actual situation and/or having a personality different from the victim's to accept. Quite often the investigator judges a victim's reaction on the basis of what he/she would do (or believes he/she would do), rather than taking into account the victim's personality, the circumstances surrounding the assault, and the fear factor involved. ([6] p 143)

Greater understanding has been gained of the ways in which fear and trauma impact on individuals, rendering many immobile and incapable of physical resistance [7-10]. The strategies employed by attackers to obtain compliance have also been researched, promoting increased awareness of tactics intentionally deployed to overpower and secure victim co-operation [6].

MR developed a style to his attacks that was designed to evoke immediate fear and achieve victim compliance. His method of assault was calculated to ensure his immediate control and dominance of the situation. Many of the women said they could tell, within the first few seconds of encountering him, that this was not a man to argue with –

he knew what he wanted and was unlikely to be deterred. When he did encounter resistance, he quickly overcame it by punching, gagging and binding the women.

Like Joseph Thompson, MR stalked his victims for some time before he attacked. Several of the women remarked that he seemed familiar with the layout of their houses, as well as the identities and whereabouts of their children. Such knowledge at times disconcerted the women into thinking their attacker must be someone they knew.

Kathleen found it unnerving that MR had observed the house intently enough to overhear arguments she was having with her partner, and was then sly enough to use this information against her during the rape.

> We had been having arguments about him [partner] seeing someone else at that stage, and that's what Rewa said to me; he said, 'This is pay back for [partner] fucking around with my missus.' So the thing is that Rewa had actually been listening to all our arguments, because they weren't quiet conversations, they were full on fights. He had been physically listening outside the windows and that is how he knew all the information he divulged during the attack. And of course, he says this to you and we have just been arguing about this and it does plant the seed in your mind that hey, maybe he [partner] has had something to do with it and I just had to take his word for it that he hadn't. Very cunning, that Rewa. Very clever that way. (Kathleen)

Another woman said it was not until the court case that she realised MR had stalked her, watching her as she arrived back from holiday:

> It was in his testimony that he admitted that he had actually seen me unloading some stuff from my car. So I figured that's what he did with all the girls, stalked the whole lot of them and worked out what they were doing. (Patricia)

Discovering that Rewa had been watching her was, she said, *scary*:

> I walked around looking behind me all the time, making sure there was nobody seeing you come into your house. (Patricia)

Accounts given by other women also provided evidence of MR having observed them for some time prior to attacking. One thought it was incredible that she was raped:

> the only night in my life that I was by myself. So, you obviously know that Rewa had a pattern of watching, following and knowing. (Ann)

When the woman had children in the house with her, MR would often close the children's door before attacking their mother. One way he learned to gain greater 'co-operation' from her was by threatening to harm the children. Shelley said she had not been worried about her daughter until MR mentioned her:

> I had my youngest daughter with me who was seven or eight at the time. She always slept in those days with the door open and that was the first thing I noticed when I walked up the hallway – her door had been closed.

JJ: Were you worried that he might have done something to her as well?

> No, it never crossed my mind because I was fighting him and he said to me if I didn't stop, he'd get my daughter so that made me passive. Up to that point I was quite aggressive.

JJ: And he clearly knew that you had a daughter there?

> He described her to me. Mm. Scary ... I knew what he was after, he wanted to rape an adult woman. I believed at the time that if I became passive and allowed him to do what he wanted to do, then he would leave my daughter alone. Now that gave me quite a lot of strength knowing that I could ... as a mother, you always hear mothers say, 'I'd do anything to protect my children' and I felt that I was clearly demonstrating that I was, that this was happening to me. (Shelley)

As well as using his knowledge of house layout and occupancy, MR used items he found to assist him in ensuring victim compliance. His modus operandi typically involved binding the women's arms and/or legs, for which he would use her pantyhose or a phone cord or other items found at the scene. He would use her pillows, or cushions he brought from the lounge, to help him manoeuvre her body into position on the bed. Bindings, mouth gags, and his sheer physicality all communicated his control and dominance of the situation.

One aspect MR could not always control was his own bodily reactions and performance. There were times when his erectile dysfunction prevented him from achieving penetration, causing both relief to some of the women while creating ambiguous questions for others regarding whether or not they had actually been raped. His erectile difficulties also prompted him to use a range of humiliating measures to increase his arousal, with some of the women expressing how degrading they found it when he engaged in such practices as shining a torch on their genitals while he masturbated.

A feature some of the women found odd was the curious contradiction in his attitudes towards them. This man was there to rape them – yet one woman commented that, when she was having difficulty breathing, MR loosened the gag around her mouth to make her more comfortable. Several commented how, after he had raped them, he would wrap a duvet round them almost tenderly, as if he was a parent settling a child for the night, before making his departure. Suzanne, in describing her feelings after getting out of the house, commented:

> He's a really violent man and I really thought for a long time that he was going to kill me, so I was pleased that I got out, but I was also really surprised at the change in his demeanour from being so violent to untying me, cutting the binds on my hands, because he didn't have to do that – which enabled me to escape so easily … It's really weird, it's like almost like a split personality, because he felt no qualms about giving me so many punches in the head and yet does something like this, I thought that was really weird! (Suzanne)

One woman said that, while he was raping her, a mosquito landed on her arm and he swiped it away – an act of caring that she found difficult to comprehend after the violence he exhibited.

Ann was also surprised by the almost contradictory tenderness displayed by MR, minutes after he had raped her:

> He left me blindfolded, gagged, my hands tied behind my back, and my feet tied up, and he laid me on my stomach and he actually put a duvet on me … I remember that specifically, what he's just done – and now he's put a duvet over me and patted it down, like I was a little kid, like 'Time to go to sleep now, thank you, bye-bye' – it was like, my God! (Ann)

Most of MR's control was exercised through threats and fear, but some women sustained severe physical injuries as well, particularly if they fought back. In describing their injuries, several women commented that his aggression intensified if the women resisted:

> Most of my bruising is to the back of my head. I've actually lost a lot of my hearing in my right ear. I had a lot of bruising around my throat when he was trying to strangle me, but I've seen some pictures of some of the other ladies and I know a lot of them are worse off. It appears the more you fought the bigger hiding you got. I did fight him quite a bit; even though he's not a particularly big guy he's a very strong guy … He can certainly 'pack a good punch', as they say. (Suzanne)

Mostly MR was silent throughout the attack, apart from telling the women to shut up. Some, however, had conversations with him, which could add to their stress.

> *After Rewa had raped me, he had asked me what I was going to do. You know, as if this is no big deal, and I said to him, 'What do you mean?', and he said, 'If you go to the police, you will be embarrassed. One, they'd never know how I got in here; two, I wore gloves; three, I wore a condom,' and I just said, 'You bastard! This is just a game to you, this means absolutely nothing to you.' So it was like, 'I'm coming for dinner and thank you very much.' (Connie)*

One difficulty faced by many was not knowing for certain when MR left the house. Had he gone? Or was he still lurking, watching, waiting?

> *My fear was that he was still there … And I actually asked the policeman to accompany me down to my bedroom to make sure that he wasn't in the wardrobe. Now he may not have thought that was a logical thought, but to me it was! (Shelley)*

How the women felt at the time of attack

MR's style of attack was deliberately chosen to shock, overwhelm, and instil fear – in most of his attacks he conforms to the profile of a 'surprise' rapist [11]. The women all described the various ways his approach impacted on them at the time. For some, the level of fear was so intense that they lost control of their bladder or their bowel. Several doubted they would survive the attack, terrified that MR was going to kill them. For most, however, it was this same fear that catapulted them into survival mode, doing anything and everything they could to get through the ordeal.

> *I know the fear I went through and the fear of thinking that you are going to die. You can't describe it, you just can't describe it. It goes through your mind that you are not going to see your family again. (Kathleen)*

Another woman described the mental turmoil she felt immediately after the attack, lying there thinking:

> *'You could have died dah de dah de dah'…there are hundreds of things going through your mind and you get the old 'why me' thing, you know, 'why do it', 'does anybody I know know him' type of stuff. (Lorna)*

Not all the women had the same apprehensions. One commented that the moment she felt most fearful related to her young daughter:

> I never thought about [daughter] until a bit further down the track and I thought, 'Shit, she's not crying, she's in the next room, why isn't she crying? What's he done to her?' ... It never entered my head that he would kill me. I was really determined that he wouldn't. (Jennifer)

The sheer fear prompted by the sudden force of the attack was what some of the women described as its worst feature. Suzanne talked about hearing an initial noise, which turned out to have been a window banging, and then the terror when this man burst into the room:

> The whole thing about the whole attack for me, even though the sexual side of it was revolting, it was that fright, when he burst into the room and kept beating me – that has been worse to get over than the sexual bit ... And the noise! My heart, I remember it going 90 to the dozen ... but I did the wrong thing, lying in bed, because I was so petrified and waiting for another noise, which was the worst thing to do. At that time I was hoping that it would go away, that's what I wanted. But it didn't, and I will never ever forget, for the rest of my life, the noise of that guy when he came in. It was so loud when he got into my room, the hitting and choking and stuff that he did afterwards. That has been a lot worse for me to get over than the sexual side, believe it or not. (Suzanne)

Another woman described feeling so terrified she feared her heart would burst, then added:

> Realistically, I guess it wasn't my time to go. The good Lord said, 'You're not going to die.' Despite my heart being at the other side of the bed jumping up and down and all over the place – it just wasn't my time. (Connie)

Similarly to some of the other women, she described feeling as if she needed to make sense of what he had done. She said:

> If I could have ever said something to him, it would have been, why me? Not why the others, but why me, why did he choose me? I asked him when he raped me, what had I ever done to him to deserve that? He said, 'Nothing, I'm just a bastard.' (Connie)

Similar questions vexed many of the women as they struggled to understand if there was something personal underlying the assault on them. Was it a man they knew, had they been targeted for any particular reason, who would want to do such a thing to them? Initially Isabel had worried about her attacker being a former acquaintance.

I had a wild guess that it would have been somebody that I asked to leave the flat, and I clung to this idea until it all became obvious that it was a mistake. So I got the poor guy hauled out of bed and no, it wasn't him, he had actually been out that night, and I'd thought, it was him. I couldn't understand why anyone would hate me that much to give me such a hard time … I went to Joseph Thompson's trial to see if it might have been him. But it wasn't him. Then it was only when they were preparing the trial that the police told me all about how they'd linked the guy [Rewa] with me by DNA. (Isabel)

Isabel felt she needed to know more about MR and why he had done this. She watched a television program about him and commented later that he was:

[A] person who superficially led what you might call a normal life. Living with a partner and going to work, they were saying on the television. He was a member of a club and then he had this secret obsession that he would indulge every month or so when the urge took him. I guess I wanted to know what sort of person would treat me like that. (Isabel)

Kathleen wondered about the links between MR's own upbringing and his actions, although she was quick to point out that this in no way excused his behaviour and the terror he inflicted:

He had a nice family, like kids and that – it's just a shame, you know. And of course, then he tried to blame his Aunty who had brought him up. And say that she was horrible to him when he was growing up and that she abused him and all that. It could have something to do with it. I don't know. It doesn't justify why he did what he did at all, especially not if he did murder Sue [Susan Burdett]. That I can't forgive, taking someone's life like that.

She said the worst part of the attack for her was:

[T]he fear of knowing that he was in complete control and that he could do anything he wanted – that was the worse part. It was really frightening that he could just do anything he wanted. He could kill me, kill the dog, burn the house down and I couldn't do anything about it. (Kathleen)

Preparation for the attack

Several women made comments indicating that they felt they had been somehow prepared in advance for the attack that followed. Raquel maintained she was able to manage in part because she had already thought about the possibility of being raped:

A couple of weeks before, my boyfriend and I had actually talked about it. We talked about how he would deal with it ... Things happen for a reason, I don't believe that there are coincidences in life. I believe that that conversation happened because it was meant to prepare me – I really do. I've often read articles in the past ... You know how everyone goes, 'It will never happen to me'? I've looked and gone, 'Okay, let's be realistic. This might happen to me one day – what would I do?' I read about the different ways of dealing with things ... it's like I prepared myself. I hate to say it but I think everyone should think about what they'd do if they got raped and how they'd handle it, because I think they'd handle it a lot better if they thought about it beforehand. It's a horrible thing to think about; it's like, hey, we all take car insurance but we don't expect to have an accident every time we drive up the drive, do we? Same thing ...

I think that had a lot to do with how I dealt with it afterwards and dealt with it at the time. As soon as I got attacked I went, 'I'm going to be raped' and I accepted it just like that. Okay, this is happening to me, this is what's going to happen, how am I going to deal with it? Straight away in the first few minutes while I was in the back seat of my car, 'What am I going to do, how am I going to do it, how am I going to deal with this?' I was very clinical about it.

Whereas if a woman always thought, 'It will never happen to me,' when it does happen, just actually accepting that it's happening could take quite a while before you actually get on to the 'how am I going to deal with it.' Like a lot of women may be in denial and in total shock, 'Oh my God, I never thought this would happen, oh my God, oh my God!' Big shock, difficult to accept. (Raquel)

Raquel was convinced that the fact that she was not denying the possibility that she could be raped helped her to respond quickly in her mind to the situation she was in, and was a significant factor in her survival.

One woman, the oldest raped by MR and one of only two Māori victims, speculated that she had been attacked by mistake, a possibility that brought a degree of comfort in its own way:

I still believe he was after my daughter. My daughter used to come every day to our house, she worked around the road at social welfare and she used to come every morning, every lunchtime and at night before she went home ... And my daughter was young, younger than me obviously, young, white, lily white, fair hair and I think he was after her. And probably had seen her maybe and associated her with the house. Hence, I guess it's some consolation that I took the brunt of it and not her – she would not have survived that ... And one of his questions before he raped me was 'How old are you?' Strange question eh? He was carrying on, 'How old are you?' and 'When did you last have sex?' So, I do believe that he possibly was after my daughter and not me. (Connie)

Resisting the attack

A curious paradox is evident in responses to women confronted with a man intent on rape. On the one hand, historically women were expected to do all they could to resist their attacker physically, with a lack of resistance being equated to victim consent. Then, if the rape was completed, victims were expected to make a 'hue and cry' immediately, and parade through the community displaying the visible signs of injury resulting from the attack [12-18]. This practice translated into the assumption that genuine victims of rape would emerge bearing injuries and evidence attesting to the level of their physical resistance. As a British detective wrote in training advice offered in the 1970s:

> It should be borne in mind that except in the case of a very young child, the offence of rape is extremely unlikely to have been committed against a woman who does not immediately show signs of extreme violence. ([12] p 1507)

The absence of visible injuries was interpreted as evidence of their co-operation or consent, and therefore the act no longer could be defined as 'rape'. Women reporting rapes without such corroborative, physical evidence were often assumed to be lying, an assumption that has helped to inflate beliefs regarding the prevalence of false rape complaints [14, 19].

Physical resistance was demanded, yet on the other hand, sexist assumptions prevailed regarding the opposing qualities assumed to differentiate women from men. Women were viewed as naturally passive and submissive, socialised to be compliant and long-suffering. As Susan Griffin noted more than 30 years ago:

> Passivity itself prevents a woman from ever considering her own potential for self-defense and forces her to look to men for protection ... Moreover, the passive woman is taught to regard herself as impotent, unable to act, unable even to perceive, in no way self-sufficient. ([20] p 33)

How, then, could such a passive woman be transformed into a fighter capable of repelling a violent male? It is this paradox that forms the background to considerations of women's capacity for resistance and self-defence.

> The irony is that when confronted with a rapist who is physically stronger and may be armed, a woman is suddenly expected to struggle, fight, and resist to a degree not otherwise expected. ([21] p 8)

Research on the reactions of victims/survivors when confronted by an attacker have emphasised the contradictory responses of acquiescence versus resistance [21, 22]. This contradiction was evident in criminal justice system responses to rape. For many years traditional police advice to women emphasised that active resistance could lead to greater violence and result in more severe injuries being received, or even in death [23, 24]. So women thought they were doing the 'right' thing by not resisting. Should the case ever reach court, however, the rapist's defence lawyer would argue that the victim's lack of resistance equated to consent, thereby increasing the likelihood of the defendant being acquitted [13-18]. Effectively this meant that, in terms of resistance, women were 'damned if they do and damned if they don't '.

International research on rape has increasingly addressed the issue of victim resistance and self-defence [9, 21, 22, 25-29]. Pauline Bart [7] was one of the first to publish material on effective rape avoidance, alleging that women who fought back were more likely to escape being raped than those who were passive. Her findings contradicted the advice not to resist, and were reflected in self-defence training being increasingly advocated as a means of rape prevention [8, 18, 26, 30].

In an analysis of rape incidents in the United States, Kleck and Sayles [29] noted that victims who resist are much less likely to have the rape completed against them than non-resisting victims, and that most forms of resistance are not associated with higher rates of victim injury. According to their research, approximately 3 per cent of rape incidents involve some additional serious physical injury, with the rape itself being the most serious injury inflicted. Research by Sarah Ullman [9] similarly found that victim resistance to verbal or physical attacks did not escalate offender violence, nor result in increased physical injury to the victim.

Much of the emphasis has been on physical resistance to a physical attack. Liz Kelly is one of the few writers to have observed:

> Women resist by refusing to be controlled, although they may not physically resist during an actual assault. Resistance, therefore, involves active opposition to abusive men's behaviour and/or the control they seek to exert. ([28] p 161)

Simply being in the presence of someone who desires to hurt and violate you can provoke a paralysing fear reaction, immobilising the potential victim. Studies have revealed the ways in which, at the time of an attack, many rape victims become terror-bound, fearing that death is imminent [28, 31]. Physical resistance may not be possible, but this should not be interpreted as a total lack of resistance, given what we are increasingly learning about mental and psychological resistance [27].

The accounts provided by the women revealed that they operated with diverse and expanded notions of what resistance and survival mean. The sense that MR was seeking to control and dominate them prompted many to respond with strategies intended to limit his power. In fact, every woman interviewed referred to ways in which she tried to take back some measure of control in the situation, ways in which she actively tried to limit his domination of her. Such strategies were evident in both women who were raped and women who he failed to rape – mental resistance and psychological survival emerged as critical to the survival process whether rape was accomplished or not.

There were five predominant ways in which the women resisted MR:

1. Physical resistance;

2. Talking to the offender;

3. Trying to alert others;

4. Doing the unexpected;

5. Mental/inner resistance.

Physical resistance

Over half of the women referred to forms of struggle and physical resistance, especially at the point of the initial attack. Shelley, for instance, said she kicked MR hard, and Gabriel was pleased she managed to kick him in the genitals – though obviously not hard enough, she complained, because there was no cry of pain. Isabel kept moving her legs around to make it difficult for him, while Jennifer simply held her legs tight together. Several tried to fight him off, struggle free, or reach for the phone or a panic button.

The women's efforts at physical resistance were typically responded to by stronger displays of violence from MR. Kathleen, for example, said her initial struggles were met with punches to her face and jaw. When she later kicked him and bit his hand, MR grabbed her by the hair and banged her head repeatedly on the floor. He then bound and gagged her, rendering further physical resistance impossible. Patricia struggled and fought with him, trying every tactic she could think of until MR's beanie hat fell off, throwing him into a panic.

Some women chose from the outset not to physically resist. Three said they were too scared to do anything; each felt she was going to die, that MR was going to kill her. One later wondered if her passivity helped to save her:

> Now what made me be submissive and quiet? Was it a survival thing, something saying, 'We don't try and kick out'? I just thought, 'Oh well, I'm going to die, that's it, close your eyes'. My father was going to come here in the morning, find me all twisted up and dead and he's going to have a heart attack; my daughter's going to come around and find two people dead. Great! (Connie)

Other women said it was clear from the outset that physical resistance would be counterproductive and that, with an attacker of MR's ilk, physical resistance never felt like a viable option. Raquel, who was attacked while getting into her car, commented how difficult it can be deciding how to react when confronted by such a situation:

> You really just have to work it out at the time and that's the hard part, whether to fight or not, whether someone has got a weapon or not. Honestly, no amount of self-defence would have ever stopped this happening to me either. I was attacked from behind, surprised. If someone comes up from behind you and if you've not seen them, not heard them, the first thing you feel is a hit, a whack to the back of the head – no amount of self-defence is going to save you. If you turn around and try and fight somebody who's a bit taller than you, a bit heavier than you, who is stronger than you and who has also got a weapon, you're an idiot. (Raquel)

Some women felt judged either by others or by themselves for not fighting back. For instance, Karen struggled with the fact that she had not fought or been physically hurt in the attack:

> I think that my rape was simple compared to a lot of the other women's. There was no violence in it, which was actually something I found really difficult to cope with afterwards. I guess I thought that rape was a violent act, and my rape wasn't violent. I didn't put up any struggle. All he said to me was, 'Be quiet or the kids will get it', and that was enough for me. I'm

pretty small and he was very strong and I just thought, 'It's not worth it.' Afterwards I actually had a really hard time dealing with, 'Oh, what if I had have done this', or 'What if I had have done that' and all that sort of shit. When I found out what had happened to some of the other women I thought, 'Thank God I didn't!' I think it would have made it difficult for my own recovery, but I think it would have been a lot worse for the kids too if I had been physically injured. (Karen)

Physical resistance against a man of MR's disposition was limited in effectiveness, prompting the women to consider and employ alternative resistance strategies, including trying to talk him out of it.

Talking to the offender

Most of the women tried talking to the offender, from a range of different perspectives. Some tried to reason, some to distract, some to deter, and some simply because they could do little else. MR's responses demonstrated that he was not there to engage in conversation. He repeatedly told the women to stop talking and 'shut up', often punching them to reinforce the point. Part of Jennifer's repeated efforts to talk to MR came from her determination not to be a passive victim in the situation.

There were times when I lay there and I thought, 'God, why doesn't he just do it and just get it over with? Maybe I should just lie here', but there was just something – every time he came towards me to get on the bed, I thought, 'You're not going to do this!' I don't know why, I don't know where it comes from, it was just an abhorrence of the fact that I didn't want him to do that ... At times I was thinking, 'This is probably really futile. How am I ever going to fight this guy off? This is ridiculous, I've got my hands tied behind my back.' But even so, I never stopped trying to untie my hands, I never stopped trying to do something. (Jennifer)

She also felt validated later in her efforts by one of the women detectives who affirmed she had done the right thing:

She said to me so often that to keep talking to them just blows them away, because they don't want you to be [a person] ... It wasn't a conscious thought to say I should keep talking, it was just the best solution I could come up with at the time. (Jennifer)

Several of the women tried asking MR questions. Shelley, for instance, asked him if he had children and urged him to think of his whakapapa (family). Some asked if he was going to kill them; others begged him not to. Several asked if he wanted money, which he often took while also making it clear that money was not all he had come for.

Others found that, if they appeared to co-operate with him, he was at least a little responsive to their needs. Thus several women spoke of how, when they asked MR to release the binds because they were hurting, or remove a pillow because they were suffocating, he did so.

> A couple of times I just couldn't breathe because he put all the bedclothes over my head. I'd say, 'I can't breathe, I can't breathe', and he'd come and pull them off a bit. (Jennifer)

Kathleen said she asked where he had put her dog and requested that he let it in to be with her when he left and MR, a dog-lover, obliged. Several women tried saying things that they hoped might put him off. Ann, for instance, told him her boyfriend would be home soon, and that she was pregnant, adding, *'I just made those things up to try and scare him and make him go away.'*

While MR was still present in the room, Lorna, a committed Christian, told him to his face that she forgave him. She said he began flicking through her Bible and 'he softened then'. She was careful not to read too much into this, commenting:

> At that point in time, well, it probably didn't mean that much to him ... It's like I give up my rights to hurt you for hurting me and it doesn't mean I am going to let you off the consequences, it doesn't mean that legally I'm not going to do something about it. What it does mean is that I am not going to hate you forever. It doesn't actually affect him, so why do it if you are only going to hurt you? For me, I knew it wasn't a personal thing, I didn't know him, it was just some guy who came in and did awful things to me. Maybe it made it easier for me to let go 'cause I didn't take it personally. (Lorna)

It is difficult to determine whether the women's questions and expressions of their fears made any difference to MR's treatment of them. What is important is that their efforts made them feel they were doing something active and positive. As one commented:

> I wanted him to treat me like a human being so I wanted to talk to him to make him aware of me as a human being, not some creature that he was using. And I held on to the notion that this had influenced him, that my talking to him about what was happening had some influence on the fact that he stopped doing it. But, I don't know really whether I did have any influence, I just wanted to feel that I had. (Isabel)

Trying to alert others

Some of the women adopted the strategy of trying to alert others to the fact that they were being attacked. This was difficult, given that in most cases MR attacked his victims knowing they were the only adult in the house. Six said they screamed initially.

> I screamed my head off, I just screamed and screamed and screamed, 'Help!' and kept screaming, and I think that's to a certain extent why he covered my head a lot as well … He just kept saying, 'Shut up! Shut up! Shut up!' I never thought about having a panic button beside my bed. I could have hit the alarm and it never even went through my head to try and hit it. In retrospect I don't think I probably could have, but it was such a logical thing to have thought about doing, and I never even made any attempt to get near it. I never even thought about it. Someone else said to me, which is a really good tip in retrospect, to break a window if you can – that will bring people, whereas just screaming and yelling might not necessarily do it. (Jennifer)

While Jennifer said she felt so panicked at the time that she forgot she had a panic button, Shelley did try to reach hers to summon help, but MR forcefully stopped her. His response when women screamed was to cover their heads and subdue them quickly through punching or gagging them. One exception was Frances, whom he attacked outside her home early one morning. He ran off when she yelled, knowing her screams were very likely to be heard and responded to. Another was Patricia, who took advantage of MR being distracted in the search for his beanie and kicked the walls of the neighboring flat. No one responded but it threw him into an even bigger panic. He left the house without raping her. While she was still in survival and action mode,

> I chased him up the road, and thought, 'What the hell are you going to do if you catch him!' So that is why I came back and rang the police. (Patricia)

Trying to alert others proved to be virtually impossible in most cases, a factor which rapists such as MR trade and rely on. Socialising women to be quiet and discreet gives male attackers a distinct advantage – women often think they are making more noise than they actually are. In a similar vein, interviews with convicted rapists have indicated that they experience women's efforts at resistance as much less aggressive than the women believe them to be. As Diana Scully noted, the meaning of fight-back to a sexually aggressive man is very different from the levels of violence most women would access.

One rapist, when asked what he would suggest victims do when attacked, astutely replied that it was impossible for him to put himself in a woman's shoes: 'Hard to say, I'm a man and can't strip myself of self-defense knowledge. I wasn't brought up to be helpless' ([32] p 177).

Fortunately, the women attacked by MR had other responses in their repertoire.

Doing the unexpected

When struggling or screaming seemed impossible or ineffective, some of the women experimented with alternative strategies. One told him he was a gentle lover in an effort to calm him down; another said she kept asking 'if he knew of any more successful ways of persuading women to have sexual intercourse with him'.

Two women faked being unconscious, Gabriel for part of the time and Raquel for the duration of the attack. MR had hit Raquel on the back of the head as she went to get into her car, late one night in a city street. Her decision was a deliberate strategy that she adopted when nothing else seemed to be working:

> *The way I analysed it was: He doesn't want to communicate with me, he doesn't want me to make any sound because he doesn't want anyone to hear. My instincts told me he doesn't want to talk to me, he wants complete and total power over me. The way I was attacked was to completely have total domination and total power over my body. Basically, I'm an object. I'm not a person – I'm an object. I was tied up, it was like, 'Don't try and fight back.' The level of violence I suffered just for him to get me to that position, I'm thinking he's not going to tolerate any kind of resistance, I'll get too badly injured ... There's no way that he would have attacked with that level of violence if he wasn't absolutely, totally intent on raping me. I thought, this is not a guy that you mess with, what he wants he will get, talking to him is a waste of time.*
>
> *I thought, he's hit me really hard on the back of the head – I could quite conceivably be unconscious or half-unconscious. If he thinks I'm unconscious he won't hurt me, because there's no reason to because I'm not going to fight back, so self-preservation ... It worked. He was very, very careful with me and that's what I found fascinating, the way he was really quite gentle with me, the way he really treated my body. I suffered no further injury after that, no further physical injury. (Raquel)*

Her decision process illustrates her commitment to survival and self-preservation. Her careful consideration of the options following such a sudden and violent attack indicates a determination to resist MR's total domination of her. For Raquel, the very fact that she successfully fooled him into thinking she was actually unconscious was hugely satisfying.

> *I fooled him, and that came out in court too – it was like, I won! ... I remember [prosecutor] saying to me, 'You did fool him. He really did think that you were unconscious because he got quite upset when the crown solicitor said, 'But she wasn't unconscious; she was conscious the whole time. She was never unconscious – that's why she remembers'.*
>
> *The fact that I'd fooled him, the fact that he really believed that and that I got the better of him. He didn't like it and that made me feel so good, it's like my little triumph, it's like, 'You didn't have complete control over me ' ... I had control over him mentally in the sense that I fooled him, I don't know how to describe that – it's really amazing. (Raquel)*

Raquel's example provides a good introduction to further consideration of the many different ways in which the women chose to mentally resist the attack.

Mental/inner resistance

Every woman interviewed described some form of mental or inner resistance, a means she adopted to help her manage and survive the attack. They may have been physically constrained, but they used their minds in highly creative and ingenious ways.

Several women, for example, adopted the strategy of trying hard not to see MR as a person:

> *I don't see him as this dreadful person that I hate. In fact, I find my ex husband harder – I have more difficulties with him than with Rewa! Because Rewa was just this faceless person that came in, did something really awful to me, and I didn't know him, I still don't know him ... He could have been an alien for all I know. It was a big black virus that affected me. (Shelley)*
>
> *I never let him be a person to me because my way of forming meaning was to associate that person with extreme evil or extreme badness ... My way of forming meaning was fighting this bizarre made up force. It was like that for me. Fighting a beast. Slaying the dragon. (Gabriel)*

Conversely, Patricia felt she needed to make MR a real person to deal with him, and said she was relieved when he became an identifiable human 'flesh and blood' being rather than 'a monster.'

Several women described using the psychological process of dissociation to help them manage the attack, mentally removing themselves in order to survive:

> *A lot of the time it didn't actually feel like I was there. It felt like I was not there, like I had gone somewhere else and I was going to come back … I was gone for a while. Whether you block it out, I don't know – it was like you split off from it a little bit. But there's only so much of that you can do, because you have to be there to survive it … I knew that I would do everything that I could and that if I did die, it was not through lack of trying to survive. (Kathleen)*

She explained how she saw this process as a choice on her part, and how even at such a terrifying time her sense of humour kicked in to help her survive:

> *I mean, even as it was happening, I remember being bound, my hands being tied back, and blindfolded and gagged with the duvet over me, and I was thinking: what would MacGyver[1] do? I mean, right from then I even kept my sense of humour, even though at exactly the same time I was thinking I might die. Like some weird things go through your mind and that is about the weirdest thing that went through my mind. How would MacGyver get out of this? (Kathleen)*

Some used their detachment to enable them to observe and mentally record details that they hoped might prove useful in apprehending their attacker later:

> *I was trying to take in as much as I could for evidence sake 'cause I knew I was going to report it … You have to be, 'I know this isn't personal and I am just going to take down every detail I can possibly remember.' You kind of disassociate yourself – well, I did. It's like, 'Okay, this isn't personal. This is my body he is doing this to. I am going to take note basically' … I don't know if it made much of a difference at all, but it was good knowing that I was doing something towards him getting caught. (Lorna)*

Another woman said she wanted to do this but was anxious her partial deafness might impede her awareness of MR:

> *I was trying to gather information in my head. Thinking if I ever survive this, use your good ear, listen, listen to his voice, see what his response is. (Connie)*

---

1   MacGyver was a fictional television action-man hero, famed for his abilities to extricate himself from seemingly impossible situations.

Patricia talked about the way in which she switched herself into work mode to observe and survive. The requirements of her particular career had prompted the development of an acute eye for detail, and her description and identification of the offender became significant factors contributing to the police's later success in apprehending him.

> I was really descriptive, because that is my skill, that is my work. And a photographic memory, being able to go back in there and picture everything and what was going on … It was almost like it was meant to be me, it was meant to happen so I could catch him, because I had all the skills whereas nobody else had those skills. They needed somebody with my skills to recall it all. (Patricia)

The strategies the women employed indicated an inner strength, a capacity to resist and a will to survive. Some appeared to psychologically inflate their own power in order to regain a sense of control in the situation. At times the women's accounts reflected an internal dialogue, a battle between action and inaction, submission and empowerment. This was evident earlier in Jennifer's description of how she fluctuated from feeling resistance was futile to focusing all of her energy into determining how to survive. Likewise, in the immediate aftermath of MR's attack, Ann described the way in which she made herself move beyond the 'Oh my God!' sense of helplessness to taking action. MR had left her gagged and blindfolded with her hands tied behind her back. She initially panicked, then she remembered a survival story her brother had told her:

> I lay there for a minute and I can remember thinking, 'Oh, I want to get these off'. And the funny thing was my brother had once told me, who was a diver, that he got stuck in a cave when he was diving and he couldn't move. He got himself in and he couldn't get himself out and if he had panicked, he would have died, but what he did was he got his breathing apparatus off. He thought, 'I've got to get this off, then I can move myself and get myself out of here,' which he did, and obviously he survived. When I was in there, I thought, 'My God, my God!' … I was scared he was going to come back and kill me. I'm laying on my stomach, blindfolded, I don't know where the man is. I don't know what I did but I just got my hands, pulled myself up and thought, 'Oh (sigh) my God!' I got my hands out. What do I do? What do I do? Is he watching me? Do I move? And then I thought, on the count of three I've got to do this. On the count of three I just whacked my legs out, pulled my feet out and jumped through an aluminium window, which obviously took heaps of layers of skin off the back of my leg because I just slid and jumped my whole body out, I didn't care … Obviously you don't care, you're outta there! (Ann)

While Ann recalled her brother's experience, Connie drew strength from her sense that the spirit of a woman who had been killed a week earlier was helping her survive the attack. Although Connie did not know it at the time, the woman whose rape and death she had read about, Susan Burdett, also turned out to be one of MR's victims. Connie said:

> From the time it had happened, from the time he tied me up and gagged me, I kept my eyes closed. I believed I was going to be another Burdett. Strange, eh?
>
> I always said, Burdett was watching over me that night. I didn't know her from a bar of soap, I just felt she must have been watching over me. Because physically I know whilst my heart was still inside my body, it was actually over the other side of the king size bed and I was trying to pull it back to survive, because I was thinking I was going to have a heart attack. The inner me was fighting and I think she was there saying, 'You can do it, calm down, do it'. That was sort of sub-consciously there. People may think I'm wrong but I really believe she was watching over me ... that spiritually she was still around, that she was connected to him some way – probably through the horrible deed of killing her, he may in fact, unbeknown, have brought her with him. (Connie)

Many of these examples suggest that the choice between submission and empowerment is not necessarily best understood as a decision to act physically, but occurs mentally, as a thought that activates a spirit of survival. Thus even when they were bound and gagged, unable to move or physically resist, the women were often making clear choices and taking control of the situation mentally. This process is powerfully apparent also in Gabriel's description of how she survived the attack, and how hard it was to talk about what actually happened for her.

> This guy had me strewn over a bed half naked, bound with blankets over my face, in position, just totally ready to rape me and he's going through the knife drawer, coming back into the room ... I thought, 'What can I do, what can I do to protect myself?' So I closed my eyes really hard and I decided to just fill up the entire room with myself so that as much of that room had me in it, so that there was no room for him in there, and it was a really hard process because I didn't have much time. Then I started praying, which is bizarre because I don't pray very much at all, but anyway God sounded like a really good idea right about then (laughs) ...
>
> I just closed my eyes to try and think about me and how big I could possibly make myself in this room without moving. Bigger and bigger and bigger and bigger, and not focusing on what he is doing out there, and

bigger and bigger and bigger and bigger. And he comes back in and he tries to rape me and he can't … It really changed my life because I started to believe that if I asked for help I would get it and it wouldn't be from people. I could do it myself. (Gabriel)

As powerful and compelling as it was, the mental and spiritual process Gabriel outlined above was not something she found easy to talk about. We had met and talked together on three separate occasions for more than ten hours before she felt ready to describe it, saying her fear of how others might react meant that she seldom mentioned this aspect of her survival experience.

It's funny how that is the most crucial experience for me but it took me all of this time to tell you … I guess I just wanted to talk about that spiritual aspect a little because I think it does come up for a few people. I mean it's a life-changing situation. You can almost feel the shift in your brain when it happens. You're off thinking on a different plane after that and anything is possible. (Gabriel)

Immediate aftermath

As well as deciding what to do at the very moment of the attack, the women had to decide how to respond in its immediate aftermath – how and when to move, where to run to, who to tell? They wondered: Had MR left the house; was it safe for them to move? This was especially so in houses where he had left the woman bound up while he searched for money, then returned to sexually assault or rape her again. The next time he wandered off, they waited, fearful that he would return.

Some of the women described how they felt they were so focused on surviving that they did not feel the terror of what was happening until afterwards.

I never actually felt any fear at the time. Fear didn't actually come into it. I was in the analytical part – what I was going to do, dealing with it. I was in survival mode. I didn't feel fear until it was over and then the fear came in right near the end after I'd been – the rape was over and I was being driven back to my destination and I thought, 'Oh my God, what's he going to do with me now? Is he going to kill me, is he going to rape me, rape me again? Oh my God, what's going to happen now?' Then I started to feel fear. (Raquel)

As well as wondering what MR might do next, the women had to decide what they would do. All of them reacted by telling somebody else what had happened, or going to others for help. Ann described opening and leaping out her bedroom window, then running straight across the road for help – to neighbours she did not know.

> I ran down my driveway screaming ... I ran, I was banging on the door 'Aaarrghh!' (screaming) and this young boy ... answered the door and I was 'Aaarrghh!', and this poor guy... His mother heard and she came in and I just said, 'I've been raped!' and they actually put, I remember, a blanket round me and I think they rang the police because I think I actually talked to the police and they said, 'Are you all right?' I was just a total fallen apart mess. (Ann)

Another woman also described leaving her house in a panic and running to the neighbour's place, even though she barely knew them:

> I was so scared that I didn't care at the time, but I was running down the street virtually half naked. They [neighbours] were really nice actually. They came back that afternoon to see if I was okay. (Suzanne)

Some of the women described their hurt and frustration when others implied they should have been able to fight off MR. It was hard not to feel criticised by such reactions, and several felt reassured later when the police showed them a photo of MR:

> I was quite pleased when I saw that photo because he's very, very muscular, a very fit man, and I was pleased in the respect that, people afterwards were saying, 'Why didn't you do this, why didn't you knee him between the legs?' and things like that. I could see then that he was a very strong man. I couldn't knee him between the legs because I was in bed when he came in. He was expecting me but I wasn't expecting him. I felt better that I hadn't been able to fight him off when I saw how muscular he was. (Suzanne)

Conclusion

What the women did to manage and survive the attack varied greatly. Some focused on calming themselves in order to be able to think and plan, while others dissociated in order to keep a part of themselves safe. Some feared dying, while for others this thought never crossed their minds. All of the women had one thing in common – they were all actively devising strategies to ensure their survival. Their accounts challenge the image of the passive, helpless victim. Even though MR was doing all he could to dominate them, they were searching for ways to keep a part of themselves separate, beyond his reach. They were resisting his control.

Resistance may result in rape avoidance or it may not. While it is clearly preferable to avoid being raped if possible, those women whom MR did rape nevertheless had their own, inner strategies of resistance. Faking being unconscious, dissociating from their body, willing themselves bigger, visualising their escape – these were all ways the women sought to access their own power and agency in the situation. Their responses challenge conventional notions of the passive victim who becomes a survivor over time; instead they demonstrate that at the very moment she is being attacked, a woman can simultaneously be both – she is a victim in survivor mode.

Such measures indicate that resistance can occur on both physical and psychological levels. It may incorporate self-defence tactics, but these are so much more than well-aimed kicks and throws. Defending the self can occur on several levels simultaneously, as the victim struggles to keep at least part of herself safe, protected from her attacker's grasp. Even if he has physically rendered her helpless, it is her body he is controlling – not her self – there is so much more of her than what can be hurt, gagged, bound or penetrated.

It is also apparent that, despite these measures, as Chapter 6 shows, the women sometimes felt it was their very selves he violated. The role of the self in rape is both complex and contradictory. It is damaged, and it also protects from further damage. It is violated, and it can also remove itself, through dissociation, to prevent further intrusion. So many different aspects of the women's lives were affected, and their sense of who they were in the world. This was evident for the women MR raped as well as for those he failed to rape, suggesting that it is not the act of rape alone that impacts so extensively. Knowing that someone intends to rape you is also injurious – that someone has been planning, stalking, fantasising –raping in his mind. Little wonder that some of the women sought to understand who could hate them so much that he would do this to them; that they asked, as Isabel did, what have I ever done to him?

Surviving police processes

Rape is not a rare event – what is rare is for the offence to be reported to the police. International research confirms that police organisations are informed about only a minority of the rapes and sexual assaults that occur [1-4]. Police responses to rape victims have been identified as a critical component of the recovery process [5, 6]. When victims turn to the police for help, they may or may not be expecting the offender to be caught and convicted. What they are often looking for is to regain a sense of personal safety, and to have their experience validated. Studies conducted from the 1970s onwards have instead revealed that many complainants feel disbelieved and judged by the police [2, 5, 7-14]. Reporting rape replicated the violation felt in the rape itself for many women, and could be experienced as a second victimisation [15, 16]. Other complainants, however, have rated the police more highly, with research results overall indicating major inconsistencies in how sexual assault victims are treated [17-20]. Such polarised accounts have been found in many countries, including New Zealand [21-24]; Australia [5, 25]; United Kingdom [1, 11, 26], and the United States [27, 28].

Research suggests that the diversity in women's experiences with the police is not randomly distributed but affected by a range of factors. The most significant ones identified concern the relationship of the victim to the perpetrator, the extent to which the victim has visible, physical injuries in addition to the rape injury, and the ways in which she 'fits' dominant stereotypes of 'real' or 'ideal' victims [1, 17, 29-33]. The chances of receiving a sympathetic police response are often linked to stranger attacks and particularly to the victim receiving visible physical injuries in the attack [29, 30, 34-36]. Evidence of the latter has been used to 'prove' a woman's resistance and lack of submission [30, 37, 38].

Questions regarding perceptions of a complainant's credibility are highly influential. Police responses can be affected by judgments made on the basis of adherence to rape myths – was she 'asking for it'? Is she lying? Is she a slut? As the gatekeepers to the criminal justice system, the police are also sensitive to how credible a victim will appear should the case reach court – what kind of background is she from? Does she come across as a victim, able to be identified with in her helplessness? Or does she look and sound 'bolshy', with too much 'attitude' to be raped?

The majority of the women attacked by MR conformed to ideal victim stereotypes [2, 29, 33, 39, 40]. They were white, typically well-educated, professional women, attacked in circumstances where few judgments could be levelled that that they had 'asked for it'. The perpetrator was a stranger, the type of predatory serial rapist whom the police prioritise in their investigative efforts, and the women's treatment by the police largely reflected such realities. Compared with accounts of rape victims' experiences of reporting to the police more generally, the majority of these women rated the police positively. This does not mean they found it easy being interviewed or partici-pating in police procedures, and nor does it mean that their treatment by the police was always perfect. The question of whether the stereotypically 'perfect' victims received 'perfect' policing has been addressed elsewhere (see [24], Ch 6). The aim here is to identify how the women coped with and survived the many police interviews and processes they participated in, from the time of reporting onwards.

Engaging with the police was a new experience for the majority of these women. For instance, in trying to recall any previous police contact she may have had, one woman commented:

I'm not sure I've had any actually, oh, apart from when I was parked on the wrong side of the road once. That was about it. I got growled at, but then I think they were traffic cops. Yeah, we had one break in, it wasn't a break in – it was a burglary, when we were at a house when I was boarding somewhere. I'm not even sure if we called the police, I think we did but they didn't do anything anyway. Yeah, apart from that, that would be about it. (Lorna)

For most of these women, the moment the attack was reported signalled the beginning of a journey into the foreign terrain of the criminal justice system. How did they experience this system? What was it like to have so much contact with the police? How was it for the earlier victims of MR when they were finally told who their attacker was, and had to decide if they would participate in his trial? In this chapter the women recount their experiences of police processes and identify both positive and negative aspects arising from these encounters.

Experiences of initial reporting and statement taking

The typically low reporting rate for rape offences is linked in part to most attackers being someone already known to the victim, maybe even someone they love. Torn loyalties, fear of their attacker, and apprehension that others may blame them for 'asking to be raped' are all factors that impact on reporting behaviour. International studies suggest that stranger attacks, although relatively rare in occurrence, have significantly higher reporting rates than acquaintance or marital rapes [35, 41-43]. Obviously MR's attacks on all the women in this study came to police attention, but how this occurred varied somewhat.

Some women rang the police themselves, most dialling the emergency number (111).

I would have never considered not doing it. It was: the first thing I need to do here is get some help. I suppose it shows I had a lot of faith in the police, it was the first person I would have rung. (Jennifer)

She added that she was also anxious that MR may still be in her home:

I wanted someone there who was going to make damn sure he had gone before I walked out of that bedroom. I was fairly sure he had, but I didn't know. (Jennifer)

One woman struggled with which number to use, opting instead not to dial the emergency number.

I went to dial 111 then I thought, I don't want to make a big deal out of it, I'll dial my mates down at the [local] police station. I don't know why I did that, just so I didn't make a big deal out of it. (Kathleen)

Kathleen's response may in part have been influenced by her own survival mechanisms, which encouraged her to cope with the attack by minimising its seriousness at the time. Since she was one of the few who were more familiar with police personnel and processes, she preferred calling the local station.

Patricia, who was the second to last of MR's known victims to be attacked, tried to catch him herself first, then rang the police. Most said that there was no doubt in their mind that the police needed to be called, and it felt like an automatic response to the trauma they had experienced and the sense of danger they still felt.

In some situations it was the women's neighbours who called the police, after they had run to them for help. In two cases, these were people whom they did not know at all, while one knew them only vaguely. In such circumstances, Helen expressed well the sense of panic some felt regarding where was it safe to run to:

> I was pretty frightened, and I didn't know who would take me in. I ran into the neighbour's and I thought, 'Oh God, it could have been him!' and ran out into the street, because I just didn't know who it was. It could have been anyone. To me, it could have been the policeman for all I knew. (Helen)

Ann also described the sense of panic that propelled her out into the street, terrified as to whether MR was waiting for her. She was scared he would come back to kill her and forced herself free of most of the bindings before leaping out the window. Ann said it was only later she realised what a sight she must have presented to the person who answered the door:

> I was just a total fallen apart mess. I think if I was the young boy that answered the door to me, I would have freaked out looking at her because there was a total mess at the door, screaming, with all these bits and pieces from when he tied me up that were all hanging off me, looking a big dishevelled mess. I thought, 'My God!' (Ann)

Lorna wanted to get out of the house in case MR was still there, or came back. She ran next door to her neighbour, whom she knew only vaguely, and who immediately phoned the police. As it turned out, a year earlier MR had raped this woman in the very house Lorna ran to for safety.

Karen also said she ran over the road to a neighbour and, when asked why she chose his house, indicated a discerning, and quick, appraisal of her options:

> I knew him as you know your neighbours, I didn't know him particularly well. The woman over the road, directly over the road from me, was a woman who lived by herself. She had prowlers a few times; it later came out in the trial that Hammer [MR's nickname] had been the prowler because [policeman] ID-ed him from photos, so I didn't want to go to [her]. You don't want to appear at a woman's doorstep saying, 'I've been raped!' at 4.30 in the morning. There was an old lady lived next door to me and the people that lived on the other side had only moved in fairly recently, so [neighbour] was my best bet and he happened to be a policeman so it was rather fortunate for me. (Karen)

Several women told their current or former husbands/partners they had been attacked and the latter phoned the police. Frances was attacked by MR as she turned into her driveway after having been out for an early morning run. She screamed and broke free, and ran into the house. Her husband immediately called the police, and she said she found it difficult coping with the rest of the family's reactions before she had been able to comprehend herself what had happened.

> My children were all there, so I was trying to act as though nothing had really happened. They'd heard me screaming too so they were quite distressed, so I was more concentrating on trying to calm them down and do what we'd normally do at that time of the morning. (Frances)

Raquel also quickly appraised her options after being raped in her car by MR, deciding to go back to the restaurant where her boyfriend worked.

> I actually went back up to the restaurant because there was nobody at home ... After what I had been through, walking into an empty dark house and being on my own and calling the police and sitting there waiting by myself, it's not really an option ... I had a choice to do that or drive one minute up the road where I knew there would be people.
>
> I didn't actually stop and consider the fact that there probably would be a few other people there, like staff members, that were going to know what had happened ... I didn't think about all the other issues. They don't cross your mind. You're in survival mode. You're just thinking about what you need. Just thinking about your immediate needs and my immediate need was being with somebody that I knew would be a comfort. (Raquel)

Calling the police did not feel like a decision so much as an automatic response. As she expressed it:

> It was sort of a given. There wasn't any question. It was obvious to call the police. There was never any thought, 'Oh, will I, won't I?' It was like, 'Of course we're going to call the police', and we didn't even need to discuss it. (Raquel)

Connie was separated from her husband yet he was the first person she wanted to call. She rang his flat but the flatmate answered so she hung up and phoned him in Hamilton, an hour-and-a-half's drive away.

> When I rang my husband, he answered the phone. I didn't even know what the time was, I just knew it was morning, early morning. I'm sobbing and he says, 'What's the matter?' and I just said 'I've been raped' (whispering). [He] said 'You get off the fucking phone', he said, 'Get off the phone.' (Connie)

He told her to call her brother, who lived nearby, while he phoned the police before driving the hundred kilometres to her place.

In Gabriel's case she had just rung her flatmates to say she was on her way to join them at a nearby party when she came face to face with MR.

> I just hoped like hell that one of them would come back and sure enough, after an hour of struggle, one of them did. One of my flatmates came back and he (MR) jumped out the window. So she actually was the first person to come on the scene ... I called out to her while he was in the house. I picked my moment and I let it rip. He got scared and took off and she went and called the police and left me in the house and I locked myself in the toilet and she actually came back in and untied me and was there when the police came ... She had a lot of problems being let into people's houses to call them as well. We live next to a retirement home and they wouldn't let her in and then someone else wouldn't let her in ... It was all just a natural flow of events for me. Like I had no paranoia about them turning up. Although I did answer the door with a knife in my hand when they did turn up! (Gabriel)

The arrival of the police was accompanied by a strong sense of relief for most of the women. Shelley described her reactions immediately after the attack:

> I rang up and said something like, 'I've been, I've just been raped,' and it was a woman I spoke to and she said, 'Is he still in the house?' and I said I didn't know. She said to me, 'We're sending a car with a dog' and she said to stay on the line, and I stayed – I didn't leave the room. She said, 'Just stay there and I'll let you know when he's in your drive-way,' which was fantastic. I was totally terrified, I was completely and utterly terrified and then she said, 'He's just told me now he's in your driveway', so I ventured up the hall ... I stood there and I made sure that it was the policeman and then I saw him there and I opened the door to him. It was quite funny actually because I did want a cuddle, I actually felt like I wanted some 'You're okay' confirmation and there was this big burly dog handler that said, 'It's all right, I'm here now.' (Shelley)

Police interviewing

As well as providing reassurance, the arrival of the police signalled the beginning of a long process of interviews, statements and medical examinations. In some situations arrangements needed to be made for the women's children or other occupants of the house, many of whom were experiencing their own distress. Karen was grateful that the neighbour she had run to went back to wake up her daughters and arranged for them to go to a friend while she went through the reporting process.

Gabriel described the police arriving and heading for the most visibly upset woman they saw:

> They went straight to my flatmate and asked if she was all right because I was making her a cup of tea. (laughs) She was bouncing off the walls because she had come home to find her flatmate gagged and bound and half naked in the toilet and she was off the wall. She'd said, 'Oh you're bruised,' and I just went to the freezer and got my ice pack and put some clothes on and grabbed a t-shirt and put the kettle on and everything was kind of automatic. And I was seeing if she was all right. It was all very strange. So when they turned up they went straight for her because she was very shocked, she was in shock. And I didn't really know what was going on. I think I was just coping. (Gabriel)

Gabriel's description of her reactions illustrates how the responses of women who have been raped may vary immensely, to the extent that they may even seem inappropriate. As she explained it:

> When I get nervous I tend to make a lot of jokes about things like this and that's my way of coping. All I wanted to do was have a coffee and a cigarette. That was my goal and I went and sat down on the couch and was making it. And they [police] said, 'We have to take you to the police station', and I said, 'I'm not leaving until I've had a cigarette.' One of the policemen said, 'Okay', and he put the kettle on and he got my coffee organised. But I didn't get a chance to have it, I only got a couple of sips and they put me and my flatmate in the car, because we couldn't touch anything. (Gabriel)

Her behaviour would have posed a quandary for the police. From a forensics point of view, she should not have been drinking anything before being examined, but from the perspective of assisting victims to regain a sense of control following such a disempowering experience, allowing her to have what she wanted was important.

The shock of the trauma impacted on the women's state of mind as they tried to respond to police questioning. Many felt they wanted someone there with them, as a support, given how vulnerable they felt. Jennifer kept trying to contact her husband but without success, and realised next morning that this was because he was 'sleeping with someone else' at the time. Although she knew their marriage was in difficulty, it was what she discovered that night that helped to seal their separation for her.

The process of reporting the attack invariably took several hours or more, and typically involved a lengthy forensic medical examination as well as police interviewing and statement-taking. Many of the women commented how difficult it was to manage the length of the reporting, examination and statement-taking process, given how exhausted they were at the time. For example, Raquel described being attacked at about 2 am, the police being called at 4.30 am, and a process beginning that she experienced as far too long. She commented:

> This is my one complaint. I got to the hospital and got checked and came back to the police station and sat and waited. I don't know where the time went but for some reason it was about midday when I got home. I'd been up all night, hadn't had any sleep and they were talking about sitting me down to give my statement. And I'm sitting there thinking, 'Ah, okay, like I've had no sleep, it's midday, no sleep' ... I remember just thinking at that point I wasn't probably capable of making a decision ... You feel you have to because the police need a statement off you. I had the feeling that I had to do what they wanted ... To be honest, expecting someone who has been up all night to give a statement, that's ridiculous ... To sit there until six o'clock at night after having no sleep and having been through what I had been through and injured, how dare they expect me to do that? I think my mother was sort of like, 'You've got to be joking!' I think they knew that I had a pretty clear idea of what had happened ... I can't remember but I'm pretty sure that I said something to them like, 'I'm not going to forget anything over night, believe me.' (Raquel)

Managing the medical examination

A critical step in the reporting process involves the medical examination of the complainant. This is important on two counts. From a police perspective it provides the means to obtain forensic evidence that could be helpful in identifying the offender and securing a conviction. From the victim's perspective, it enables her to have any physical injuries treated as well as a sexual health examination, and to be provided with medication to prevent pregnancy.

Forensically, it is vital that the victim is examined as soon as possible, ideally before she has urinated and particularly before she has bathed or showered. The closer the time of the examination to the incident's occurrence, the more likely it is that forensic evidence may be obtained, particularly semen traces, pubic hairs, and skin tissue (especially if the victim scratched him). These examinations are now typically conducted by predominantly women doctors in clinics or premises away from the police station, a far cry from earlier times when a male police surgeon would examine the woman in a police cell [21].

The examination itself is a lengthy and often difficult procedure for the victim. Other studies have indicated how invasive and exposing the procedures can feel, especially when the victim is in shock and trying to manage the invasion of the rape [44-47]. Careful examination of every orifice is required, pubic hair needs to be combed, and all this has the potential to feel as invasive as the original rape. That is why the attitude and sensitivity of the examining doctor is so critical, and most victims prefer to be examined by a woman doctor [22, 48]. Following the examination they are able to shower and put on new clothes.

From the victim's perspective, it is difficult to have to wait such a long time before washing and cleaning themselves. Connie, for instance, described being attacked in the early morning and it being two or three the following afternoon before she could shower.

> I found that really hard. I just wanted to get this filth off my body. It was a relief in the end. I found that really disturbing, it was a long time, even having the photographs. I know they needed it, it's pretty degrading ... I did the normal thing that people usually do in the shower afterwards. I didn't want to get out. I mean, it's pretty standard, you want to scrub and scrub because he's had his hand everywhere. With me it was his mouth and whatever. It was like, 'Oooh, I don't want him on me anymore.' (Connie)

By the time she was interviewed, she said she felt:

> Absolutely shell-shocked. And I was so tired, so worn out, just drained, completely drained, I just wanted to go home and go to sleep. (Connie)

Seeing the photographs of herself later was also a shock.

> I looked at myself. It was a picture of devastation, disbelief at what had just happened. It was quite sad to look at it because obviously it was so bad I didn't want to remember that part, and I had to look at a photograph to remember. (Connie)

The women interviewed reported mostly positive experiences of how the medical examination was conducted, once it was arranged. Shelley said of the doctor who examined her:

> She was absolutely fantastic. She was just wonderful. She was just so gentle and so sympathetic but also time wasn't important to her and she

just explained things really well and let me take my time. She was fantastic … When the medical finished they said I could go and have a shower and that was the time that I actually became really upset. I stood in the shower for about ten minutes and let all the water wash over me and cleanse me. It was the first time I cried. It was nice to be on my own but feeling safe and just letting this water cleanse me – it was really nice. (Shelley)

Karen also felt very positive about the woman doctor who examined her soon after she was raped:

She was just really lovely. She was very, very calming and caring. I felt well looked after by her. She rang me a couple of times afterwards to see how I was, which I thought was nice. (Karen)

Despite her praise for the doctor, she said it was a difficult procedure to manage:

I felt like it was hard even though I had a really good doctor and a good support person with me. It's like the last thing you want to do really. It's something that has to be done. (Karen)

There was overwhelming support for having women doctors perform the forensic medical procedures.

I can think of nothing worse than having a male doctor do that examination after you've been raped, I don't think they should be allowed to do them. I'm not particularly squeamish about having a medical examination, it's not something that really worries me, but at that point, I can remember being there with my knees up and my legs were going like this (shaking back and forth), I was a mess by then. (Karen)

Not all of the women were referred for medical examinations, a point which some bitterly resented later. At the time they trusted the police to do what was necessary, but variable levels of police knowledge and understanding occasionally resulted in poor decision-making. Suzanne felt sorely aggrieved when the insensitive detective interviewing her failed to have her medically examined. Suzanne said that later, when she had a fuller appreciation of the procedures that should have been followed, she struggled to understand how this detective failed to hear the signals that should have alerted her to the situation and confirmed the need for an examination.

I said to her, 'I feel so dirty and revolting' and she said, 'You'll have to stay here for the meantime,' and I said, 'Well, can I go to the toilet?' and she said, 'Yep', so I went to the toilet at the police station and I said, 'Oooh yuck, I feel really yuck and I stink'. She never ever did anything about it, she never sent me for any tests, she told me to have a shower when I got home and I did. I even told her, 'Couldn't they have some DNA,' I would say, 'whether it would be hairs or anything?' I should have probably insisted but then, given what I've been through, it's their job to remember that ... I would have been really furious given everything I'd been through with all the statements and police interviews and everything if it had not stood up in court. (Suzanne)

Jennifer was not referred immediately for a medical examination. She decided to go and see her own general practitioner straight after she had given her statement and had a police detective ask her if she could possibly get her own doctor to do the forensic examination. This was problematic.

He (the doctor) really didn't know. He was asking me what they wanted and I had no idea what they wanted ... It was a bit of a balls up, their part in that. I think they were hoping that my GP would know what to do, but he didn't know what they were after. (Jennifer)

Two or three days later Jennifer was finally taken for a forensic medical examination. She said she appreciated the way in which the doctor explained so fully what she was doing and why, but this doctor also was annoyed at the delay in having her examined, and the potential loss of forensic evidence.

Gabriel was attacked in her flat by MR at about 11 pm, three days before Christmas. She told the police she was in a lot of pain and having trouble breathing so they called a doctor in to examine her at the police station. She was not impressed by either the doctor or the environment and became assertive in her efforts to manage the situation.

This is quite terrible, but I was examined in the first aid room next to the cell block in the central city police station ... They called in this nut ... She started to give me this medical. She was bloody annoying ... The first thing she said, she was checking measuring the bruises on my back and she said, 'Oh, that's a nasty melanoma, you really should get that looked at, have you been to a doctor?', and I just went off my tree ... Then they [police] found out I had been penetrated and they screwed up the piece of paper in front of me and said, 'We can't use this now, we have to take you to hospital', and I was so angry that they hadn't checked that out before the medical examination. I was really annoyed. (Gabriel)

She said that she had been insistent she had not been raped but this had been accepted by the police with no further question about other forms of penetration. She was transferred to the hospital in the early hours of the morning, having difficulty breathing and her feelings of vulnerability exacerbated by not being able to sit up without assistance. By 6 am she was transferred to a room to sleep, and given drugs and a panic button because of her high distress levels, then woken three hours later at 9 am to talk to the police.

> *It started off by taking my statement at the hospital and then they had to clear the bed so I needed to get up and go back to the house. And then I had to go right through the entire house and pinpoint everything that was mine and everything that was touched and that was just really disturbing. My flatmates were there and that was the first time I cried, I think. I found it really disturbing, going back there, and then we went to the police station and all my flatmates were interviewed as well and myself. And then I got taken for my medical. (Gabriel)*

It was now 1 pm, 14 hours since the attack, and a support person had been called in, arriving as the medical procedure commenced.

> *That was the most hideous experience I've ever had – that medical examination. And that woman [doctor] was very, very rude ... I think she had a time limit for how long my medical examination would take and she was just very blunt and not sympathetic. 'Right, I have to measure your bruises, now I have to do this'. Everything is measured, saliva and your pubic hair is cut. When I was having my medical examination she said, 'Your pubic hair has been cut in some areas'. And I said, 'Yes, it has' and she said, 'Why?' And I said, 'Because I trim my pubic hair'. And she said, 'How ridiculous, trimming your pubic hair!' And I said, 'Why?' And she said, 'I've never heard of anyone doing that before.' And I said, 'Quite a few women do that'. Even the support person was quite shocked. And she [support person] said, 'Of course some women trim their pubic hair'. She [doctor] said, 'I think that's silly'. (Gabriel)*

Gabriel found this doctor's attitude very insensitive, a point reinforced by the pressure she felt to do everything quickly for the doctor's convenience.

> *It took me a very long time before I could open my legs for my internal because of the nature of my attack, which was that my legs were prised open. Part of her touching on the inside here was not somewhere where I was able to go because I had been forced against my will. She kept saying, 'You've got to open your legs' and I just couldn't. I just wasn't ready to do it. And I said, 'I know, I'm trying, but I just need to take as long as I can'. It was very hard ... She kept going, 'The quicker you do this the*

quicker we get out of here'. I felt like she was angry because I was taking so long. (Gabriel)

Finally the two of them came to an impasse:

She wanted to give me an internal and I refused one and she got very angry about that and told me that I had to have one. I said that I wasn't raped and no, I wouldn't have an internal because why should I if I wasn't raped? I couldn't understand the purpose of it. And she said, 'But you had manual penetration' and I said, 'Yes, but fingers don't ejaculate'. I couldn't understand, it you know. She was very intent on this internal and I was very intent on not having it. In the end it was, 'No, it's my body and you can't do it. I won't let you!' I couldn't, I was too distressed. She got quite shirty about that. (Gabriel)

Gabriel's experience reveals the traumatic nature of such an invasive examination as well as indicating her need to retain some control over proceedings. One way she sought to protect herself against the doctor's impatience and lack of sensitivity was by asserting her own will and refusing to become a pawn in the hands of the system. Other women chose to manage the examination and protect themselves by dissociating, allowing whatever needed to happen to occur.

Describing in detail the nature of a sexual assault is something most victims find difficult. Some of the women suggested ways of trying to ease its impact:

There were some things I didn't feel comfortable saying that had happened because I didn't want to say it. What I think would be helpful is if they had like a checklist and they went through and asked you if things happened. There are some things, like when he ... the oral sex bit, I didn't know how to say what had happened. It was just uncomfortable, horrible. It wasn't until one of the nurses actually asked me, 'Did he perform oral sex?' that I said, 'Yes'. Otherwise I would probably not have come out and said that. It made me feel very uncomfortable talking about that. It's all very well saying that you've been raped but to go into the itty bitty, nitty gritty details is really quite difficult. (Kathleen)

Other women felt that they might have managed the examination better if the different aspects were explained more fully:

The funny thing is, when you do get to have your examination, no one actually explains to you what you're doing. I was pretty traumatised. I don't know whether I would have wanted it explained, but nobody gives you the option to explain to you what they're doing – they just go and they examine you. When you first get there, they're eager to get you to eat.

Well, they got me to eat a piece of gum, and I wondered for years why I actually got to eat that gum. They were looking for different parts of your saliva, but no one told you. They just said, 'Can you chew this gum, can you chew this?' At the time it was like, 'Yeah, whatever.' Perhaps things like that could change. (Ann)

In Ann's case there was further embarrassment because of confusion over her ethnic identity.

When they took me to this clinic, because of my name, they actually thought I was an Islander and they got me an island interpreter in case I wanted to speak my own language. With my sister being there and this lady starting to speak to me, even though I'm Māori, in Samoan, it was like, 'Umm, I'm Māori, I don't know what you're talking about!' (laughter) So that was a bit of a bummer. (Ann)

A more appropriate support worker was found and the examination continued. While Ann felt the procedure was managed well by the doctor, nevertheless she still found it difficult.

It's pretty traumatising. By the end of the day you're just so zapped out because emotionally you've been drained, in every inch of your body, you feel violated, you feel unbelievable that sometimes you've thought, it wasn't me. I suppose you have a mechanism in your body that kicks in to say, 'This didn't happen to me' because I can't cope anymore because I'm on the edge of cracking. After my shower, I don't really remember a lot after that. I remember my sister saying, 'Ann, you have to get out.' (Ann)

Several women commented that they found it difficult to manage follow-up health checks when these required them to see a doctor at a sexual health clinic. Shelley said going to the clinic at night following the rape felt quite different from returning in the daytime.

I had to return there to have further swabs and tests and I found that quite distressing. First of all to have to go there – I mean, it was the sexual health clinic where all the prostitutes and various people go for their VD checks, and I felt that was really quite insensitive and inappropriate for me to actually be there in a waiting room sitting round with all these people.

The doctor was lovely. It was just actually the surroundings that I was in, so it was that environment. I was saying to myself, now don't be snobbish about this. But I felt that I wouldn't have been there in my ordinary life and I felt that I shouldn't have been there for so many public people to see ... I just felt it was really too open for me to be there. (Shelley)

Karen also described struggling with going back to the sexual health clinic:

> I'd never go to an STD clinic. Why on earth would you go to an STD clinic, even if you had an STD, wouldn't you go to a doctor? It was horrible! I felt like I was a sex worker ... I felt quite dirty. I don't know why I didn't say, 'I'm not going there. I want to go to my doctor.' It was like I had to follow the procedure, and that seemed to me what the procedure was. I didn't like going there at all. (Karen)

After the medical examination, many of the women returned to the police station to give their statement.

Interviewing environment

The physical environment within which a rape victim is interviewed may also be important to her sense of well-being and safety. Many of the women were critical of the rooms and facilities available. Police organisations have been criticised for interviewing victims in the came cell-type rooms used to interrogate criminal offenders [22, 24]. Kassin and Fong [49] observed that such interview rooms were designed to intimidate and enhance feelings of sensory deprivation and isolation – the converse of establishing a safe, comfortable environment within which to obtain full accounts of highly sensitive and personal experiences.

One woman said the detective interviewing her acknowledged this to be the case:

> As he [the detective] said, their interview rooms are really for interviewing criminals, and they don't go to a great deal of effort to make them too comfortable. They had to find some tissues for me, but they looked after me quite well. (Karen)

Another described her shock at the state of the room she was interviewed in:

> It was absolutely disgusting. The chairs were falling apart ... We had to use our mobile phones. The window was broken, the air conditioning was half hanging off the wall, I mean it was third world, something you imagine you'd see in Istanbul or South Africa. And that actually had a huge impact on my mental alertness. (Shelley)

Gabriel also felt strongly about the interviewing environment at the police station:

The whole place is set up for you to feel as uncomfortable as possible in my opinion. Well, just look at the environment, and the decor and the fact that you've never been inside a police station before in your life, and nothing about it is there to make you feel better. (Gabriel)

She felt uncomfortable being questioned by a uniformed officer, and felt that the layout of the room was important:

I don't think they [interviews] should be done behind a desk. Do you know what I mean? It's like going into an office and someone going, 'Okay, well tell us about your rape thing'. It's like the power is in that person's hands because they've got their desk and their pen and their box of tissues and you're sitting there in this chair that you've never sat in before, in a room that you don't know … And then if they sit next to you it's even weirder because you're in their office and they're sitting next to you and there is no-one behind the desk! I just think there needs to be some kind of safe place that is used specifically for sensitive complainants that has things that they can touch, like pillows that they can hold, or tissues there … Or a room with a couch, or something that is positive, like positive colours in a room, for example. But a room that is specifically put aside for people who are feeling vulnerable … Being in an unfamiliar environment can probably stop a lot of people from giving really good evidence in their statement because they want to get the hell out of there really quickly … There are no resources available that are positive for the complainant – I think that's terrible. (Gabriel)

The need for safety and comfort is exacerbated by the ordeal victims have been through. The trauma of the attack may be experienced and responded to in different ways, and some women described feeling they could hold themselves together in certain contexts and not others. Karen, for example, described how she felt when she needed to stop the interview and go to the toilet:

The toilets weren't very far. I said, 'I can go by myself.' I went into the cubicle. I can remember sitting there and being so fucking scared, just so 'What's happened to me? I can't believe this has happened!' I was really in shock. When I came out of the cubicle, this young woman walked in. She was probably one of their admin staff or something, she wouldn't have been a police officer, and she went to say something to me, and I just screamed at her, 'I've been raped!' I just broke down. This poor kid, she must have just got such a shock. But I had no control over what I was doing. I could keep myself together when I was being interviewed, but it was like this moment of not having anybody with me, thinking I'm okay, I really found out that no, I wasn't okay. We had a break after that. They said, 'You don't have to continue if you don't want to.' I said, 'I just want to get this done.' (Karen)

The lack of comfort was noted by many of the women, who found the station an impersonal and at times intimidating environment.

It's in the middle of the night and there's no one around in the police station for a start. And you've got a cold cup of coffee, a cup of coffee in a plastic cup, not very nice and warm. You probably need a bit of support and comfort at that time really. You're not feeling too good, you've been bashed up a bit as well, you need a bit of comfort. (Helen)

It was a long interview process and she later went to get herself another drink:

I went to make myself a cup of tea and the only place to make a cup of tea was in the officers' mess, so there's a lot of people around. Again, it would have been nice to have a little room that had a sofa in it, and a coffee cup, something so that you've got a bit of privacy. Because again you've got this room full of men, big bulky men, and you're feeling pretty vulnerable at the time. They weren't offensive or anything, it was just you're feeling vulnerable, you think everyone's looking at you, you've just been attacked, raped, you feel yuck, and that just makes it worse really. You want to hide, so why not let someone just at that time, just give them the comfort they need? (Helen)

As she said, to assist the recovery process there needs to be more consideration of what is needed from the woman's point of view, given all she has been through.

Some of the women described their growing unease as the police kept questioning them about the likely identity of their attacker. One woman, for instance, said she found it difficult:

[T]hat they kept probing me, for me to think of who this guy was and I found that quite disturbing because it went back to 'Have you ever had anybody do this or do that?' and it started to fill me with this paranoia of potential people that I knew who could have done this terrible thing to me. Because it was repeated to me quite a few times by various different ones, 'Are you sure you can't think of anyone?' And I found that very disturbing, being asked that all the time. It's like trying to pin someone that you know up for some heinous crime. (Gabriel)

The lack of privacy was a factor mentioned by several of the women, who found it difficult when other police personnel kept coming in and out of the interview room or area. This aspect has also been highlighted internationally as an issue of concern [22, 25]. Helen said that while she felt positive about the woman officer interviewing her, she hated the lack of privacy.

> There was one point when these police guys kept bursting in to the room. She [detective] didn't have her own room to do the interviews in, and she was sharing with some policemen. I just felt really stared at by them, so that wasn't nice. I could tell that [she] was pretty angry about them. She'd say, 'Excuse me boys, but I'm conducting an interview here. Do you think you could leave?' And they were like, 'Got this work to do'. They knew what I was there for, so that was not good, I felt very degraded by that. (Helen)

Connie talked about the police wanting to take her down to the station immediately after she had reported the rape.

> They took me down to the police station in my nightie, exactly how I was dressed, in my nightie ... I can't remember how long I was there, it seemed to be ages. I was not in any particular private area because it must have been the start to the change of a shift because people seemed to be coming and going and sort of staring at me.

JJ: How did that feel?

> Lonely, just lonely. (Connie)

Having one's home turned into a crime scene

After having being medically examined and interviewed, the women were usually returned home, which was for most the scene of the attack. Some arrived to find their house was still the centre of a major forensic examination. Shelley described the difficulties:

> Actually, I couldn't go home because forensic had everything taped off and I couldn't actually go in because I would have contaminated the area. So before I went to the police station, fortunately one of these two young police had enough nous to say to me 'Go and get some clothes to wear afterwards', but I couldn't go into my room, back into my bedroom, so I went into my daughter's room who's the same size as me and I got her jeans and a top. And I had to wear her clothes for a day. (Shelley)

After she had given her statement, she said:

> My brother attempted to take me home and we couldn't get in. It was swarming with police. These big yellow police ribbons they have round the scene, and police cars up and down the drive and down the road and it

certainly showed that there had been an event there that involved the police! There were so many police there! They were all measuring and doing different things ... I was quite shocked. I was shocked for several reasons. The first one was that every single person in the street from here to Hamilton would have known that was my house. I felt shocked that I couldn't be in my own home. Even though I'd been attacked there, it was still a place, a sanctuary for me to go back to it. Fortunately as I was with my brother, I could go back to his place. (Shelley)

On another level, she said it was reassuring returning home.

It was actually good for me to go back and I'm glad I did because one policeman said to me, 'Do you know how he got in?' and I said, 'No', and he pointed out to me where – and that was really good. I was filled with a great relief when I saw that because I hadn't done anything wrong. I hadn't made a mistake which I could have blamed myself for. I hadn't left a door open, I hadn't left a window open. He had crow-barred a skylight open to get in and my house had just recently been painted so it was very clear from the marks on the window where he had got in. (Shelley)

While some women, like Shelley, were keen to retreat to their home afterwards, others felt they could never sleep there again. Gabriel talked about her reaction to seeing her flat and the road outside swarming with police officers:

It's bloody embarrassing, because our house was right on the street and any of our friends could have gone past and found out and heaps of them did. But everyone would know that something was happening with that kind of stuff going on. And the fact that none of us could stay. There was inconvenience to my flatmates because they couldn't stay in the house that night and they all had to find alternative accommodation. We all moved out. No one would stay there after that because he was still around there and I had two female flatmates and he could come back. Everyone moved out, we all lost the flat. I lost bond money from a smashed window out the back which [flatmate] smashed to come in and save me. They wouldn't give me my bond money back. (Gabriel)

She also described a sense of reassurance from seeing police swarming over the property:

I was pleased to see them all there really, I was, because it made me feel good that they were doing something. I was important, you know. (Gabriel)

By the time of the trial, most of the women had moved house, with the judge acknowledging the financial strain this had placed on some.

Many of the women had been attacked in their bedrooms, while wearing night attire, and these garments also needed to be examined. Retrieving replacement clothes for them to wear was problematic when their bedroom was the crime scene, leading to situations some found disconcerting.

> *I remember them taking [my daughter] over to get me some clothes. My room had been closed off so they couldn't get my clothes so [she] brought me an old tracksuit of [my partner's] to wear, I looked very glamorous for the day! My glasses, which I always kept on my bedside table, had somehow mysteriously found themselves way under my bed where I couldn't find them, where he purposely put them because he would have known that I wore glasses, but that was something that we made sense of later. So I couldn't see. I didn't get my glasses until about 11 o'clock that day, I suppose, which was awful because I'm blind as a bat – as if I didn't feel disorientated enough I didn't have my glasses, which was quite big for me. (Karen)*

Identifying the attacker

The majority of the women did not see their attacker clearly. It was typically dark at the time, and he usually wore a balaclava or beanie over his head. It was also later revealed that MR intentionally tried to change his appearance often during these years, alternatively growing and cutting his hair, wearing it different ways, having a beard sometimes and being clean-shaven at others.

Not knowing who it was who attacked them was particularly frightening for many of the women. It meant that any man they saw could possibly have been their attacker, a suspicion that was profoundly disconcerting. Only one woman saw him clearly. This was Patricia, who unsettled MR by making a lot of noise, causing him to struggle violently with her, in the process losing his beanie. He panicked and began scrabbling round on the floor trying to find it, knowing he dare not risk leaving it at the crime scene. Patricia ended up chasing him from the house. She was attacked at about 5 am and said that by 11 am that morning she was sitting with a police officer trying to do an identikit picture of the offender. The questions came fast and furious:

> *'Does he have a wide mouth, a medium mouth, a medium wide mouth or a small mouth?' I said he had a wide mouth, so they click on wide mouth. I go, 'That's not a wide mouth.' So here is this guy, 'What kind of a hat did he have? How was his hair? Was it parted?' I would say, 'It was parted in*

the middle,' and he looks this up, 'Sorry, no hairdo's parted in the middle.'
They had an American profile program in there, it had not one Polynesian,
not anything, the closest thing to an Asian was an Eskimo. They didn't
have anything that was slightly conducive with a Māori or Polynesian that
you see on the street.

So this poor guy, who doesn't use this machine much, is trying to
draw in the lines and all the cragginess around, and he is trying to chop
this Canadian woodchopper hat down to a beanie ... The closest was the
Canadian woodchopper's hat, so we kind of sliced the top to make it sit
on his hair. (Patricia)

It took several hours of concentration and patience to achieve an
image resembling MR, and the detective, whom Patricia said had been
pacing the floor behind them all this time, was relieved when she
rated the picture a nine out of ten in terms of its likeness. When this
picture appeared on the front page of the newspaper and on posters
all round her area, however, she felt exposed despite all the support
she received.

The police later asked her to assist them in various procedures to
try to locate the offender. On one occasion, for example, she was rung
and taken to a gym after a member of the public rang to say someone
fitting that description was there. She and one of the police went in
posing as gym clients, using bikes and treadmills, while she observed
the other clientele. Through all these procedures and the identification
parade, what Patricia said she both feared and hoped for was that she
would recognise someone she knew as her attacker.

Another time the police asked her to look at a range of photos of
potential suspects. She recognised MR instantly.

There was absolutely no doubt in my mind. You get it at such a feeling
level and of course they couldn't believe it. I said, 'That's him!'... And they
said, 'What?' I said, 'That's him there,' and they said, 'Okay, well, we will
just put that there and you just keep going'. And I looked at another and
by this time everything was starting to go and I said, 'There is no point.'
He said, 'We will have two piles – the maybes and the nos.' They were
trying to undermine my confidence ... I said, 'Look at my hands.' The
palms of my hands were sweating. I said, 'There is no point going on. It's
that guy there.' So in the end we did go through all the rest until they said,
'Well that's fine, it's that guy.' (Patricia)

Participating in such an intensive process was difficult but also
brought some relief to her at the end:

When I had identified him, it was a hell of a lot better for me. He became a person. I hadn't become scared of the unknown, so if this person was hiding behind the bushes when I walked out the steps of my house then I would know it was him, not somebody else. The time there [with offender] is so intense, this relationship is formed ... You walk around looking for him all the time, just checking people all the time. The thing that was scary was I knew that if I saw him, I would know it – but shit, he would know it was me too! (Patricia)

Despite her confidence, however, Patricia worried afterwards whether she had in fact chosen the right man.

When I walked out of the police station, after I identified him, I drove out into the car park and my next-door neighbour was there with her baby in a pram and I just about ran her over! And I still didn't know. I got home and rang her a little while later, 'cause it went through my mind, 'Was it or wasn't it him? Look what you have just done.' Because one of the scariest things you go through in identification is knowing that that is the one. You don't want to dob the wrong guy in. Then I think, 'Yes, this is the person,' and I get home and I calm down a bit ... I thought, 'Yeah, I have got it right.' I rang up my neighbour to tell her and she said, 'You just about bloody ran me over!' She had banged on the car and I didn't even know, so that's how much you know that they are the right person' (Patricia)

Trying to work out who their attacker was and why they had been chosen as victims was an issue that worried many of the women. Some of the later victims/survivors obtained some comfort from the knowledge that a serial rapist was responsible, although there was also horror at the thought of any such attacker existing. As Gabriel said:

It is helpful because you think, oh well, he's sick, it's not personal. There is obviously some sick guy out there who sniffs around people's backyards, stares at women and climbs in their bedroom and does terrible things to them. I was horrified, but it was more the sense of there being someone prowling around and I started to feel like he was everywhere. That there was a serial rapist out there and I had never heard of him and there he was. There could be hundreds more out there. Every person was a potential serial rapist. All of a sudden the environment that you feel safe in becomes incredibly unsafe and quite scary. (Gabriel)

The notion of a stranger breaking in and raping them was terrifying, but so also was the possibility that someone they knew might do this to them. In Karen's case, she said about the man who raped her:

> *I didn't find out who he was until six months after the attack, I didn't recognise him, but he was a friend of a really close friend of mine ... So I had the experience of both, of it being just an intruder rape, where you have all that doubt about why me and has this person been watching me and all that sort of stuff to finding out that it was him and just feeling even more devastated and betrayed. (Karen)*

This was a man who had visited, sat round her table drinking coffee, and returned to break in the night before she was due to move house. She had no idea it was him at the time.

> *I still can't believe that he actually let me see his face. How did he know that I wouldn't recognise him? I saw him well enough to know that it was someone familiar to me. I've always just found that so weird, that he actually let me see his face. I used to wonder what I would have done had I recognised him. Would I have gone to the police? Because I knew him as this 'You don't fuck with Hammer' sort of thing, would I have rung up the police and said, 'This man has just raped me'? When I found out that it was him, I just felt like I had been raped all over again. (Karen)*

Karen was fortunate that the mutual friend she shared with MR chose to believe and support her, and this helped in her own process of coming to terms with the rape.

Managing variable police attitudes

Rape complainants in other studies have often described feeling as if they were swept up in police processes in ways that reassured some and frightened others [22, 23, 25]. Several of the women talked of various ways in which they sought to retain a sense of control. This was not necessarily a conscious act on their part, but by their actions they showed a determination to assert themselves and have at least some of their needs met. Police procedures are typically oriented to meet police investigative needs rather than the needs of victims, although the two are not mutually exclusive. Ensuring the victim is well supported and cared for would ideally be highlighted as a priority for the police, given the extent of their reliance on victims for information and support in catching the offender.

> A good detective soon realizes that the victim in a sexual assault case is by far the most important piece of evidence you have, and that if you trample on that evidence, it is much worse than trampling on a crime scene. (Barry Burkhart, quoted in Epstein and Langenbahn [27] p 17).

At times the needs expressed may seem quite basic, but being responded to positively can convey to the victim/survivor a sense of her being viewed as a person, not simply a case or evidence-provider. One woman, for instance, recounted how she had to remind the detective that she might need sustenance during the lengthy interview procedures:

> *I had to make a request of them [police] because by this time, I'd got quite hungry. I said to them they had to give me some breakfast because I was really needing something to sustain me, so they had to go out and get me some takeaways. I did have to ask for it, but when I asked for it they did something about it. (Isabel)*

The attitude of the interviewing officer can be a significant determinant of complainant satisfaction with the police [44, 50, 51]. The extent to which victims/survivors feel supported and understood can also affect the quality of the information they provide, and the amount of detail conveyed. Sensing a lack of belief or respect can impact particularly heavily on someone who is already in a state of shock. Suzanne was angry about the way she was interviewed by a detective, and aggrieved especially that it was a woman displaying such insensitivity.

> *She took me up into this room that had about a dozen desks that the police work in and sat me in one of these and started doing my statement. She took three personal phone calls while I was doing the statement with her. One of them she talked to for about 15 minutes while I was sitting waiting, talking about something that she'd done the night before. She was laughing and joking, didn't even say, 'Look, I've got somebody with me, can I ring you back?' Just kept on going. I was sitting there, people were coming and going, in and out of the room, I thought, 'I can't believe this!' If I had been in my normal state of mind and not been through what I'd just been through, I would have said, 'Excuse me, what the hell do you think you're doing?' I just couldn't believe that she was doing it, especially for a female to do it. She should have known how I felt and she obviously didn't care. (Suzanne)*

Although she said she told the detective in detail what had happened, not everything was written down and recorded in her statement. Suzanne herself was struggling to understand what she had just experienced, and says that initially she thought that she could not be viewed as a rape victim since MR had failed to have an erection and penetrate her fully. She described all this to the detective but none of this detail was recorded, even after Suzanne called her friend in to the interview room and repeated it.

It was trivialised. I really just don't think she was interested. To her it was just a minor assault because that's the way the statement ended up being ... I remember telling her about how he (MR) was pushing himself in, he couldn't get into me and it wasn't until later in the court that I realised that that wasn't recorded ... She was just in a hurry, I think she might have been going somewhere for lunch or something, because she was in a hurry to get rid of me anyway. (Suzanne)

She felt that normally she would have been stronger and able to challenge the process but having been through an attack, and sitting in such an environment, without having had a chance to wash, or to wear her own clothes, all she wanted to do was get home, and it seemed easier at the time to simply sign what had been recorded as her statement and leave.

This detective's dismissive attitude continued the next day, angering and distressing Suzanne further.

There was her and a male constable took me into town for the photos that they get done in central. The whole time [driving] in there she was laughing and joking ... She was talking about guys that she knew and parties that she'd been to, and they saw this uniformed car going the other way on the motorway, so she leans across and she's beeping the horn and waving out – just so immature, I just couldn't believe it ... She was not focused on her job at all, very unprofessional. It was almost like she thought, 'Here's another one for today – just chuck her into the car.' That was her whole attitude. And yet it was so nice that I had these others, for the court trial and pre-trial – all the other police that I dealt with were exceptional. (Suzanne)

Suzanne felt other police later validated her experience by acknowledging to her that MR's actions constituted rape and that she should have been treated as a rape victim from the outset. She was relieved when offered the chance to redo her statement with another woman detective, correcting mistakes she had let go on the first occasion.

I was so fed up with the way it went the first time, I had to have it exactly how I knew it to be, exactly, right down to things that probably might not have been here nor there really, but I wanted it right this time. (Suzanne)

This time she felt she was questioned in a constructive manner that helped her to focus her memory and recall more fully details she might otherwise have neglected to mention. The fact that two, slightly different statements now existed unfortunately provided MR's defence lawyer with ammunition to use when she took the stand:

> *He's [defence lawyer] got a job to do but even so, he did make a very big issue of it. He insinuated that I'd been coached by the police. He kept saying that 'I put this to you', and then he read out parts of the statement and I thought well, what can I say here, I wasn't going to have a stand up argument so I just said, 'Well, this is the truth and I can't say any more, this is the truth', and he said, 'But this wasn't said in your initial statement, I say to you that the police have put these words into your head.' I said, 'No, what I have in the second statement is the truth, parts of it had been missed in the first statement,' but he really pushed on with it. I think he was trying to break me down. I thought, 'No I'm not going to', so I stood my ground and obviously the jury went in my favour with it too. (Suzanne)*

Despite these mistakes and impediments, MR was convicted of the sexual violation by rape of Suzanne.

Patricia was also concerned at the quality of the statement police obtained from her. When she read it later, she felt some bits were different from how she had expressed it, especially the summary at the end. She felt that the detective interviewing her was too young and not good at sensing what she was trying to say, writing down his version of events rather than enabling her to give hers.

> *They write the conclusion and you are so exhausted at that stage that you go 'Oh, okay,' and you don't actually realise how important what you are putting your signature to is. You want to get the bloody thing over and done with at that stage. Possibly it's a bit like reading your rights, possibly an explanation of what the statement is for and what it's about and what it's used for would be really helpful. Like what you say has got to be 100% and just take your time and make sure that you do and that it is all correct and all that, and right the way through none of that happened. And I would say that that is a huge fault that they put things in their words and then get you to sign it. (Patricia)*

Other women also commented that they felt they were interviewed by officers who were inexperienced and uncomfortable with the process. Gabriel was disappointed when a different detective from those she had seen the night of the attack interviewed her the next day.

> *It was the first time he had taken a statement like that. He said it was. And I think I would have preferred someone who had done it before. He was awkward with trying to find replacement words to avoid being embarrassed, and I didn't feel embarrassed. I felt he was embarrassed and that made it awkward for me. (Gabriel)*

She also felt the police photographer displayed insensitivity:

He just came in and said, 'Oh, you don't look that bad. You got off okay.' I think he was trying to be, you know, 'Ha ha.' I was pretty pissed off with him.

JJ: *How did you feel when he said that?*

Like killing him. Like I've just been brutally sexually assaulted and so I'm not missing an arm or anything but I felt like it was a big thing. (Gabriel)

The issue of belief is a defining feature of the police-complainant relationship in rape cases. Internationally concern has frequently been raised regarding the 'culture of scepticism' that exists within the police towards women rape complainants [2, 24]. Research with rape survivors elsewhere has confirmed the importance of feeling believed [1, 25, 26, 28, 52].

The majority of the women faced no such doubts regarding the veracity of their allegations. The circumstances in which they were attacked, by a stranger who over time was recognised as a serial offender, automatically enhanced perceptions of their credibility by police.

I don't know whether I was just lucky, but I never felt disbelieved, and that was really, really good because it must be incredibly difficult. You hear about it all the time, and I don't know whether it is the circumstances of mine that made it obvious that there was nothing to disbelieve, the fact that I went to a policeman's house afterwards probably helped! (Karen)

There were, however, several exceptions. One was a woman attacked in 1987, Wendy, whom I was unable to interview. Her case was widely reported later, however, when it became evident that she had recognised MR through her own gang associations, and had named him to police as the man who raped her. They were sceptical of her testimony, influenced to some extent by their own perceptions of her as having dubious credibility as a victim. The police did attempt to check her story out but her boyfriend, who was also a mate of MR's, provided him with an alibi that was accepted by police at the time, despite its flimsy nature. She told a reporter later:

They weren't treating me seriously. As far as they were concerned, I was just some bimbo. I wasn't important enough for them to go to any trouble. But I was a decent young girl who'd got in with the wrong crowd. And it wasn't as if I was out at a party with him when I was raped. I was home in bed. ([53] p 22)

This woman did finally see MR take the stand more than ten years later, charged with raping her, but by then he had sexually assaulted at least 26 other women.

As MR's modus operandi became better known, and the frequency of his attacks increased, his victims were less likely to have their allegations doubted. This was obviously reinforced by the fact that most of these women had no prior relationship with MR and were attacked in their homes. On occasion, however, doubts were still expressed by the police, and impacted hugely on the woman concerned. Kathleen described how this process affected her:

About three days after it happened I was up at the station talking with [the detectives] and they turned around and said, 'Come on Kathleen, we know you were making all this up. We know you were having an affair and you were having sex that morning and it got a bit rough and you made all this up just so your husband doesn't find out.' My God! What I said to them I probably can't repeat but I told them what to do with themselves! So I walked home with them literally following me in the police car saying, 'We're sorry, we're sorry, blah blah blah', and when I got home they were hanging off the phone saying, 'We know that's not what happened and we just had to see what your reaction was and if you hadn't reacted like that the we would have been a bit suspicious.' I felt like punching them! (Kathleen)

She said it concerned her particularly that up until this point she was sure they were getting on with the investigation and moving closer towards finding her attacker. She felt aghast when she realised:

I'm not even on the same planet, you aren't even as close as I thought you were, or as far into the investigation as I thought you were. (Kathleen)

Her partner, to whom she was engaged at the time and later married, was also regarded suspiciously by the police, and accused by them of knowing who the attacker was, possibly even of putting him up to it. Her parents said the police told them he was not suitable for their daughter and she could 'do better'. Detectives spent hours questioning him until they were satisfied he had not had anything to do with the attack.

Kathleen also said she felt judged by the police when they commented on her choice of night attire.

I had worn just a camisole top and underwear to bed and I remember one of them saying to me, 'Oh, is that all you wore to bed?' That sort or attitude, that sort of male attitude: 'Maybe if you had worn a winceyette nightie it might not have happened.' (Kathleen)

Connie also felt initially that maybe the police did not believe her. She felt acutely aware that her lack of visible injuries made her claims of having been raped seem dubious to the young officers attending the scene.

I basically thought that what was happening was that they didn't believe me. In hindsight you feel lonely, you feel absolutely filthy, you want to go to the toilet but you can't go to the toilet because they want specimens and they keep on saying to you, 'Look we'd love you to go to the toilet but you need to be examined, you need to give specimens.' I thought maybe that they didn't actually know what to do with me. I wasn't sitting there cut to pieces, there was no sign of being raped, my face wasn't bruised or battered, I wasn't bleeding, there was no physical sign at all. I think they actually didn't know, I don't think there was anyone there that actually knew. And no one was talking to me. (Connie)

Gender of the interviewing officer

An issue long debated involves whether or not it is preferable to have women police officers available to interview female rape victims. On one level it seems as if this would be obviously desirable and preferred by complainants, but the research has been less clear-cut [54-57]. While some victims/survivors have indicated a strong preference for female police officers, most consider other attributes to be more important. These include an officer's knowledge and professionalism, as well as the extent to which they convey sensitivity and empathy for the victim. As the experiences of many women have shown, there is no guarantee of being treated in a caring manner simply by virtue of the officer's gender. In fact, some rape victims have complained that police women may be more judgmental and harsher in their attitudes than police men [55-57].

Blaming and judgmental attitudes are more likely to be expressed in situations where victims are perceived as being at risk of 'asking for it' by their dress, drinking or behaviour. Most of MR's victims were immune from such judgments, given the circumstances surrounding their attacks by this invasive, stranger-rapist. Most said it was irrelevant to them whether the police officers they interacted with were male or female. One woman, for instance, said that when she rang the police to report the attack, it mattered little to her who answered the phone – as she said:

> *It didn't matter at that stage – as long as there was a human being at the end of the phone, that was fine. (Kathleen)*

She did add, however, that she began feeling uncomfortable as more and more male officers arrived on the scene:

> *There were heaps of people. There would have been, maybe three detectives, plain clothes and half a dozen, maybe more ... There were about three or four cars. Talk about not wanting to make a scene! Bombarded with them, yeah. But there were no women, no women policemen.*
>
> *At the time, I probably didn't worry too much but as the questions kept coming it did hit me that I would rather be speaking to a woman, and I never had that ... I didn't feel that comfortable 'cause I couldn't say a lot of the stuff I wanted to say or that I felt I needed to say. I couldn't, I just couldn't. I felt embarrassed, yeah, that's the word for it, I felt embarrassed. (Kathleen)*

Raquel maintained that it was being interviewed by a woman that helped her talk without feeling embarrassed.

> *There was no embarrassment, there was no shame, there was nothing like that. I had no problem talking to her. It was probably easier having a female police officer, and yes, I would say that did make it more comfortable for me. I can only guess because I've never experienced giving the statement to a male so I can't compare ... I honestly don't believe any male, whether they're a police officer or not, is going to feel completely comfortable hearing a female talking about the details of rape. I think a female is going to be able to deal with it a lot better. (Raquel)*

Several women commented that being interviewed by a male detective interview felt totally inappropriate, with one stating:

> *A man interviewed me! Now that was ridiculous. It was ridiculous having a man there because, he was totally embarrassed, really embarrassed. I don't think he asked me the right questions ... I just remember him not wanting to ask me any questions that were sensitive, but not because he was being sensitive to me, but because he was too embarrassed to ask.*
>
> *I think it would have been a sensible thing to do [have a woman interviewer]. You've just been violated by a man, I suppose at the time you're in shock, but you don't trust any men. Luckily a friend of mine was with me, and I don't think I minded too much, but I think the most sensible thing to do would have been to put me with a woman ... They probably would have got more out of me, if they wanted to get the story straight out, fast ... He obviously didn't get what he needed to get out of*

me, because I had to go and do it again the next day ... he didn't get the nitty gritty that he needed to get. (Helen)

Being interviewed again the following day, by a woman detective, was a completely different experience. As she described it:

She was more compassionate and tried to make sure as much as possible that I was comfortable and got what I needed. (Helen)

She also felt she was in a better space to provide the information needed the day after the attack. She described how she responded to the immediate impact, and how that affected how she could manage being interviewed:

I felt that I'd left my body and I don't think I'd come back. I wasn't really there, you know. I was just going through the motions and stuff. But by the next day, you're back and you realise it's reality again, and in my case, I probably thought, I want to give the police as much as possible to find out who the hell this is, who did this. But that night you're just not there – well, I wasn't anyway. (Helen)

Marie, who had been attacked by MR in 1975, said she had specifically asked for a female detective at the time but was told there were none available. Explaining why this was her preference, she stated:

My father died when I was young – I was only nine. There was just my sister and myself and my mother. I'd lived in an environment with mainly women. I had a lot of male friends, but I wasn't really talking on that sort of level with people. It just would have been easier with a female. It was really my first sexual encounter with anybody. I wasn't naïve but it was just really difficult to talk about all that, and with a male. (Marie)

When she was contacted by the police 20 years later to see if she would consider appearing in court at MR's trial, she was relieved that she could deal extensively with female police detectives.

It felt very different. I don't think I would have probably gone through with it if I hadn't had a policewoman. She had more empathy. She shared part of herself with me as well, she told me things about herself, how her husband had died in the police helicopter and I think one of the interviews was around about the time of the anniversary. She told me about that and how she felt and how people had treated her. She was easy to relate to, I had a rapport with her, but if it was a man – I can't imagine a man doing that. (Marie)

In contrast, another woman felt completely satisfied with how a male detective interviewed her:

> He was really good, you know. He looked really sympathetic, without being pitying. I found him really good ... I didn't find him condescending or blaming or any of those things. He was soft, I suppose. (Lorna)

She also valued the opportunity to have a positive experience with a man:

> I think having a guy was good actually, because you have just been through this horrendous experience by a guy and having a nice guy there sort of counteracted it. You could easily end up with an attitude that they all suck ... I think it was actually helpful in some ways. I saw that they can be decent. Before that, I knew there were good guys out there but I hadn't seen many of them. So in some ways it was good for me to release some stuff, it was good having [male detective] there instead of a woman – in my case I could have ended up screwed up for years! (Lorna)

Suzanne was impressed with how the senior police involved in the investigation were able to relate so well to the women. She commented:

> Although they were guys they still put themselves in our shoes and thought about it from our perspective. They were good like that. And they pushed me along when I started having doubts through the trial about how my case was going to stand up. They were great, really supportive. (Suzanne)

Managing police errors and oversights

Despite the positive treatment most of these women received from the police, mistakes did happen which at times had potentially serious consequences. One that affected several women resulted from their not being sent for immediate medical examination following the attack.

Jennifer had not actually been raped but the chance of forensic evidence being obtainable existed in her case, since she had scratched MR. She said the woman detective who later interviewed her was really angry that she had not been sent for a medical examination:

> As [she] said to me, whilst I hadn't been raped, they weren't to know I wasn't just saying that because I didn't want to admit it. (Jennifer)

The detective's concern is fully supported by research evidence showing that one of the most common responses to a sexual assault is for the victim/survivor to minimise what has happened, and to struggle with defining herself as a victim of rape [42, 58].

Raquel felt the police who arrived on the scene that night made a grave oversight in not immediately having her physical injuries medically examined. She had been hit hard on the head and lost a lot of blood.

> It's probably a little bit slack on their part. If I had been really badly injured they would have taken me to hospital, you know, but because I was walking and talking fine they didn't concede that there was anything wrong with me. God, I could have collapsed an hour later! (Raquel)

As a result of what she called a 'mix-up' with her papers, Shelley said MR was charged with only one count of rape in relation to her when in fact he had raped her twice.

> I was quite annoyed but I mean not enough to sort of rock the world because I knew that really would make no difference to the outcome. It was just that it wasn't acknowledged really that it was more than once that it happened to me. (Shelley)

Another 'mix-up' resulted in Gabriel's case almost not being proceeded with because of confusion over whether or not she had been raped. It was months after Gabriel had been attacked that the police were re-interviewing her when the detective realised that technically she had been, because she had felt MR's penis between her labia.

> I was quite shocked, especially in terms of the word 'rape' and what it implies. The difference between sexual assault and rape. Just the word was quite a shift. And the fact that it was taken so much more seriously. Like, 'Oh God, this is much more serious, because we have to change the charge' and, you know, all this kind of thing. It wasn't attempted rape anymore, it was rape. Like more of a violation. (Gabriel)

On the other hand, she struggled to use the word 'rape' in relation to her experience and felt this was 'false':

> I didn't feel like I had been raped. Because I wasn't totally penetrated, I wasn't entered. So I felt a bit funny about this big heavy rape charge for myself. Before it was attempted rape and I could handle that. It felt like a lie in a sense. Strange. It felt very hard for my family to understand too, that it went from an attempted rape to a rape. They say why and you go, 'Well ...'. It was very confusing for everyone. (Gabriel)

In Shelley's case, she made a mistake that could have had serious repercussions later, then felt it was compounded by the actions of others. When she was shown photographs of the items found in MR's possession, she thought she saw a camisole of hers there. She made a statement to that effect, then a month later found hers in her daughter's drawer. She found it difficult deciding to tell the police:

> They were disappointed but I felt really bad disappointing them and I thought, 'Will I tell them or not?' because they were so pleased they'd actually found something that had belonged to me. (Shelley)

She did and hoped the issue was resolved, but this statement still found its way into defence counsel's hands.

> I felt a little bit let down by the police that there had been a communication problem and unfortunately the defence had that information. He really hassled me on that. He'd say, 'You were wrong with the camisole, are you wrong with anything else?' I felt that they'd [police] exposed me unnecessarily to that sort of questioning and I found that really, really hard. I felt like I had to claw my way out of it really. (Shelley)

The attack on Patricia was initially viewed as a robbery, something that she said she accepted, in part because she compared what happened to her with another woman she knew whose attackers had sodomised her for five hours. It was not until she was in the witness chair describing photographs from the crime scene that the prosecutor said he realised they demonstrated that MR's intention had been rape. There were such clear linkages with the other women's cases showing how he gathered and used cushions and pillows beforehand to use in the attacks. Next day in court further evidence was presented as to how MR had stalked her and she finally realised, with somewhat of a shock, how close she had come to being raped.

Patricia felt aggrieved that the police lost a scarf that she believed MR to have left in her home. She said:

> So I've got this scarf and finally they [police] came to pick it up, to take it away for forensic evidence. It was so smelly and horrible. Whatever they look for, there was nothing there, they couldn't find anything, so then they delivered the scarf back to me. I went, 'Listen, I don't think that I am supposed to have this. What am I going to do with it?' So finally they picked it up and took it away again, and then they lost it! (Patricia)

At times those close to the victim/survivor intervened to ease her management of police processes. This occurred in Raquel's case, where she was attacked after midnight and up with the police all night before finally going home to rest. At 8am the police rang wanting her to go and give her statement:

> My mother was really furious … she felt that ringing at 8 o'clock in the morning was a little bit off. They wanted her to wake me up, they were expecting me to be woken up. She said, 'I'm not going to wake her up, she's still sleeping, I'm going to let her sleep so no, you can't speak to her.' (Raquel)

Connie's anxiety about whether the police believed her was triggered by another incident. She had only just arrived at her parents' place after giving a long statement when the police were on the phone asking her to return to the station.

> I went back, they took me upstairs and I said, 'Before we go any further, don't you believe me?' They said, 'Yeah, we believe you, why?' I said, 'So what am I doing here now?' What had happened was that the typist or whoever was doing the typing had spelt a particular word wrong in the statement … She must have been proofreading her typing and she thought, that's not the word she said, it's the word 'velcro' and she had spelt it wrong. It was just one page of my statement that she had retyped up and I had to go back in and sign the paper. (Connie)

She also described the impact that the police not believing her would have had.

> I probably was in a state in my head when they called me back that I was going to just say, 'Forget it, if you don't believe me, forget it. I'm outta here, eh. I've been through enough today, it's been a long day and I'm worn out.' (Connie)

Her reaction enhances our understanding of why some rape complainants later decide to retract their allegations – not because the allegation was false but because they fear others doubt their veracity [24, 31].

What is interesting is that although there were mistakes and errors made, some of which clearly angered the women, they usually felt able to forgive the police for these oversights if fundamentally they had a positive relationship with them. As one commented:

> I had a very positive relationship with the police and accepted a lot of their downfalls as well. In fact, I know that their processes weren't often wonderful and having to deal with 30 of them [victims] at different times, I

kind of accepted that, because each one of them as individuals were really nice to me. And that's why I could accept it. (Shelley)

Isabel said she felt empowered as a result of how the police relied on her for help with the investigation.

Okay, so they run the system, the police and the lawyers run the justice system, but they needed my help to do what they needed to do and they let me do it my way, a little bit. (Isabel)

The issue of post-interview care

An important aspect raised involved ascertaining how the victim/survivor is managing by the time she has completed her statement and ensuring she feels safe as she ventures back into the world. As one woman expressed it:

I think if the police are taking somebody's statement then they really need to ensure that that person is feeling safe before they go home, and that should be part of the procedure. You know, after five hours of giving a statement, 'How are you feeling right now? Are you okay to go home? Is there anyone I can call for you? Do you want me to arrange some support?' I think that is really important. We all too naturally assume that if people don't say anything they are okay ... I had to think about where I was going to live, how was I going to get my furniture across town, do I have any clothes for this evening, I need to talk to my mother, does [flatmate] know about this, is she going to come back to the house and find it cordoned off, has everyone been contacted? In times like that you are thinking so much about everyone else, you need to be sure that you are safe and that you feel okay and people need to ask you that all the time. (Gabriel)

In terms of their initial contact with the police, while most of the women felt they were well treated by the officers involved, some felt fuller explanations and consultation would have helped their management of these procedures. This was not aided by changes in police personnel.

Every single person would tell you a different story. Because a staff member would be there and then they would have to bugger off because there would be some crime somewhere and they would go off and someone else would come ... I mean, they were nice people and they were helpful when I spoke to them, but they were off doing other things. (Gabriel)

The case re-opened

For many of MR's earlier victims, years lapsed between the time they were attacked and initially reported it and the time when they found out who the offender was and heard he had been arrested.

Frances said it was several years after she had been attacked that a detective phoned her at work:

> I was really quite taken back because as soon as he said he was calling from Operation Harvey, I knew exactly what he was ringing about. But I never thought that the person that attacked me was responsible for all of those other attacks. I was quite shocked. (Frances)

Isabel also said when she was contacted, more than five years later, the call came through at her workplace, something she found difficult.

> It brought back bad memories. [Woman detective] was very good, I was glad to be working with her. It was a bit tricky having to do it in working hours. The other detective would come to the house at night but [she] wanted to see me in working hours and I didn't want to tell my work-mates, I couldn't really tell them what was happening. (Isabel)

Many of the women expressed their shock at discovering their attacker was a serial rapist, especially given the media publicity regarding the hunt for this particular perpetrator.

Raquel, however, said she was not at all surprised. Even though the police at the time had suggested she was the victim of a spontaneous street assault, she always felt otherwise.

> I knew when he raped me he'd done it before ... He knew what he was doing, he's a professional criminal, he was well prepared. I knew he was a professional criminal because he wore gloves and he had something to tie me up with, he was obviously carrying them, he was out with intent. (Raquel)

Shelley was relieved also because it meant an end to what she called her 'gloomy' mornings:

> I'd wake up in the morning and I'd feel really gloomy and I knew that he'd attacked again. And when I opened the paper it was, 'Serial Rapist Attacks' and I always knew that it had happened. It was a really awful feeling, just this totally black cloud oppressed feeling and once he was caught it was a fantastic feeling to know that it wasn't going to happen again. (Shelley)

One of the women who was most shocked was Marie. She had seen her attacker jailed 20 years previously, and had absolutely no idea that, following his release from prison, he had become the serial rapist now at the centre of such a massive police investigation. The police traced her through a former nursing colleague, who suggested they inform Marie's husband first and let him break the news:

> I was totally blown away. My husband had to tell me on the phone. I was actually at a ladies group ... He rang me there. He was really cagey and said, 'What time are you going to be home?' He didn't come out right and say, so I said, 'Well, what's the matter?' I thought something had happened. He went quiet. In the end he just had to tell me. I just dropped the phone. I couldn't talk to him. I was just totally shocked, that he [MR] could carry on doing that. I think that's what I found so hard to cope with, the fact that he didn't stop with his however many years he had in jail, he just got out and got worse. (Marie)

She was not at all pleased to have this part of her life dragged to the surface again.

> As far as I was concerned, I had dealt with it. It was part of my life that was behind me. I had been through several lots of counselling and I felt that I had really dealt with it ... I felt that it was where it should be and to drag it all up again – I just couldn't cope with that. I really wished they hadn't told me, but because they had I felt then that I had to follow through with what they wanted. (Marie)

The police were considerate in arranging to visit when her husband could be present, and having a woman police detective involved in the meetings. It was still a hard process to manage, especially having to read her initial court statement again.

> I found that very hard, to actually have to sit down and read through what I'd said. I did that with a counsellor – she was there for that first interview, but then I felt quite comfortable with [woman detective], so I was quite happy going through further interviews with her, just one to one. (Marie)

She found it difficult trying to recall details so many years later.

> I found it really difficult to remember. I felt that I should have remembered. I really felt, well, I'm not giving them what they want. As it progressed I could see where they were coming from, that I was sort of baseline and what I was saying was setting the scene for what he did in the future. I really felt I wasn't really giving them the information they wanted but I couldn't do any more than I could remember. (Marie)

One aspect appreciated by the women involved the improved communication. The high-profile nature of this investigation helped in motivating the police to consider the best ways of maintaining positive contact with the women and supporting them during the lead-up to MR's trial. Waiting for the trial is a difficult time for victims/survivors, particularly so in rape cases. In part this is because of the publicity given to the gruelling nature of rape trials and the low chances of securing a conviction. It is also difficult for victims given their own healing and survival journeys and the way in which the trial can interrupt this process, with the potential to retraumatise.

The officers involved in the investigation were committed to seeing MR convicted and understood the need for the women to be fully supported. The fact that there were multiple victims meant that the women became a force to be reckoned with, especially since so many of them were well-educated, professional women, highly articulate and assertive.

What frustrated some of the women was the long period of time waiting for the trial, particularly when there were long intervals with no communication.

> *After I identified him they didn't keep me informed. They rang me and said, 'Don't leave town as we've got him' and then they never kind of rang me so there I am not leaving town and I am having to ring them all the time with, 'Okay, what's going on now?' (Patricia)*

When some of the women complained that they were not being kept informed of trial developments, the police responded positively and began sending letters out. Helen said one of the hardest aspects was waiting to hear when the trial was going to commence, and why the dates kept changing.

> *In the end I initiated it and said, 'You've got to send us more letters, tell us what the hell is going on', because there were times when they'd say, 'Look, the trial's here', but then you didn't hear and then you're waiting to go to trial and then someone phones and says, 'Oh no, it's not happening for another six months'. You're going in like a roller coaster here, there was no communication to say, 'No, it's not actually going to be happening'. That was really hard, I actually suffered every time that happened. Emotionally you do, trying to prepare yourself for it ...*
>
> *I said, 'I know this is only another job to you.' For some of them it wasn't, they were really involved, but I said, 'I'm thinking about this every day. You've got three that you're thinking about. Every single day' ... They probably felt that they were doing enough, but when you live with*

something day by day, it's not enough. You need to know this guy is going to be put away or whatever you're feeling, and he's not going to be out there. Just those little silly things: are you making sure he can't get out? He can't get bail, can he? Because you don't know ... It would have been nice if there was someone to answer those questions and not feel silly about it. (Helen)

She said she did feel that the police listened to her and responded well, quoting them as saying to her:

'Well, thank you for having the courage to come forward and go to court. Thank you for telling me that about the communication. I understand it from your point of view now and we'll try and do something about it, however, understand we've got this skeleton staff, and dah dah dah.' (Helen)

Patricia also noted that once senior police involved with the case appreciated more fully what the women needed, information was much more forthcoming. Initiating the sending of newsletters with updates indicated willingness on the part of the police involved with this case to listen and learn from the women, a fact acknowledged directly by some of the detectives involved. They felt that this group of women were quite extraordinary in their intelligence and forth-rightness and while some police may have felt threatened and become defensive, these particular officers seemed willing to listen and enhance their understanding of how these processes impacted on victims/survivors.

Jennifer said there had been a big break in contact after MR was arrested and the women had been asked if they could identify any of the belongings seized from his van, and then the letters were useful as a way of keeping in touch.

Once you've been through all that stage of identifying things, there was a letter that came and said, 'This is what we think is going to happen blah, blah, blah.' Leading up to the trial, before they actually got in contact with you, there were another two letters I think. It was good, it told you what was happening and when they expected it to happen etc, etc, and always a 'Please feel free to contact us if you need anything', with numbers. (Jennifer)

She appreciated the police's efforts to keep them informed, laughing as she commented that it was *quite professional really – that's not like a government department at all!*

The police appointed dedicated officers to be available to the women in the lead-up to the trial. These were women detectives who made themselves available to answer queries, provide information and support the women through the build-up. Initially there was one such detective appointed, and after she left two others took over the role to support the women through the trial. Measures such as this, and the positive attitudes of the investigative team, impressed Marie in particular, whose earlier experience with the police had been much less sympathetic and supportive.

Property retention and return

As well as the women's bodies being forensically examined following the rape, objects from the crime scene are often collected and sent away for forensic testing. Most of the women had at least some items of clothing or bedding retained for examination, a fact they generally accepted as necessary to further the investigation. Difficulties often arose, however, in relation to the eventual return or otherwise of those items. What many of the women expressed was the need for fuller explanation regarding what these items were needed for, and what choices they had about their possible return.

Some felt somewhat aggrieved at the disappearance of expensive or favourite items. Gabriel had her only pair of boots retained by the police and said they were returned three months later, and only *because I kicked up such a bloody stink*. Other items, such as her bedding, and the extension cord MR used around her neck, were never returned, and nor did she think they were used in the trial.

One woman's duvet, pillows, dressing gown and night attire were all retained, with little explanation offered by the police.

> They may have said to me, 'We're taking it for evidence,' but that was all and there was certainly no clear explanation that I wasn't going to get it back and that actually surprised me. (Shelley)

Afterwards it was all destroyed, which she was upset about as the duvet was part of an expensive set. Her insurance company initially turned down a claim she submitted until the police provided a letter of validation. Another item retained was a pair of her pantyhose that MR had used to bind her during the attack. These she heard nothing about until she saw them displayed on television news, and felt 'horrified' when she recognised them as her own.

Following MR's arrest in May 1996, the police showed the women photographs of items found in his possession, in case they could recognise any of them. This was also a difficult process for many to undertake, and some said they appreciated being asked if they were willing to do this, rather than being forced to look at these images. Gabriel said seeing these items impacted on her greatly.

> He [MR] took souvenirs from women, so you would be looking at some-body else's underpants, photographs of women's bras, women's personal jewellery, women's photographs and ID shots, and at the end of it all I just felt sick. There was nothing of mine, but it started to make it a bit more personal for other women and that was horrible. (Gabriel)

There were diverse responses to property being retained without further word from the police. Some of the women felt these were not items they would particularly want to see again and accepted their loss. Those whose property was returned were often aghast at how insensitively this aspect was managed. In some cases an unknown police officer suddenly arrived on the doorstep with the items in question, without the woman being given a choice regarding whether or not she wanted to see these items again. The police did not always seem to appreciate how traumatic it could be for a woman to see the clothes worn on the night she was raped. From the police's pers-pective, it was simply time to return the property so it was returned. The condition of some items meant that, ideally, complainants would have been warned about the state of the goods in question. Isabel, for example, found it distressing when her property came back with crosses marking the spots where semen stains had been found.

> They took away all the clothes that I'd been wearing when I was attacked and they gave them back sometime later, but I don't know why they bothered giving them back because they all had little holes cut out of them. They came back in those evidence bags. (Isabel)

Raquel had the pair of jeans she had been wearing returned to her, without any advance warning, and with a big hole cut out of the crotch area where material had been removed for forensic analysis. She had been attacked and raped in her car; when the police had finished their examination of the vehicle, she was told to arrange for it to be collected.

> When [boyfriend] went to pick my car up he was really, really upset seeing the seat down because it made him think about everything, and the first thing he did was put the seat back up ...

Raquel's parents were shocked that her blood was still in the car.

The police should have said, 'Look, the car, there's still blood, it's a bit of a mess. Why don't we just get it valet-cleaned and we'll just give you the bill?' Honestly, giving someone back a car that's got their daughter's blood everywhere in the backseat, because I'd been bleeding from the head injuries – that's not very nice ... (Raquel)

As she observed, as far as the police were concerned, they had completed their examination and were returning the victim's property, a task that may have been procedurally correct but which also needed to be handled with empathy and sensitivity.

Reaction to news of MR's arrest

The arrest of MR was a potentially momentous event – finally their attacker had a face and a name and could not come after them again.

I was really relieved, relieved that he was caught and I could put a face to it. Up until then I was always wondering. I never saw him through the attack so I didn't have a face to go by or anything. It sort of put a full stop there. (Kathleen)

For her it settled an uneasy sense that had persisted since she was raped. The police had initially been suspicious of her complaint and challenged her story, then later queried whether the attack was linked in some way to her husband and his associates, whom they viewed as 'undesirable'. This suspicion was further fuelled by comments MR made during the attack implying involvement by her husband, raising doubts even in Kathleen's mind. It was clearly important to have this issue resolved, for both of them.

[Husband] was relieved as he knew he was innocent all along and he had to cope with all these people thinking that maybe he did and even me thinking that maybe he did. It went on for a long time, so it was really just a relief, yeah ... (Kathleen)

Gabriel also described the relief she felt at the news:

The sense of relief was overwhelming. That other women weren't being attacked. I was so excited. I don't think anyone could really understand how exciting it is to hear that. He didn't keep going. Initially, when you are attacked, you have this sordid sense that he is coming back to get me, which is all part of the shock and everything else, because he is out there on the streets. I would have these nightmares, like, 'Oh God he's seen my car registration and he could easily find out where I'm staying', and stuff like that. So I was relieved. Especially since a lot of my friends lived in the central city. It was just a worry. Every weekend you would be worried. (Gabriel)

Again, not all the women reacted the same. Shelley expressed surprise that she seemed relatively unmoved by news of MR's arrest.

Oh yeah, he's been arrested. It was like confirm or deny. It was just like, oh well, that's good. One of the beneficial things was that it was good to be able to tell the children because initially the children wanted him caught that night. There was a fear, which I shared with them, that he was going to come back. So my reaction, even though it was a ho hum reaction, I felt safer, that he was locked away and that he wasn't going to come back. (Shelley)

Another woman described her reaction to the phone call informing her of his arrest:

It was okay, but it really didn't mean anything because all the damage had been done. It was good to know that this person, thing, had been, if it was him, found and put away, but by that time, the damage had been done. And although it's probably selfish, I would have thought, 'That's great', because other women weren't going to go through what I'd been through. I think at the time it was like 'So bloody what? I'm not feeling too good about it. He's done it.' So it wasn't like 'whoopy doo', it wasn't like, 'This is celebration time'. (Helen)

Conclusion

Researchers in an Australian rape study in the 1990s identified the potential conflict between the victim's needs and police procedures:

A common source of concern is the perceived failure of the police to strike a consistent and compassionate balance between the victim/survivors' needs and the demands of investigative and administrative priorities. ([5] p 12)

In the aftermath of rape, women struggle to regain power and autonomy, a process that can be either enhanced or undermined by the police response. The police may feel a professional responsibility to retain control of the proceedings, and their own struggle may be in relinquishing a little of that control. As well as being what the victim/survivor needs, responding empathically to the victim is of paramount importance if her trust and co-operation are to be secured.

To my knowledge there has been only one other review published of police investigations into a serial rapist that retrospectively considered the victims/survivors experiences with the police. This was the Bernardo Investigation Review [59], assessing the investigation of Paul Bernardo for 18 known rapes and sexual assaults, plus three homicides, in Ontario, Canada. In recommending what was needed for 'A Strategic Defence Against Serial Predators', Justice Campbell included reference to the importance of sound sexual assault case management systems and sexual assault investigation training. He emphasised in particular that this case reinforced the need for 'sensitivity to the special concerns of sexual assault survivors and the potential for their revictimisation through the investigative, prosecution, and judicial processes', as well as stressing the importance of such factors as employing interviewing techniques enabling full disclosure of the assault, keeping victims informed, providing officer continuity, and utilising victim support services. It is apparent that Justice Campbell recognised these aspects of victim care as important features within the coordinated case management system he recommended overall.

Large and complex cases such as this one can provide good training for police organisations. In New Zealand this became apparent during Operation Park [60] and was extended during Operations Harvey and Atlas as the police closed in on MR. Detectives involved in this investigation told me afterwards how much they learned from these women about the most supportive and appropriate ways of interacting with them.

Some of the women commented also how important it was for them that a positive relationship was established. Several observed that there was a clear need for a special unit of trained detectives to interview rape complainants. In part this was because some felt that they were dealt with by officers with little understanding of rape, or empathy with the victims, yet in the lead-up to the trial became aware of how supportive other police could be. This prompted one woman to say:

> I think they actually need a team for this sort of work, because you get the wrong people and it can shut you down. (Ann)

Some of the women were aware that the high profile of their attacker undoubtedly resulted in the police prioritising them in terms of victim care and support. As Gabriel observed:

When I was attacked the police already knew that there was a serial rapist out there and had a very good idea that this was part of it. And perhaps I did get a lot of special treatment and then definitely throughout the trial, in fact all of us did because it was so unusual and it had to look good because shit, everyone was looking at them. It had to look good. Imagine if it wasn't handled very well. I mean, God, how would the country feel to find that there was a serial rapist and the police force were all over the place and didn't give a shit? It had to be handled very well because it was in the limelight. (Gabriel)

As she alludes to here, it was in the preparation for court that many special measures were implemented. The next chapter considers how the women managed and survived the gruelling process of testifying in court against the man who sexually attacked them.

4

Surviving the trial

Going to court is invariably an arduous experience, particularly for victims of rape facing cross-examination in the stand. In an adversarial justice system, such as that in the United Kingdom, Australia and New Zealand, the victim appears in court as a witness, and can be questioned by both the prosecution and defence. The system is oriented primarily around the legal requirements involved in bringing an accused person to justice, with victims often feeling marginalised within court proceedings. Many find it difficult to accept that the personal harm sustained by individuals is not the over-riding concern of the court, and that the defendant is the focus of the case. As one major study conducted with the victims of sexual and domestic violence concluded: 'For those who sought redress in the criminal justice system, the single greatest shock was the discovery of just how little they mattered' ([1] p 581).

Rape trials are particularly notorious for the way in which the credibility of the victim is attacked in court, with the emphasis typically being placed on showing how she may have 'asked' to be raped or in some way brought the attack upon herself. This is often argued by the defence raising questions designed to suggest that she is dishonest and inconsistent in her testimony, and of dubious moral character. Victims have often described feeling that the trial is experienced as a re-victimisation, echoing in many ways the trauma of the initial rape [2-8]. An Australian researcher who followed 150 rape cases through the courts concluded: 'This is state-sanctioned victimisation' ([9] p 125).

Since most rapes are committed by men already known by the victim, sometimes men they have already been in an intimate relationship with, the case typically rests on the question of consent. Assessing the victim's credibility becomes pivotal, and defence lawyers become experts at insinuation and innuendo – the more they can diminish the worth of the complainant's testimony, the higher their client's is elevated. For example, a woman who enjoyed writing stories for children had this ability twisted into a negative by a defence lawyer who suggested that this implied a fanciful imagination and tendency towards story-telling – how could the jury possibly know if this allegation arose within her factual or fictional life? [10]

The opportunity for such attacks to be mounted by the defence is significantly reduced in the minority of cases involving stranger rape scenarios, where less scope exists for implying that the woman 'asked for it'. Most of MR's victims were violated after he broke into their homes while they were sleeping, providing little scope for suggesting they had provoked their own attack.

Following his arrest, hopes were held by some of the women that he would plead guilty, as Joseph Thompson had done, and spare them the ordeal of the trial. Others, however, rightly predicted that MR was not the sort of man to be cooperative and the police who arrested him were also not surprised that the only cases he admitted were the six for which compelling DNA evidence existed. Thus one woman said the police:

> [M]ade it clear to me that Rewa was basically going to use the system to his advantage and be a 'Hollywood', if you want to call it that – 'Oh gosh, I'm on the news, I'm a big man.' (Connie)

Gabriel was furious that MR's actions subjected them to a court trial in addition to the rapes. When she heard he had pleaded not guilty, she wondered:

> How long is it going to take now and why is it dragging on? Another two years of my life, another year before I have to go to court. God, I wish I could get over it and I wish he had pleaded guilty and gone to jail and that would have been the end of it. And the fact that he was so cocky enough to deny all of that! (Gabriel)

It was as if MR was still 'calling the shots', still exerting his influence over the women's lives. The trial lasted three months and was held in the High Court in Auckland, before a jury comprising six men and six women.

Hearing the charges

The women attacked by MR all experienced multiple offences for which he could, technically, have been charged. These were reduced to 45 charges on which he eventually stood trial. Such a process is undertaken on the basis of ensuring representative charges are laid and the more serious allegations adequately covered, while more minor offences are 'counted in'. The ways in which charges are reduced and plea-bargains entered become familiar to those involved regularly in the criminal justice system, but from the outside may appear confusing and unfair [11].

Having offences 'counted in' felt, to many, as if specific offences against them had been 'counted out', and they felt aggrieved that MR was not charged for other offences he had committed against them. For example, one woman expressed her feelings forcefully when she described how angry she felt about this process:

> (M)ine just became one charge of rape and I was really pissed off about that. I thought he should have had to face every single charge. (Karen)

Raquel also said she was outraged that he was not being charged for the money he stole from her:

> Why he isn't he being done for theft? He stole $100 off me. I think they just dropped it. I said to them, 'Why? He committed a crime, why isn't he being done for it?' (Raquel)

Raquel was one of the six women for whom DNA evidence existed and who could have been spared a court appearance. She and the others chose still to go to court, motivated by a desire to support the other women involved.

> The main reason I went to court and went through with it all was for the girls who were not DNA linked, because we knew he was the one. I just wanted to do everything within my power to give them a bit more support because I am just so thankful that I was DNA linked and in my case it would have been just so much harder. I really felt for the girls that weren't and I just wanted to make it a little bit easier. (Kathleen)

Some of the women expressed the hope that since he was DNA-linked on some of the charges, MR would plead guilty to the others. Unfortunately for the women, he refused and so one of the biggest trials in New Zealand's criminal history commenced. Karen expressed the outrage of many:

> Because he was going to go down for the six that there was DNA for, if he was going to plead guilty to them, why not plead guilty to all of them instead of putting us what he put us through? (Karen)

Connie, who had felt such a strong link to Susan Burdett when she was raped, said in many ways she decided to go to court for her:

I could have died, we all could have died. I could have got beaten up, I didn't and possibly what was I saying to myself? That a woman that I didn't even know, died from this? By the same hands, by the same indivi- dual. And really, what was wrong with me? I was still living. I wanted to die, sometimes I wished I had of, but she died, she didn't have a choice ... [She was] someone who couldn't speak; we were all given the opportunity to speak. I guess I really went for her, and I hope in some way that some of the other girls did too. I know I did. (Connie)

Also asked to appear in court was Marie, who had been attacked by MR in 1975, since she could provide similar fact evidence from early in his criminal career.

Preparing for court

A difficult time was spent waiting for the trial to commence. Twenty-two months passed between when MR was arrested and the trial began, and before this there was the time lapse between when each woman was attacked and the offender was apprehended. For half the women interviewed, more than five years had passed since they were attacked. Victims/survivors typically describe the period before a trial commences as an anxious time, where their lives feel as if they have been put on hold. Such long delays can impact negatively and inter- rupt the recovery process [6].

Several of the women observed how difficult it was waiting for the trial, with the following comment being typical:

Waiting for the trial, you felt like you couldn't really move on until it was over. (Jennifer)

It is difficult to plan trips away or move on with life generally knowing that a major disruption is scheduled at an indefinite time in the future. Many of the women expressed dissatisfaction with the constant changes to court dates, and likened this process to the highs and lows of an emotional roller-coaster.

There was that whole year from when they caught him till when the court case started looking like it might happen – this huge void. We didn't really get that much contact with the police, there was a long period where it seemed like there was nothing. (Karen)

Other women also talked about how difficult they found this period, with one of the hardest aspects to manage being the lack of certainty regarding when they were likely to be called. Not only did they feel they were at the whim of a system much bigger than them, but they could not advise those who were going to support them as to when they would be needed. Such experiences could trigger in the women a sense of their ongoing powerlessness.

In the aftermath of rape, the victim/survivor looks for ways to regain a sense of her own power, yet enters a criminal justice system oriented around its own processes and agendas [1, 4, 6, 7, 9, 12, 13]. These women were not unusual in experiencing frustration with the delays and lack of information they were given; being part of such a large case was unusual, and may have helped to strengthen the women's resolve to be more proactive in asking for what they needed. The police and prosecutors also had a large investment in wanting to see a repeat serious offender like MR convicted, and knew they needed the women's cooperation. As several of the police said later, they also found this particular group of victims were highly articulate and used to working with professionals, and the women were not afraid to challenge them when they considered it necessary.

A responsive partnership evolved, with the women letting the police know what they expected or needed and the police endeavouring to provide that, resulting in this group of complainants receiving fuller support and preparation than is usual. When the women voiced their dissatisfaction with the delays and lack of information about what was happening in the 22 months between MR's arrest and the commencement of the trial, the police responded positively with several measures designed to better meet the women's needs as they struggled to manage their anxiety. A senior detective later commented that he and his colleagues were on a 'learning curve' throughout this process as they endeavoured to understand what the women needed and provide them with optimal levels of support. His conclusion: 'The kind of treatment these women got was the kind every woman who's been raped should get' ([14] p 181).

One of the measures introduced involved the police assigning two female dedicated officers whose primary role was to provide on-going support and liaison with the women during the lead-up to the trial and throughout its duration. Attempts were made to keep a sense of continuity, and when one of these detectives left the team, she was replaced with another. A second measure involved the issuing of written news bulletins, which the police sent out periodically to keep the women in touch with developments and explain delays. During the trial a room was set aside for the women at the court so that they had access to private space, although in practice many said they felt welcome in the room used by the police team.

For most of the women this trial marked the first time they had stepped inside a courtroom and they were understandably nervous. Their apprehension was heightened by media interest in the case and the sense of responsibility many felt for ensuring their evidence would help to convict this rapist.

Many spoke highly of the efforts the police and prosecution team went to in order to help in preparing them for court. A further special measure saw the women being asked to come in individually to meet with the senior police team and the prosecutors several months before the trial began. This meeting was also useful in enabling each of the three prosecutors to be assigned those women with whom they established a positive rapport.

Organising these team meetings in the chambers reflected a strong commitment on the part of the police and prosecutors and was greatly appreciated. It was also, as Gabriel expressed it, *hellishly intimidating,* an occasion which many of the women shuddered about as they recalled the anxiety it provoked.

> *I'm quite a confident person, I speak to large groups so it didn't really worry me but I thought, 'My God, if you're sort of a teensy bit shy or not used to being with people who are wearing suits and in positions of power, it would just be a totally daunting exercise. Totally daunting.' (Shelley)*

> *There were way too many people there. Although I could see what they were doing and the intentions behind what they were doing were right, they'd allocated us all 45 minutes so we weren't rushed, you had time to ask questions, they had a little patter going of exactly what was going to happen, who was doing what and whose job was what, but it was like, 'Wow, who are all these people!' (Karen)*

Shortly before the trial the women were given the chance to view the courtroom and hear how it would be set up, an opportunity rarely extended to witnesses. Procedures such as this conveyed to the women the fact that this trial was being treated a little differently from the usual. Suzanne, for example, said she was given a depiction of the court's layout and found that reassuring:

> *They gave me a map of where everyone was sitting a few days before so I could study it. I knew exactly who was going to be sitting everywhere and it was good, it made me feel heaps easier. (Suzanne)*

While such measures helped, they also reinforced the fact that the women's day in court was approaching. Frances said she was so anxious in the lead-up to the trial that she almost hoped the charges involving her would be dropped. She had been attacked while out running, and had not been raped, and said:

> Leading up to the trial, I kept thinking that come to the crunch, they won't need me. They had all these women that had had such awful, awful attacks. Often I'd think they'd decide that they didn't need my information anyway. When I met the prosecutors, Simon Moore said. 'You're probably wondering why we would want you as a witness', and then he said again the similar fact thing helps tie a lot of other bits together, other things that happened in other cases. It would have been around then that it really hit home that we were going to go ahead with it. (Frances)

One question many were anxious about concerned where MR was going to be in the courtroom and how securely he would be held. Ann found being given this information both useful and harrowing:

> She [policewoman] took me to the court. She took me into the room, told me where I would stand, where my sister would be, they told us where Rewa was going to be, she even sat in there and pulled out the handcuffs and said, 'This is where he's going to be.' I was thinking, 'Could he ever get away and get me?' and she showed me, 'This is what it's like once he's in here. He's going to have to lift up the whole wooden plank to get out of here. He's going to be flanked by three prison officers, Ann', she said 'and one of them is really big!' But when I did go in they had a replica of Rewa which was, 'Oh God!' Like how he looked and how he put his balaclava on ... They showed it to the jury to show how it's scary and how he looked to a woman ... His face was sort of covered, but you saw like the height and everything, and the pants, and I was sort of like, 'Oh my God!' (Ann)

As the trial unfolded, each woman was brought in to court for a briefing with the prosecutor immediately before they would present their evidence. The women appreciated the intention behind this but not all felt it occurred in ways that would best meet their needs.

Gabriel found the latter process difficult and disturbing:

> I was annoyed that I wasn't briefed on the procedure of testifying until the day I testified. I came in in the morning and he [prosecutor] said, 'You'll either be on this afternoon', and I just about leapt out of my chair, 'or you could come back tomorrow, it all depends if we can slot this person in or not.' It was all just a bit of a nightmare ... I said, 'Well, I don't feel very good about the fact that I've come in here thinking that I'm just going to

be briefed and now you're telling me that I could be testifying in a matter of three hours time. I haven't got time to prepare myself, or psych myself up for this or arrange proper support.' And he said, ' But we've found that for most women it is better to be briefed in the morning and then go in the afternoon.' And I said, 'Well I'm not most women, I'm myself! And my support person needs notification so that she can get time off work and I'm so not happy about you just assuming that everything will fit into place and I will go in there. This is a really important time for me and I'm really pissed off with you!'

He was shocked. This is the second time I've met him and he just kept talking, kept talking and put his foot in his mouth and talked about procedure and all the rest of it until I said, 'I'm not interested in the procedure right at this second, I'm more interested in my mental state of well-being than your procedure actually.' Then he said, 'Oh God, of course you're upset and who can blame you.' And then he was very understanding about it. (Gabriel)

Helen also felt it would have been better to have been given a little more notice before testifying, saying of the briefing she received:

It came a bit late, because I had dreams about it and what it was going to be like and it was very scary for me because you've no idea ... As soon as I knew I was going, you got the letter, then you start dreaming, it's like, 'Oh my God, he's going to be able to come across there and kill me!' You know they're not logical but you still want to know that there's ten people between you and him. Because if he can do it once, he can do it again. How do you know he hasn't got a knife, how do you know?

Maybe it might have helped me a bit to know, there's two body-guards on either side, there's all these people there – which I was told two days beforehand and that's great, but it would have been better if I had been told when I was actually starting to think about it. (Helen)

While the women all appreciated the efforts taken to equip them for court, some aspects were neglected that they wished had been covered. Marie, for instance, felt distracted at the level of movement and activity within the courtroom.

What really did throw me was people could get up and walk around while you were giving evidence, I found that very rude. I wasn't told to expect people to pop up and down and give out bits of paper. (Marie)

Frances wished the briefing had included more direction on how she could provide additional information. She felt a wrong impression was given when she said she had gone back out running after MR had attacked her while she was on a run one morning, without having the opportunity to comment as to how difficult this had been for her and the additional security measures that had been employed.

> *I was asked one question, 'Did you keep running?' by [defence lawyer] and I said, 'Yes,' thinking that he would come back with something about, 'Well, didn't you feel safe?' so I never got the chance to say that we took dogs and we bought alarms. We changed a whole lot of things – we didn't just carry on running. (Frances)*

How the courtroom was changed

Part of the preparation for the trial involved considering ways to promote a sense of safety for those testifying against MR. The court was rearranged so that the witness box was not in a direct line with the defendant, and special security measures were employed. These followed an incident that occurred earlier:

> *At the depositions hearing the little Japanese girl gave her evidence and at the end of it, he suddenly jumped up. No one knows what he was going to do but he jumped up and yelled and the detectives just grabbed him – they couldn't wait to get their hands on him, no doubt! ... I remember when I heard it [on the news] I just totally lost it. All I could think about was this poor little kid that was in this foreign country, that had been raped by this animal and at the depositions hearing this had happened. I was just so angry, but I guess the good thing that came out of that is that obviously they'd decided there was no way he was going to have the opportunity to do it again. They had him manacled into place every day. (Karen)*

As well as being handcuffed to the box, MR was escorted and kept in place by three prison officers. Several of the women said they were appreciative of the judge's flexibility in allowing such modifications:

> *In cases like this, if you can do things like what he did, allow the court room to be moved around to be sensitive to us – it was brilliant ... I think that having a sensitive judge was really good. (Lorna)*

At least one woman, however, felt that although the rearranging of the courtroom was well intentioned, it posed other difficulties. She struggled at how the witness box was now right alongside the jurors, making it both difficult to see them while nevertheless being acutely aware of their proximity:

> *I hated where I had to sit ... You're standing there giving testimony about the most intimate details of being raped to 12 total strangers. They're like*

this *(holds out arm)* far away from you. They never asked any of the victims, they just rearranged it to what they thought was right ... The thing is, they made a decision for a whole lot of women without asking the women. It's like, you're dealing with rape survivors here, ask them what they think, it's common sense. *(Kathleen)*

How the women experienced the prosecutor in court

The extensive preparation clearly paid off in the sense that the women felt better able to manage being on the witness stand and answering questions. Several of the women referred to the 'human' face all three prosecutors put on what could have felt like a large, impersonal case.

You'd walk into a courtroom and they'd straight away know you by name. I thought there's so many people involved in this case, but they still knew who each of us was. *(Frances)*

He [prosecutor] was really very professional but just put that little bit extra into it, treated you as a person, never as a case – that's how well he does his job. If you ever need a lawyer, he is the one! *(Kathleen)*

The efforts made by the police and prosecutors to know and relate to each woman individually were greatly appreciated and experienced as reassuring by many of the women:

Even the crown prosecutor said, 'From seeing you people we've realised that we're actually dealing with real people here', rather than, 'We've got a mass of 27 bloody women we've got to try to get through court.' *(Helen)*

She also said it was clear that the women challenged some of the police and prosecutors' perceptions about rape victims:

It was even brought home to me the perceptions held, even amongst these people, that women who get raped are not very intelligent, come from lower class backgrounds, are asking for it, are either prostitutes or dah, dah, dah ... and they're saying [about us], 'Actually, there's a lot of intelligent women coming through here.' *(Helen)*

Gabriel felt validated by the prosecutor and described what happened when she went in to have him show her round the courtroom.

When we were standing in the courtroom he said, 'I've been looking forward to meeting you so much.' And I said, 'Why?' And he said, 'Because of what you said to Malcolm Rewa.' And I said, 'What did I say?' And he said, 'Fuck off you idiot!' And I said, 'Did I say that?' And he said, 'Well, it's in your statement, bloody good show! I thought that was *fabulous. Hundreds of women thought it but you said it. Well done!' ... So it was nice to have that sense of him being familiar with my case before meeting me and him knowing all of that. (Gabriel)*

Marie said she felt all was going well during her briefing with the prosecutor until:

About halfway through he said, 'Well, how did you feel?' I wanted to say, 'Well how the hell do you think I felt, blindfolded with a gag in my mouth!' That sort of threw me, that question. I thought what a strange thing to ask me, how did I feel? I just said, 'Petrified.' (Marie)

She appreciated the prosecutor responding sympathetically when, after several hours of meeting into the evening with no dinner, she became tearful:

By 9 o'clock I just had had enough and I cried and I think that threw him a little bit. He said, 'Do you really feel you can go through with this?' He was quite concerned about me and gave me his home phone number and said, 'Look, you just give me a ring any time.' I really appreciated it, not that I used it, but it was nice. (Marie)

How the women experienced the police in court

The support of the police during the trial was positively commented on by all the women. The high profile of this case, and the number of victims and witnesses involved, resulted in a good investment of resources by the police to assist with trial preparation and management. A team of senior detectives was heavily involved throughout, providing good continuity for the women and enabling positive and trusting relationships to develop. Comments from the women attest to the importance of this:

They were all very caring and respectful. They all got on with their job, as far as I was concerned, very well. He was convicted and they won, the goodies won and the baddies lost. It was probably reassuring more than anything to see people like that in action. (Jennifer)

You weren't just a witness, you were actually a person to them, which was nice, so they were good, I can't fault them. I was pleasantly surprised really. (Helen)

They're all so matey, the police. It's a real boys' thing. They're all joking and carrying on. We had [head of police team] making up cups of tea – he's probably never made a cup of tea for a woman in his life, I'd say!

They looked after us. I didn't feel like I was up there by myself or that I shouldn't have been there or that I was in the way or anything like that. I felt that if I wanted to be there, they were happy for me to be there. (Karen)

Some women described specific incidents where they felt reassured by the police.

[Detective] used to accompany you in and out of the trial during the breaks, you'd have to walk past this area where Rewa was and I said to him, 'What would you do if I just ran over there and had a look at him? Would you stop me?' And he just turned around and said, 'He is such a piece of shit, who cares what he looks like!' And for me it was the right thing to say at the time, it was like, 'Yeah, it's true, he is a piece of shit!' (Jennifer)

As for the police, the Harvey team, I felt that they became like a caring little family. A lot of detective men are really hard, but the ones that I met came up when they saw you, 'Hi, how are you?' The detectives' wives came in, the superintendent's wife came in, they really cared. Their partners were working on this case and they wanted to come in and see what sort of man did this to these women. One of the detective's wives came in with their little baby, and some brought cakes – just to take the edge off what was happening ... I think they tried to make it as easy as they could for the victim – they looked after you. At a time like that, what more could you say, what more could you do? (Ann)

It was the acknowledgement from the police and prosecutors that validated the women and conveyed that each was important in her own right. When [prosecutor] wrote one woman a letter, saying why he had been keen to have her as one of his complainants, it felt significant and had a big impact on her:

He really acknowledged me for personal things that were my own in that letter, that were me, that were personal to me, and that made me feel less like a victim and a pawn of the justice system and more like a person with my own individual strength and courage and humour. (Gabriel)

Being seen as a person, recognised and valued as an individual, was very important to the women, and they respected the efforts made by the police and prosecutors involved in the case to communicate this to them.

There was a huge shift in that people became real and we started to relate to each other on real terms ... Not only did they acknowledge us as

people, but it made me realise how important it was for me to acknow-
ledge them as people and how horrific it must have been for them as well.
(Gabriel)

Gabriel also described how even the head of the police investigative team went out of his way to acknowledge the women:

[He] was amazing, he was fantastic. He knew everybody's name, he
remembered everything that was happening in your life. They would all
follow up where they left off when you saw them next – how has tech
been going and how have your marks been going and how is your part-
ner? You know, it was really amazing that they did that with so many of
us, astounding.

It is all about acknowledging that your experience was important. It did
happen, it is valued, you are valued, you are respected for your
experience. (Gabriel)

Small slights or omissions, however, could quickly erode this sense of being special and valued:

The only thing that ever happened that upset me, and it was something
really silly, was I rang up once and said, 'It's Karen here, I'm one of the
women involved in the case,' and the guy said, 'What's your name?' I
said, 'Karen' and he said, 'Oh, you're number 61, aren't you?' I said,
'Yeah, lovely!' It was a small thing but it was like, 'Oh yes, thank you very
much!' I don't think he meant to offend me or anything but I just felt a bit
off. (Karen)

Support in court

A key issue for many of the women involved deciding who they would have in court with them as a support person. While it may have seemed automatic to choose the person closest to them, many became aware of the disadvantages that could come from doing so. How would partners or family members manage hearing the details of the attack? How also could the victim herself concentrate on the task at hand if she was worrying about the reactions of others? Shelley explained it this way to her parents:

'It's like you being present at the birth of my child, it's nice to be there at
the end and to mop my brow from time to time but not to actually see or
hear the nitty gritty.' (Shelley)

Often it seemed easier for the women to have as their support person somebody completely 'neutral', a professional whom they could rely on to manage hearing whatever was said. The obvious choice for several was to have one of the policewomen who had been helping to prepare them for the trial accompany them to court. Marie, for instance, decided having [policewoman] in there was a better option than her husband.

> I felt it was better to have [policewoman] because she knew everything that happened and I didn't want to be giving evidence and thinking, 'I wonder how [husband] is feeling listening to this?' I felt it was better to have somebody neutral ... I just felt that she was the right person to be there. (Marie)

Suzanne also thought it would be difficult for her husband:

> There were reasons why I didn't want him to go through that, for him to have to sit in there watching what I was going through and to get cross examined and then have Rewa sitting there without the guts to look at anybody – it could be quite frustrating from a guy's point of view. (Suzanne)

Some of the women opted to have the policewoman in the actual courtroom but liked having their partners waiting nearby.

> My partner came with me but didn't come into court with me. [Policewoman] was my support person in the court ... I needed someone who was completely objective. But it was really nice when we had a break to go out to where my partner was and have a cuddle and then talk, and talk to the police and the prosecution and then go back in with [policewoman]. (Shelley)

Raquel also had the policewoman in the courtroom while her mother waited outside, but found it very difficult telling her mother what she wanted:

> It was a nightmare. I could tell it was a big thing for her. For her it was like she wanted to be there for me, and I denied her that, I put myself first. It was a choice of either do it for her and not be happy myself, or do what was right for me and not let her have the satisfaction of being in court. That was a hard decision to make. (Raquel)

Karen's teenage daughter had to give evidence and Karen felt focused on supporting her as the court date approached. While her daughter took a friend in, Karen decided not to have anyone accompany her into the courtroom. As she expressed it:

You're in such a hugely emotional space when you're at court to give evidence in your own rape trial. I'd chosen not to have a support person with me because I didn't want anybody connected to me listening to me giving evidence, because I knew what I was going to have to say ... So I went into the courtroom alone. (Karen)

This view was also shared by Kathleen, who said she felt it was very important that family members try to understand and accept that the woman may not always want them there.

One of the ladies I work with, her daughter was raped recently, like a date rape sort of thing. The mother was saying to me, 'I can't wait to get to court and be there for her', and I said, 'Look, just ask her whether she wants you there. Don't just assume.' I think most people just feel like they have got to be there for you all the time. That was the last thing I wanted, was to have anybody there that I would have to worry about, worry about how they felt all the time. (Kathleen)

Other women did choose to have family members or partners accompany them, decisions that produced mixed results. Some felt they needed the support of a loved one close by, while they went through such a challenging and personal process, and appreciated their presence in the courtroom.

Lorna chose to have her husband accompany her, and for her this was the right decision.

He knew all the stuff before we married, 'cause I told him. When we first started going out I told him little bits and when we were married more would come out as he was ready to hear it ... He wanted to go in anyway to support me, and yeah, I could have had anyone but it was good to have him there. I don't think it would have been good to have others from my family as they are still really angry, so I don't think that would have helped. My sister probably would have dived in and beaten him [MR]! (Lorna)

In Frances's case she asked her sister-in-law to accompany her to court.

She is such a supportive person to me, she always has been. We had to wait a long time at the court before we got called in, so it was really good to have her there and not just be sitting there by myself ... And it was really good afterwards to be able to sit down and talk to her about it. (Frances)

She felt her mother was disappointed not to have been asked. At the time MR assaulted her, her mother was overseas:

I know she would have liked to have come with me as my support person, but it was more important for me that my sister-in-law came because she was with me 10 minutes after it happened. She went right through everything with me. I actually needed to have her there, but I think mum was a little bit hurt about that. (Frances)

Ann also opted to have the family member who had been immediately available after the rape be the person who accompanied her into court:

My sister was with me from the time it happened. I couldn't handle my mum, 'cause it was dirty. The pain in my mum's eyes, 'This is my baby daughter, look what happened to her.' It was just too much for me. I felt like I didn't want my mum to see me because I felt so dirty. (Ann)

Most of the woman felt they had made the right decision. Patricia, however, took a girlfriend along and regretted her choice somewhat. This person had been good and supportive on other occasions, but Patricia found her difficult to cope with when they went to court:

I thought, 'Shit, why do I have her there?' It would have been better to have just [policewoman] because she just sat there and wanted to rip his head off. Well what sort of support is that for me when she wants to rip the guy's head off? She is not there to do that, she is there to support me. I just wanted to tell her to shut up and get out of there. (Patricia)

The clearest message to emerge from the women's experiences is the need for them to be the ones to choose whom they have, and ideally to be able to give guidance as to how best to support them. While on the surface it may seem as though the person closest to the victim is the one who 'should' be there, for the victim/survivor herself this can promote additional anxieties. A conflict can arise over whose sensibilities she stays attuned to, potentially adding to her stress levels and affecting her ability to testify. It is a difficult situation for all parties involved, and no one 'solution' is right in every case. As several of the women commented, whoever is in the role of supporter needs to be willing to focus on what the victim/survivor needs rather than venting their own emotions.

Giving evidence

The actual experience of testifying was a terrifying ordeal. It was also a challenge the women were determined to accomplish, despite the many fears and anxieties they wrestled with along the way.

It's probably the biggest challenge I've ever had to give myself, to make myself do it. (Frances)

I was very determined to do it really well. My biggest fear was getting things out of sequence – two years down the track you tend to forget some of it ... If I'd been raped then I might have felt differently about it, but I never had to give anything that was really, really personal. (Jennifer)

There were times when Jennifer felt she had relayed the order of events wrongly, but found the prosecutor understanding and helpful:

At one stage I was very sure that I had things out of sequence but I didn't realise until afterwards. It was just before a break. I went out and said, 'I stuffed that up, didn't I? Had it out of sequence.' He was really good. He said, 'It doesn't matter, doesn't matter, those aren't the essential bits, it's the other bits that he did that make all the difference.' (Jennifer)

Others also expressed how fearful they felt before taking the stand:

I was totally scared, totally out of my tree, shaking, going to the toilet every two minutes before I went in the room, and it was sort of like, just get this over, I need it over. I thought oh God, they're going to ask me questions, I'm gonna forget it, because you're trying to recall everything and you're under such a stressful situation and it's really hard to recall, and I said, 'What if I say something wrong, or what if I can't remember?' They said, 'Fine, don't worry about it.' I remember crying in there and things like that. (Ann)

Some adopted a pragmatic approach to the challenge:

My personal experience of going to court was okay, it had to be done. No, I didn't want to be interviewed by detectives for seven hours but it had to be done. No, I didn't want to go and give my evidence in a crowded court-room, even if it was a closed courtroom, there was still plenty of people there, but it had to be done. (Karen)

One issue several commented on was the strangeness of 'court speak', and the requirement to talk slowly.

I found it really hard, especially from the point of view that you just can't go ahead and talk, you have to stop for the court whatever-she-is-called. Because I have quite a quiet voice too, sometimes I need to repeat things, and if I am nervous I tend to talk fast ... Yeah, there was the odd time there you felt like crying. (Lorna)

They (prosecutors) may have said you have to speak slowly but I didn't really realise how slow. I probably needed a demonstration about how you speak. (Shelley)

In Jennifer's case, the prosecution wanted to get her description of MR noted, because she had, like others of the women, not thought her attacker was a Māori. The defence counsel were wanting to suggest it therefore could not have been MR, but in Jennifer's case he had actually admitted to being there.

I thought he was white, but he's actually a very fair Māori and so in the limited light that we had I said no, he wasn't a Māori, he was a pakeha. The reason why the prosecution wanted to get it in was to say, here's someone where we know it was him and she didn't describe him that well or she described him as such and such, so therefore these other people that describe him like that, they must have been right, you can see how the error can happen. (Jennifer)

Frances found court intimidating, and to make matters worse felt she had said something wrong:

When I was giving evidence the other lawyer stood and argued and said, 'There's a point of law here,' and the jury just got up and walked out. Rewa was taken out. I thought I'd said something really wrong, that there was going to be a mistrial or something. I had no idea what had happened. (Frances)

Once outside the court, the police explained that the defence lawyer had not wanted part of her evidence presented to the jury.

It was used in the end, but the police said, 'We knew he was going to do that.' I thought, 'I wished you'd told me!' (Frances)

Rape victims in international research have often commented that, although the defendant is supposedly the person on trial, when they appear in court it is they who feel like the accused ([3, 4, 13, 15-18]. Judith Herman, for example, described the ways in which victims struggle to survive the rigours of court processes and concluded:

Indeed, if one set out intentionally to design a system for provoking symptoms of traumatic stress, it might look very much like a court of law. ([1] p 574)

Even in a case with so many victims, and an offender who had already pleaded guilty on multiple counts, some of the women felt like they were the ones whose lives were under scrutiny. As Karen said: *You feel like you're on trial when you're being cross-examined.*

She also felt no amount of preparation could be enough to prevent the experience being gruelling:

> Nothing can actually prepare you for doing that. I prepared myself, I searched the Internet, I got in touch with people, I read journal articles and I did whatever I could to prepare myself for going to court, but nothing actually prepares you for having everything stripped away from you – and that's what it feels like. You are there in a courtroom, you can be asked anything that they feel like asking you. (Karen)

She decided to focus her attention on the prosecutor in order to feel less vulnerable. This was a strategy adopted by many of the women to help them to manage the ordeal of testifying. In turning their attention to whoever was asking the questions, they effectively screened everyone else out.

> I think I almost forgot that there were other people there. I remember at one stage answering a question and the judge saying something, and I got quite a fright. I thought, 'Oh, you're there too, that's right!' (Frances)

> I was a bit nervous to start with, as I think anyone would have been. I just told my story. In reality, I suppose I could have stood there and told the judge because the only person I was really aware of was the judge. I figured, well if I'm going to focus on anything, I'm going to focus on him. I guess I told myself I had to focus. Block out and get in there and get out in one piece. (Connie)

Although Marie's case was the historic offence for which MR had already served time in prison, nevertheless, the experience was still a terrifying ordeal.

> It was actually having to go in there and say what had happened in front of all those people … I didn't sleep that night because I just went over and over what I'd said: 'Oh, why didn't I say that differently, why did I say what I said, I could have put that differently or I could have said this, I could have said that.' (Marie)

She had been told how important it was that the court see the links between what MR had done back then and his more recent rapes, a responsibility that weighed heavily on her.

> They did get through to me how important it was that I was there. My main fear was that I was going to get in there and be a blubbering mess and that I was going to stuff it up and not be able to tell them what they

needed, that was my main fear ... It wasn't until after that I had given evidence that I could then feel for the other women ... I knew I was one of 27 or something, but the way I coped with it was not to focus on them. I just had to focus on me and doing what I was doing. (Marie)

Some of the women described almost enjoying aspects of giving their testimony, especially when their statements humiliated MR. This became another way of taking some of their power back:

Apparently whenever people testified against him to say that he used to wank himself because he couldn't get it together, he used to get really annoyed – there was no way he was going to admit that there was anything wrong with his performance! And when I said that [about him], the guards started laughing. At the time I was quite put out actually. I thought, 'Don't laugh at me.' Afterwards. [prosecutor] said to me, 'Didn't you hear him?' I said, 'No.' Apparently he [MR] sat there and said, 'Oh bullshit, fucking bullshit, what are they talking about?' (laugh) That's actually why the guards were laughing. (Jennifer)

Karen had additional issues to come to terms with, once she realised that the person who raped her was not a stranger but a friend of one of her friends, and someone who had visited her home and socialised with her previously. MR probably heard she was shifting house, which was why he came and attacked her the night before she moved. Given the darkness and the glimpses she had, Karen initially thought her attacker was European until, after doing a compusketch, the detective suggested to her that she had in fact drawn a 'Polynesian' face. She was shocked when she was told that her attacker was the man she knew as 'Hammer'.

It was: how come I didn't realise before, how come I didn't recognise him? Thank God I didn't recognise him! I'm so glad I didn't recognise him because I don't know what I would have done, I really don't know. I like to think that I would have done exactly what I did do, but I don't know. Maybe it would have been different if I had have recognised him – I'm glad I didn't.

I knew he was a tough bikie. 'You don't fuck with Hammer', that was the sort of person, that was the sort of reputation ... It worked out for me in that I didn't recognise him. The other thing of course too is that I may well have been killed if I had recognised him, because what would he have done too? (Karen)

She described how this strengthened her resolve to see MR in court, although also acknowledged how terrifying the prospect was for her:

I wanted him to see me, I wanted him to know that I was there … Although I must say when I was in the courtroom, Rewa turned around and I honestly just about shat myself! … I just felt such intense fear go through me – it was horrible, absolutely horrible. (Karen)

Each woman survived the trial process in her own way, often exhibiting positive energy and creativity in her coping mechanisms. Helen described how she prepared for court with the help of her girlfriend:

We did a lot of mental stuff. There was a lot of spiritual stuff that I got into that gave me strength and whatever. With this friend of mine the box where I was going to be, we glit up, with the glitter of courage. We also put it into his [MR] box. We went over there and so we showed it my strength – this was my room, this was my space. So a lot of that was very much, 'I am the Goddess of Justice', very much setting it up for myself. (Helen)

She said she had asked for permission to sprinkle the 'glitter of courage' around before she took the stand, and been granted it.

It's great to know that he [MR] probably wouldn't know what the hell all this glitter was on the floor or around his box! And all the girls after me knew that this was the strength glitter, which was really nice. They knew it was there. I left my little thing of glitter so they could put more in there if they wanted to. (Helen)

Helen said she carried things into the courtroom with her to help her manage the experience.

It's pretty horrific, pretty horrific. Pretty degrading experience … I was very lucky to have my friend around actually, because there were just little things she did. She gave me a stone and a feather, a stone to earth me which I had in my pocket. Teeny weeny things that were actually really, really powerful to me. (Helen)

For some women going to court brought them face-to-face with particular aspects of the attack for the first time. For example, when Patricia went to court she was expecting to be used primarily as an identification witness, having seen MR clearly on the night and selected him subsequently from photographs. In court, however, the emphasis shifted when MR admitted the charge against her, and the prosecutor began questioning her about other aspects, including how MR had moved cushions from her lounge to the bedroom. This behaviour mirrored the ways he had acted in other women's homes, using pillows and cushions as props in the rapes he committed. Suddenly and unexpectedly, Patricia felt she had to come to the terms with the fact that the evidence suggested MR had broken in to rape her.

> I said to [policewoman], 'Well, I don't think he was there to rape me,' and she said, 'There was nothing clearer, there was no clearer cut case that I have seen that was attempted rape, that he would have raped you if he could.' (Patricia)

She felt it would have been preferable to have had it explained to her why, given their knowledge of rapists' behaviour, the police were so sure of this, instead of letting it all unfold while she was on the witness stand. It was only there, as the questioning from the prosecutor proceeded, that she in fact realised that MR's intention that night was rape.

Reflecting later on the trial, one of the women explained how all-consuming the case had seemed at the time, then how it diminished once MR had been convicted and sentenced.

> It doesn't seem huge now, in fact it seems very small. It felt so huge at the time but now it's over and it's behind us and old bum-face is in jail, it all seems quite small, like it's taken its place in the whole scheme of things. (Gabriel)

Seeing and hearing Rewa

A difficult aspect for the women to contemplate was how they would feel seeing MR in court. This is well recognised as a potentially re-traumatising aspect of the court case [8, 11, 19] and the women were offered the option of having a screen between them and MR. None of them opted for this, however, which is a choice consistent with the findings of other studies. The opportunity to confront one's attacker is often taken by victims/survivors, with many wanting 'to be able to face the perpetrator with dignity' ([1] p 594).

Most said they had little hesitation, although some of the women described how weird it felt to be finally seeing the man who had been in their homes, raping them in their beds.

> I didn't see the man until the day I went to court. I didn't have any idea of what he looked like. I nearly shat myself when I saw him. I thought, 'You ugly bastard!' (Connie)

> I was scared shitless too, seeing him, face up like that – it was really nightmare stuff and having to go to court again and sit in the dock and sit in the courtroom and pick him out, God! I was scared he would have a

gun and shoot me or something! And when I took the stand, shit I was scared. (Patricia)

For Raquel it was the initial moment of walking in to court that felt overwhelming:

I was walking in and all of a sudden it was like this huge sensation. It was almost like this hot and cold, really incredible sort of sensation. It completely overwhelmed me and blanketed me ... It was almost like fear itself just came and completely wrapped itself around me and then just went again. It's like I could physically feel fear and then it was gone ... But it did touch me for a second. (Raquel)

Despite their fear, most of the women expressed their annoyance at the way MR crouched over in the box, keeping his face hidden. Some felt strongly that they wanted to be able to see him and even look him in the eye, a way of making him confront their own strength and power. Jennifer's account shows clearly both the women's anger at his efforts to hide and their anxiety about being seen by him:

More than anything, I was annoyed that he wouldn't look up at you. I thought, 'You wimp, come on!' He never looked up ... [I felt] quite angry really, it was like, 'Come on mate, get your act together! You were happy enough to come and attack me, now you won't even look me in the eye!' (Jennifer)

She wanted to know more about the man who raped her, and during the trial asked the police to let her know when MR was testifying. They rang, and she went in:

I got as far as the court, I got up to the court and walked up to the front door, I had this sick feeling at the bottom of my stomach, that if I actually saw him and knew what he looked like, he would become more real ... I got to the front door and chickened out. (Jennifer)

Next day she decided to try again:

I actually went, and I'm pleased that I went because I think I would have always looked back and thought: should I have done that or shouldn't I? You actually feel quite empowered to see him, because you can see what a wimp he was, because he knew a lot of us were sitting in the front there and he would just not look at you. I was quite pleased, it made him a smaller person, he wasn't even brave enough to look you in the face and admit what he'd done. Now I don't even really think about him that much, the guy is locked up. (Jennifer)

Frances described how MR delayed court proceedings by refusing to leave his cell the morning she went in. When he finally did come up, she still could not see him because of the way he crouched over. She said it made it easier for her that he behaved like he did, so she did not have to look at him. However, she also felt:

> [A] sense of anger that he had absolutely no respect, no respect for anything, no respect for a court ... Anger that people like that have got that arrogance about them, that they do whatever they want to do. (Frances)

Kathleen was also angry that MR kept his head down, preventing her from having the *eye contact* she wanted:

> When I walked passed him I said something to him I probably shouldn't have and I got a thump in the back from [policewoman]! I'd said, 'You gutless prick!' (laughs). (Kathleen)

> I wanted him to see that I was there, that I was standing up there. It was really important to me, but he didn't look up at all ... You think, 'Can't they make him sit up? Can't they put him in a fucking straightjacket? I've got to be here, he should have to be here! (Karen)

Gabriel also felt MR should not have been allowed to hide his face:

> I had to sit up on a big bloody stand with a microphone and everyone gets to stare at me and hear personal, explicit details about some ghastly event that happened to me – and he gets to sit down and stare at the floor. It sucked ... It is your time to look at him, and for us, I mean, he got to strip all our clothes off, tie us up, leave us in any position that he felt like and have a really good look, you know, and all I got to see was the top of his head. And that didn't seem fair, that he could do that. (Gabriel)

She described how MR was kept secure within the court:

> He sits in a kind of dock and at the back there is a chain that comes through and he's handcuffed and chained to the handcuff, and three huge hefty guys would sit by him. And his head was down. I think I was hoping that he would be like some caged animal, wild and horrible. He just looked like this pathetic little man. It was almost hard to believe that he had done, exercised so much violence over so many women, because he looked so frail.

> I wanted him to look big and strong and powerful and scary, so that it would be like, 'Haha, look where it's got you!' I wanted people to see that sense of rage and power that obviously was sitting in there, to fit with the

story, but instead there was this shrivelled little man sitting down there. And you are going through all the details of having your head bashed against the wall and being thrown against this and all the rest of it – and there is this little guy! (Gabriel)

True to form, however, MR tried other means of asserting his dominance:

He would stay in his blocks right until the very last minute. Sometimes the trial would have to wait for him because he would refuse to come out of his cell. He did it right up until the very end. I think it was a chance for him to take some personal power back still. (Gabriel)

Seeing him and being seen by him were two different things. She had some awareness of him when she gave her evidence:

Rattles his chains every now and then (laughs) and a few swear words under his breath possibly. I looked at him quite a lot when I gave evidence. I didn't feel intimidated by him. I don't know, on the other hand, how I would have felt if he had been standing up staring me in the face as soon as I walked in. I don't know because that didn't happen. I actually went back for quite a lot of the trial in the hope of seeing him. I would get in before so that they could bring him and I could see him before he sat down, and then I would stay there right until the end and watch them take him out and I really enjoyed it. I really enjoyed seeing him all handcuffed and in chains with three people. It was so weird. Especially going into the courtroom beforehand and seeing the box with the handcuffs and the chains, thinking, 'Oh my God, this guy's an animal.' (Gabriel)

Raquel said she felt fine about MR being there:

To me, I felt I was the one in control because he didn't want me to see him so he had to put his head down so I was controlling that in a way. I didn't feel like he had any control over anything. (Raquel)

Suzanne also desperately wanted MR to see her looking at him.

When I went in and gave my evidence, as he did with everyone, he kept his head down. I wanted to look him in the face. I kept looking at him virtually the whole time. Once he looked up and I glared at him and looked him in the face as if to say, 'I'm not scared of you mate!' ... I was glad, and I know a lot of the girls felt the same way – they just wanted to show him that they're still standing there still strong. It's like, 'You're there now and I'm still here.' Yeah, it was important to see him. (Suzanne)

Helen said she found it personally empowering to be in a different context with MR, one where he no longer had control of her. She thought her attitude may have really rankled him:

> I wouldn't call him, 'him,' I called him 'Monster'. He didn't like it. 'It' or 'the Monster.' It's quite fun really, no, it wasn't at the time. I just felt he wasn't a man. I wanted to make sure I separated the two, because if you don't separate the two, then you associate all men with this animal behaviour, so it was better to change the name for him ...

> After the break he basically said he wasn't going to come back into the courtroom because what I was saying wasn't the truth, or what I was saying was upsetting him, or something. So basically he didn't come back into the courtroom and I caused a bit of a fuss. Well, I didn't get much choice when he was in my house. I didn't get much choice that I wanted to leave then – why the hell should he get a choice that he wants to leave now? Because for me, there's two reasons for being there. One was to give my evidence and obviously get him put away, but it was also to tell the story to him. It was also for him to hear how it had hurt me, so when he wasn't there, I felt cheated ... However, I also felt that I had won. He was so pathetic that he couldn't even stand there in front of me. (Helen)

Everyone in court became accustomed to MR sitting with his head down, so much so that the police reassured some women that they did not need to worry about him confronting them.

> They said, 'He's had his head down all the time, he's not looking.' My day, he chose to look ... I looked up and I thought, 'Oh my God, he's looking at me.' Rewa was looking at me! ... I went as white as a ghost and nearly dropped dead. After that he didn't even put his head up. (Connie)

Even though most wanted to see him, the prospect was still terrifying for many, and they did not know how they would react.

> I was nervous about seeing him. I was worried that I'd cry ... I was aware of the fact that what the jury had been hearing before my case was so much worse than my case as well. I was worried I'd cry and they'd think, well, it wasn't that bad in comparison to what they'd heard previous to my evidence. (Frances)

Seeing MR was one hurdle to overcome; another was testifying in front of him, speaking about him knowing he was there, listening. I asked the women how they felt:

> It didn't actually worry me that much ... If anything, I was quite pleased, I would have been really angry if he hadn't been there, because I figured

that he needed to hear what I had to say really. Also, the other thing that I felt quite good about was the fact that he got to sit there and listen to it all. (Jennifer)

Having him hear what they were saying was challenging:

That was scary, it was freaky. There was one moment though where I felt a slight bit of empowerment when I was asked about the size of his penis and I can remember thinking, 'Right, this is my one moment.' I said it was very small or something and I can remember him going, 'Oh no!' That was funny and it was kind of like, 'Yeah I've got one over you!' (Shelley)

Testifying in court was important for some of the women for the chance it offered of confronting their attacker and exerting control of their own over him. Several said they relished seeing MR reduced to a cowering, mumbling, shackled and powerless being. Even those who felt the most desperately terrified of him still found the courage to stand in court and testify against him. What frustrated some of the women was how the media continued to portray MR as the powerful offender and the women as the helpless victims.

And the worst thing was that the media who were so happy to cover every little detail about the distressed women in the witness stand and all that crap, nobody said, 'and the defendant hid underneath the whatever you call it and never showed his face!' I was astounded by that – if I was a journalist I would have made it front page news! (Karen)

Hearing Rewa

Several of the women went in to the courtroom while MR was on the stand, so determined were they to see him. Their reactions to what he said varied.

Frances found it difficult at times hearing MR testify:

I felt quite sick about it. The part I heard was particularly questioning him about quite a brutal assault that he'd done. It was quite graphic and the questions that were asked, he blatantly answered saying, 'Yes, I did do that.' He admitted to breaking in to this property and to assaulting this woman quite viciously. He did admit to that, arrogantly. (Frances)

Patricia went to hear MR but soon left: *I ended up going home – he was so boring.* What Patricia found particularly boring were the excuses he was making and lies he was telling. The 'reasons' MR gave to explain his actions seemed preposterous to the women, who were often amused at the way the prosecutor would expose MR's lies. How did the women feel about his attempts to assert his innocence?

> Laughable, it honestly was, it was a joke. He had to give an excuse as to what he was doing in my house. He told them [court] that the reason he was there was that he'd been to a party around the corner and some of the people at the party had decided they wanted to burgle my house, so he had come in, not to burgle my house but just to open it up for them! Can you see why I thought it was laughable? (Jennifer)

> I felt that he was making matters worse for himself. Even though the police said he was quite intelligent in his own way, he didn't come across at all intelligent to me. In fact quite the opposite. Some of the things that he said almost immediately after another one were contradicting the first thing, I just felt the longer he talked the worse he made himself look ... Every time he felt like he was backing himself into a corner he said, 'I'm not answering that, I don't have to.' He might as well have said, 'Guilty'. (Suzanne)

The impression Helen received of MR was:

> That he was very pathetic and very weak, which was a good feeling. Also, though, you could tell he was evil. That came across to me – that he was evil ... (Helen)

What some women found difficult in court was the growing awareness of how they were viewed by MR. Gabriel expressed it this way:

> When you go to court, it is all in your face. I really felt, just having all these images of what Malcolm Rewa must have seen ... I was thinking, 'Uggh.' Hating, really hating being looked at like that and that is a violation in itself. Allowing yourself to look at yourself the way he might have seen you is just sick-making, absolutely sick-making. I mean, I don't really want to go there, but I do want to. I do want to acknowledge that I've been sexually violated by somebody I didn't know, like somebody else's body parts touching mine. 'Get out, ugggh!' It's been really easy for me to look at it on this level and underneath that is the violation and the humiliation. (Gabriel)

Karen said she was very keen to see MR on the stand, *particularly since I hadn't seen him, I really wanted to see him*. She asked the police to ring and let her know when this was happening, and described the overwhelming feelings she had upon entering the courtroom:

> I just wanted to kill him! I felt so overcome with emotion and being so close to him, I just wanted to kill him. I just wanted to scream, I really

wanted to just abuse the hell out of him. As I was standing there, feeling all this anger come up and threatening to overtake me, [the detective] appeared, grabbed me, walked me out and said, 'It's not worth it. If you yell out, it would be you that gets removed from the courtroom, not him. The bastard's not worth it.' It was like it kind of dissipated, it was like, 'Thank you!' So, then I went out and had a cuppa tea. (Karen)

Some of those who did not go to hear MR testify regretted it. Gabriel said she was sad to have missed the experience:

Especially since a lot of the women said it was just so funny. They got quite a good sense of what a dick he was, and that they all laughed together and I felt a bit sad that I missed out on all of that. I was also terrified of him testifying as well. Of actually hearing his voice, because he talks to you while you are attacked, so I was a bit nervous about hearing his voice again in case it had repercussions for me. I felt that if I had have gone I would have had this big sense of hatred towards him whereas if I left him at a neutral space then I wouldn't have that. (Gabriel)

Shelley wished she had gone also, but was prevented partly by work commitments and also by friends and family having advised her against it. She felt she had missed out on what could have been a positive experience with the other women. Her parents, however, did go when MR took the stand, as did her partner.

It wasn't helpful hearing my parents report back and I wasn't really happy that my mother went ... One of the ones that she [mother] went to, there had been an incident where he had used handcuffs on his victim and she came back to me and said, 'Oh, did he use handcuffs on you?' And I just felt that it was all bit too close to her and I felt that it was a bit like watching an operation on your own family member. I don't think it was helpful for her to know exactly blow by blow what actually happened. (Shelley)

Other women also recounted how family members and partners had come into the court to hear MR testify. Some were quite keen for them to see how the trial was being conducted and meet some of the personnel involved. Karen was prompted by seeing a man whom she thought was Shelley's father into asking her own parents along. They were very keen:

He [father] said, 'Oh yes, your mother and I have both been wanting to go up but since you hadn't asked us we thought you didn't want us there,' so we [Karen and her partner] took them up with us as well. That was actually good for them in a lot of ways because I'd told them about how good the police had been and the lawyers and all the rest but they'd never been in a courtroom, had no idea of what it was like ...

[Criminal profiling detectives] had produced this huge chart and took hours going through this chart with dad showing him how it all fits together, telling him all this stuff – dad just found it fascinating. So they saw him [MR] giving evidence too. They had tea and coffee and mum was saying, 'Are you sure it's all right to drink that coffee?' 'Yeah, yeah mum, of course, it's for us.' it was really good for them in that they found out just how well supported I'd been ... (Karen)

Would the women like to have spoken to MR?

Having to be in such close proximity to MR raised the issue for some of the women as to whether they had anything they particularly wanted to say to him. They were divided on this issue with half thinking it was better not to, while the others wanted either to try to get him to see their pain and fear, maybe experience it himself, or find out why he chose them, why he did what he did.

Some were clear that they had nothing to say, that he was not worth their speaking to, a perspective sometimes reinforced by the police:

I've got nothing to say to him. There's no point asking anybody like that why they did it, because it is obviously a power thing. (Suzanne)

Others felt they did have things they wanted to say:

It would have been very spur of the moment. Something along the lines of, 'You're obviously a very disturbed person and I don't hold any of this against you – but I do.' Well, I don't know, something. 'I do think you are quite revolting and hope you are listening really hard to the effects of what you have done to people and I hope you rot in hell'. Probably something like that. Something very direct. (Gabriel)

I would have liked to have just gone wild at him. I would now, I don't think I would have done at the time. I don't think it would help, but I think I would just like to let him know what I'd like to happen to him ... The visualisation of what you'd like to say is almost therapeutic for me ... Obviously you'd have people with you, because I don't feel secure with him on my own, and even to have the bars and be there and be able to scream and scream and scream at him would be just wonderful! (laughs). I don't want to kill him, that's not the way I feel. It's just being able to release that anger back on him, that he causes you to feel that anger and that fear, to be able to get a hold of it really ... So that he'd realise what he'd done and what sort of pain, what pain and fear is, what real fear is. Which obviously means I haven't forgiven him yet! (laugh). (Helen)

Helen was one of MR's more recent victims. While her anger was still very much to the fore, women attacked several years before her often expressed different emotions, being at different stages in the recovery process.

I would just like to know why really. What would make him do that and what is worse – admitting you have a problem and seeking help or just being total scum and hurting totally innocent people? I would be interested to know where it came from – it's no excuse but it makes it more understandable. (Suzanne)

Wanting to understand MR's behaviour was a concern of several of the women.

I can't understand how anyone could do what he did. People that [husband] worked with, they knew him and all his dogs. They just couldn't believe that he could do what he did. He came across as being just a normal citizen, a nice person. (Marie)

Hearing about MR's sad childhood was both explanation as well as no reason at all:

If I could have ever said something to him, it would have been, 'Why me?' Not why the others, but why me, why did he choose me. I asked him when he raped me, what had I ever done to him to deserve that? (Connie)

Facing judge, jury and defence

Managing the trial process inevitably meant finding ways to handle exposure in court, and being able to manage speaking not only in the presence of MR, but also with the judge, jury and defence lawyers present. Judges in rape trials have often been criticised for displaying a lack of empathy with women victims [13, 16] or, more rarely, applauded for recognising the courage of victims/survivors [9]. In this case, with so many victims and a notorious offender, the women generally felt well supported during the trial and even more so at sentencing.

Some of the women valued acknowledgement by the judge:

I thought he was wonderful. There was always a nod of recognition from him, like when you'd read your bit you would get a brief nod at the end and 'Thank you, Gabriel' or whatever they say. I felt like he was objective but I said a couple of good lines, some funny lines, when I was giving evidence and I saw him smile a couple of times. They said one thing like, 'So you kicked Malcolm Rewa in the testicles, how hard did you kick him in the testicles, tell me how hard you kicked him in the testicles?' And I said. 'Well, not hard enough unfortunately'. And they kind of laughed. He smiled and I had recognition and I felt really safe with him. I didn't feel intimidated by him at all. (Gabriel)

Lorna also felt the judge displayed feeling for the victims

I found him really good, the fact that he was considering us. Like beforehand he allowed the court room to be moved around – that showed us how straight up he was, not just some superior dude that just because he has a degree and this, that and the other thinks he is wonderful – he was human. (Lorna)

Some of the women felt validated by the ways in which the judge intervened when either MR or his lawyers overstepped the line.

The judge was fine, I thought he was really awesome. Rewa acted like a pig sometimes in court, wouldn't answer questions, he was terrible. The judge was, not comical, but he was like, 'Mr Rewa, would you please answer the question?' (Ann)

The intentionally impartial nature of a court of law felt cold and impersonal to the women at times. Kathleen said she found it hard imagining the jury listening and judging:

The one thing I never did was look at the jury. I just couldn't do it – they all looked like my mother! They didn't but they did! (laughs)

A lot of people think you deserve it for some reason … If you get raped, 'Well, you are walking down the street, you shouldn't have had your dress so short,' and things like this. A couple of the old guys at the rest home had actually said to me – I don't know if they actually knew that I had been raped but as the trial was coming up it was always in the paper – and they would be talking about it amongst themselves and say, 'Oh this lucky bastard, he's had a few.' … A friend of my husband's came over the other day, 'All women fantasise about being raped,' he says. This is the sort of people … and I'm wondering you know, 'Should I have worn this? Should I have worn less make up? Should I have had my hair up? Should I have …' It's just people (sigh), you've always got to worry about what other people are thinking. (Kathleen)

Defence lawyers in rape trials are notorious for the ways in which they attack the complainant's credibility and manipulate jurors' possible adherence to rape myths [2, 4, 7-9, 20, 21]. In this trial there was limited scope for such tactics, given that this was a stranger, serial attacker and there could be no debate over consent. Some of the women said they knew they were relatively fortunate in not being attacked as viciously on the stand as other rape victims could be. Nevertheless, they still expressed high levels of vitriol towards the defence lawyer who questioned them, variously describing him as *a snake* (Suzanne), *a slime ball* (Patricia), *a smarmy little creep* (Karen), and *a little weasel* (Frances).

Some said they felt as angry, or even angrier, towards him as they did towards MR:

> He just makes me cringe, more than Rewa actually. (Frances)

> I think he's the most horrible man in the world, the second most ... He actually comes across like Malcolm Rewa was his mate! (Karen)

> He is an ant – I want to stamp on him! (Patricia)

Shelley felt retraumatised by the defence lawyer's questioning of her in court:

> I felt almost back to that day that I was actually raped. That's how dreadful it was.
>
> He was like a dog with a bone. He laboured a point and laboured it and laboured it and laboured it, and I was actually almost at screaming point, like wanting to tell him to shut up and move on to the next point.
>
> But I did sort of have my own strategies and one of them was, when he asked me a question, I'd look him in the eye and say, 'I'm sorry, I don't quite understand what you're getting at. Can you repeat it in another way please?' So that was something that empowered me to get round that. (Shelley)

She said that while she had nothing to say to MR, she would have liked the opportunity to address his defence lawyer:

> I would have liked the last word. I would have liked to have said something to him like, 'You, Mr [lawyer], and your questioning have violated me almost in the same way as the man you represent.' (Shelley)

Other women also said it was the defence lawyer's manner that they found so repugnant.

> He seems to almost look down his nose at you and question you as though you're stupid, all that kind of thing. (Frances)

Karen said she still recalls the feeling of relief when his questioning of her was over:

> I can remember getting off the witness stand and looking at [police-woman], 'Is that it?' and she's saying, 'Yeah, c'mon.' I stepped off and I just burst into tears, I just totally broke down. (Karen)

The verdict

Waiting for the jury to reach a verdict is always a tense part of any trial. This jury went out on a Tuesday and did not return with a verdict until Friday night, after midnight. Late Friday afternoon the police told the women they thought the jury would shortly reach a decision. As the night went on, some went to bed, others waited up at home to hear, and some went into the court to wait.

Connie's former partner went to the verdict and phoned her at home when it came through.

> Quite a few people said to me, 'How do you feel now?' and I said, 'I still don't feel any different.' It wasn't important. Putting someone in prison is important, I guess, for all the others he could have raped. At least we've stopped that. But hearing the word 'guilty' or 'not guilty' is not going to take away what happened to you. It's not going to take away any other sort of losses you've incurred. So what, we're all paying him to be there. We are paying for him to have three meals a day, watch TV, build his body up in the gym, blah, blah, blah. How ironic is that? He's probably got a better life than what we've got! (Connie)

It was when some of the women went to court to wait for the verdict to be announced that they met up with each other for the first time. Finally they could speak with each other, now that all the evidence had been presented.

> It was good to have that comradeship and be allowed to talk to these people, which you weren't allowed to do beforehand, so there was a bit more of a, 'Hey, we're in this together.' (Helen)

Unexpected connections were also made as the tension mounted.

> While we were waiting for the verdict, I turned round and saw Malcolm Rewa's daughter standing there crying and so I asked her if she wanted to come downstairs and have a cup of coffee with me. I said to my mother, 'I'm going downstairs to have a cup of coffee with Malcolm Rewa's daughter' and she said, 'Jesus Christ, what are you doing?' I said, 'Look at her, she's got nobody here, she's by herself, standing there

crying. The police aren't looking after her.' I just turned around and said, 'Do you want a cup of coffee?' and she went, 'Yes.' So I took her down and we had a cup of coffee and the police came and sat with us and we talked about shit, which was very easy to talk about. And we talked about her kids and I was talking about [study] and we talked about everything else but. We walked up the stairs and she said, 'Why are you here?' and I said, 'I'm a complainant' and she said, 'I thought so', and I said, 'It's okay'. And it was. She wasn't there to support her dad, she was just there because he was her dad. She wasn't pleading his innocence ... There are moments like that where that whole day defied every role that everybody was in. It didn't matter if you were a lawyer or a policeman or a complainant or Malcolm Rewa's daughter, it didn't matter – we were all the same. That was why it was such a shock when it all finished because it was like this really magical moment you have in life where everyone is the same. It's like it doesn't matter where you are or where you come from and what your age is. Everybody was there for the one thing and it was all good. It was a very powerful day for me. It was the first time that I had connected with those other women and that was very powerful, very, very powerful. (Gabriel)

Karen spoke of going up to court after work, with her partner, where she met up with Gabriel and Helen.

We were all so nervous about the verdict and so uncertain. This was the fourth day that we'd been waiting for a verdict. Those four days were horrendous, waiting, waiting, waiting ... Parts of it were quite funny as we discussed things that had happened to us, our reactions afterwards. We had a lot of similar experiences – like he'd taken my wallet and I'd thrown a big tantrum at the bank because they wouldn't give me a new cashcard. I think that had happened to Helen as well, there were lots of similarities. It was like, 'Wow, this is really amazing! Here's someone who knows exactly what I've been through.' They've had their own experience of it but it was a shared experience.

At the verdict, the three of us sat together, Helen, Gabriel and I. Our cases were just about chronological. When they finally gave the verdict, they used our case numbers. Wendy's case had been first, Wendy wouldn't sit with us, she wanted to stand at the back. We knew that Wendy's was going to be a real indication of whether or not he was found guilty. When they said guilty to Wendy, the three of us just went, 'Yes!' and the judge went 'Silence in the court!', and Wendy went out screaming, hysterical. We sat there ... When they said, 'Guilty' [to mine] I have never felt so relieved in my life about anything. I just felt that it had been worthwhile, the horror of going through a court trial, an indescribable horror, but it was worth it. (Karen)

Gabriel also said it was very important to her to meet the others.

I was astounded by these women, just considering the horror of Malcolm Rewa and the incredible intelligence that so many showed in their encounters and the way that they handled him, the way that they spoke to him, the way that they protected their children. I just thought they were pretty cool.

Karen and I and my mother went out for dinner while we were waiting. Karen and I would talk, 'Did he masturbate for you?' and it was, 'Oh yes', and my mother was like, ' Ohhhhh!' She had to step outside and have a big breath of fresh air. A bit much for her to handle! (Gabriel)

When the three of them went back to court after dinner, she said:

We came back in and everyone was having pizza and wine up in the chambers upstairs and that was weird. My mum was still with me and we got to all sit around and laugh and talk to the police and the detectives. It was like a closing down period for us because it was the verdict and we were talking about all the things that had happened and how we felt about this and that. It was really amazing, so amazing to be able to do that and [prosecutor] said, 'God, I've never done this before!'

[Afterwards] I just went and sat in a corner by myself and realised that I was desperately upset ... It was like. 'Yeah he was guilty, he did do that to me. Oh my God – that person in there did that to me!' That sense of being believed and having someone convicted was totally huge and overwhelming for me.

It was weird because it was like everyone said goodbye. You had spent three months involved with these people and had been drinking and eating pizza up there and then it's like 'bye' and you go back home. My mother followed me home and I just cried and cried and cried. I couldn't cope, couldn't sit still. My partner was away. Because it was three years of my life to get that 'guilty' and there was no one there who could have possibly understood what that felt like, to have it end. I found that really upsetting. (Gabriel)

In all, MR was convicted of charges against 24 of the 27 women. The jury found him not guilty of two charges of Assault with Intent to Commit Sexual Violation, and could not agree as to whether he was responsible for the rape and murder of Susan Burdett. Understandably, those for whom guilty verdicts were returned were relieved, whether they were in court or not.

I actually went to bed because I thought I'm not going to stay up all night and at 7 o'clock the following morning, a detective who I don't know phoned me and told me, which was really neat. I was pleased that they rang me early and told me rather than me hear it on the radio ... I was rapt. (Suzanne)

To be one of the only two women about whose cases the jury declared, 'Not guilty', was devastating. Frances had gone through all the same preparation and procedures with the others, but now, right when they were starting to link up and affirm a sense of group identity, her case resulted in a different outcome.

I was shocked. By then I just thought that he'd be found guilty for everything, so I was quite shocked. I was angry. Initially I felt angry with the jury. A lot of me felt angry with myself. I wished I had said more. For days after I would be, 'I should have said this', almost reliving giving my evidence, doing it over again in my head. (Frances)

She said she really wished someone had spoken more with her afterwards.

Perhaps just to sit down with [prosecutor] and maybe for him to say why he thought I got that verdict. I think I was quite surprised too, leading up to the trial they seemed to be going out of their way so much to make sure everything was going to be okay for all the witnesses, and then afterwards there wasn't any contact. That was it, it's finished, it's over.

When we had a thing a few months later, I spoke to [prosecutor] about it there, she came up and she made me feel better about it. She said, 'We have no doubt in our mind that he was the one who attacked you.' I actually really needed to hear that, but I needed to hear it sooner. It would have just given me that affirmation that I needed at the time. (Frances)

How the women felt after court

The women expressed a strong sense of relief and sometimes a sense of finality once they had testified.

As far as I'm concerned, closure is when I walked out of that courtroom. For me, it's over. (Raquel)

I felt that it was kind of an ending, a closing. It was very much part of the healing process to actually physically get it out there and close the door on it. (Shelley)

I felt really good after I had given the evidence, I guess like a personal challenge thing to me that I'd done it, I got through it. So it was quite a good feeling to have that. I did get very nervous leading up to it, so it was a really good feeling that it's done now, it's not that thing in the future, it's that thing in the past. (Frances)

Frances's story reflects the highs and lows that testifying in court can be. She moved from feeling so panicky about testifying that she hoped that day would never come to feeling proud at the way she coped:

It was a real challenge. When I came off the witness stand and walked out of that room, it was a real sense of achievement.

This sense was short-lived, for soon she was to be devastated by the 'not guilty' verdict.

The women were generally very appreciative of the investment of time and energy put into preparing them for the trial and supporting them to give evidence. What many found hard, however, was that as soon as they left the stand, it was the next woman's turn, and so the police and prosecutors transferred their energies to this person. It was at this point that some felt a little as if they had been used and were now abandoned – they had done their bit and were now surplus to requirements. While they could appreciate the need for the next woman testifying to be supported, nevertheless they often felt as if their own need for support had not evaporated. They left the stand feeling a range of emotions and wished they could talk over what had happened, as well as receive validation.

For Marie it was a different situation, since MR had been convicted and served time for his attempted rape of her many years earlier. Now, more than 20 years later, she was pleased she had accepted the difficult challenge of returning to court:

Because it was brought up again for me, I really had to see it through. I was really torn between whether I should or shouldn't go through with it ... Going through the trial has helped me to end it. I'm pleased I did it. Partly because of where [MR] is. But also the fact that I met the challenge and worked my way through it and I think because of that I'm a stronger person in myself. I couldn't have pulled out half way because I would always have those question marks. Now I know I've done it. (Marie)

Coming back to present evidence about him so long after the event was still a traumatic and disturbing experience, and like many of the other women, she felt strongly that she needed some kind of follow-up or debrief after testifying.

I was quite happy with the way things went. The only thing I would say, I wasn't prepared for afterwards. After I had given evidence. I actually had a dreadful time over the next 2 or 3 days, just the let down. I don't know whether it was all the build up to get me there, but afterwards I felt there was nothing, I was just left high and dry … I got the impression that it was, 'You've been there, done your bit, goodbye now, thank you very much.' I just felt there was no follow up … nobody really was there for afterwards. (Marie)

Marie's openness about her experience is useful on several fronts. It demonstrates well the way in which events many years after a sexual assault can trigger similar feelings of vulnerability to those provoked by the initial assault. The old adage, 'time heals', has both some truth in the sense that pain and fear will decrease over time, particularly with good support, as well as showing how healed wounds have scar tissue covering them, and events in the present can cause them to re-open. In returning to court to testify about her own experience many years earlier, old feelings were reawakened as another stage in the recovery process was undertaken.

Marie also felt as though she was dropped as soon as she had completed giving her evidence.

I don't know how it could be done differently, but I just felt that I was being cast aside. 'You've done your bit now, thank you very much.' Which is probably not the way it was, but that was how I felt. … I knew that they were really busy, they still had their case to proceed with. I felt that I was being really selfish, but that was what I needed. I actually rang a counsellor and I went back into counselling. (Marie)

Her sense of abandonment was also experienced by other women, who expressed a need to be debriefed:

There was no debrief and I think that's really important to have some system of debriefing. I just felt absolutely ghastly after I left … It was about a week before the headaches went and the sleeplessness went and just the constant thinking about it. (Shelley)

One reason no such follow-up occurs may be because from the police perspective their job is done, and it may be hard to fully appreciate how big an event it has been for the women to go through. Shelley spoke of how important and 'special' she had felt to the case as she prepared to take the stand, contrasted with the aloneness and abandonment she experienced immediately afterwards – as if she was simply *a disposable witness*. In relation to what she thought might help in terms of a debrief, Shelley said:

113

It needed to be reasonably immediately after the case and it needed to be a one on one or even with a couple, it would have even been good to have a couple of the police there. I think I needed affirmation. Like, 'You did really well, you just gave such clear evidence and this is what will happen next and this is probably what you will be thinking'. I mean, I needed all that … As a nurse, I laid out bodies and that was my job and I didn't need debriefing after that. But if you had to lay out a dead body and it was quite out of your sphere of work, then that would be very traumatic and you need to debrief on it. And it's the same for a court appearance for me. (Shelley)

Gabriel also felt like this following jury deliberations, and spoke of:

[T]he shock of the verdict, after the build-up. There was no debriefing afterwards, there was no 'Come in on Tuesday and we'll just have a chat about how you are feeling'. You never get to see those people ever again. That was it. (Gabriel)

After such intense involvement, it felt to some as if all the supports had been swept away. After having been part of a major team effort for all the months leading up to and during the trial, now there was nothing. Life was supposed to return to 'normal', but after such extraordinary experiences and roller-coaster episodes, what was 'normal? Just as they needed a process or passage into the court arena, they needed a passage out as well, a procedure to acknowledge all they had been through and accomplished and assist them out of the system.

It was particularly hard afterwards for Frances, given that the jury decided MR was not guilty in relation to the charges involving her. The only other case for which he was found not guilty involved a woman whose calls for help following the attack Frances had actually answered.

It sort of felt like the two that I had anything to do with were both not guilty. But she never saw him, she couldn't identify him. I did see him and I did identify him – that was the bit that really got me. (Frances)

Whereas some of the women on whose charges MR was found guilty had not expected such an outcome, Frances had felt it was being treated as a 'foregone conclusion' that he would be convicted for her attack. She expected MR to be found guilty, and did not feel prepared for any other outcome. It was only when she rang the court the night of the verdict that [the policewoman] gave her the news. While she did this sympathetically, it was one in the morning and did not feel like the right time to discuss it, but Frances was disappointed that this, as far as she could remember, was her last contact with the police.

> *I did feel angry with the police. I suppose I was thinking, 'Why didn't you just leave me out of it altogether? You had enough women with enough evidence without me anyway.' It was never really given as an option, right from the start. It was just, 'This was him and he's going to trial and we'll need your evidence.' (Frances)*

Frances ended up speculating with others outside the case as to why this verdict had been reached on the charges involving her. She wondered if the reason was linked to MR having been charged with 'assault with sexual intent', when the jury may have felt that 'intent' was difficult to prove.

Despite the negative court outcome and lack of debrief, Frances did feel as if her experience had raised her respect and appreciation for the police overall.

> *I certainly do have a higher respect for police than what I had before. Perhaps it's humanised the police a bit more for me, actually getting to know some more.*

A positive move appreciated by many was the letter they received from the police.

> *After the trial, after I'd finished testifying, about three days later I got a letter from [the Officer in Charge] to say, 'Thank you very much, you did a great job, blah, blah, blah.' It was actually a really nice letter. (Jennifer)*

It felt anti-climatic to have the verdict and the case over.

> *'Ta ta' It's a bit of a blow to the old system. This terrible feeling of being supported through this for all this time and all these people telling you how strong you are and how great you are, who know your case inside out, who know the difficulties that you went through, who have spent two years getting inside all of it. It was the first time I really felt like people had understood and acknowledged my experience and that is what the guilty was: yes it was real, yes it happened, yes it is important, this guy is going to go away for it. It was an acknowledgement and then of course if you take that away, where else do you have that in your life? (Gabriel)*

Sentencing

One of the most powerful aspects of the trial process was the sentencing of MR. About half of the women went to the court and were seated together in the front. Shelley said she was keen to go for several reasons:

> *I knew that there would be some summing up and I wanted to hear the summing up of both sides. I knew that there would be other women there. And for me personally it was a finishing off to the process. It was an ending. (Shelley)*

The judge was emphatic in his denunciation of MR and his praise and respect for the women. In his opening remarks he said:

> Prisoner,
> Over the past several months you have been the focus of public and media attention to this case. I intend this morning to diffuse the focus on you and consider the cases of the women you have so cruelly violated. My comments are taken from the victim impact reports which are expressed with dignified understatement. I wish to record my admiration for the dignity and the courage with which each of these women gave her evidence before this Court in the harrowing course of the trial. [22]

The judge then read out a summary of each woman's report, referring to each woman by her initials only, summarising what MR had done and how it had affected her life. All of those I spoke with, who heard this summary, said it was an amazing and moving experience, a sentiment echoed by the police personnel present. At the end he turned to MR and ordered:

> Rewa, those are the wounds you have inflicted on these sisters in the legion of the brave and now you are going to pay for it. Stand up. [22].

He referred to MR's 'entrenched pattern of violent predatory sexual offending' indicating 'a remorseless compulsion to commit sexual crimes of a most violent nature,' and condemned:

> The sheer brutality of your attacks, and their premeditation, which involved lurking, stalking and hunting of victims at vulnerable times. [22]

After referring to MR's upbringing, lack of remorse and likelihood of persistent re-offending, Justice Anderson sentenced him to preventive detention with a minimum period of imprisonment of 22 years before he could be considered for parole.

How did the women experience this process? Gabriel recalled feeling overwhelmed at the extent of damage to so many women's lives encapsulated in such a short space of time:

What a ghastly four hours that was. It was victim impact reports summarised by the judge and read out individually. [Prosecutor] did about an hour and half worth of summary as well. It was just, oh my God, like nothing you have ever heard in your life. It was just hours worth of women who can't sleep at night, women who had to sell their houses and move somewhere else, women whose relationships broke up, self-mutilation, eating disorders, hating your own body and your image, moving countries, shifting town, leaving your partner, not being able to stay in your house, burglar alarms, paranoia, moving back to your mother's, putting furniture against doors, walking around with knives, unable to go jogging anymore, unable to flat anymore, unable to live in this area or that area, paranoid for your children – the list of things for each individual. It was grotesque and horrible. It was truly horrible. The judge decided to read every single woman's one and he summarised them personally himself. He did that because, and he put it quite nicely, he said, 'All we've heard is what you've done, Malcolm Rewa, and now it is time for you to hear from the women.'

[MR] was snorting a little bit and uttering the odd swear word. For each one, I think, I cried. For every single one. It was devastating. Especially because we were all there – we were all there and we were all crying. Most people there were crying because it was terrible. I had this sense of rage that I had never felt before in my life. And sickness – I felt sick and just angry as hell. I thought he should have been shot! (laughs). I had this concept of, my God, this guy gets to do all of this damage. For each individual you've got years and years worth of damage and pain and it changes your life forever – and he gets to go to prison ... I got really angry and I just wept for all the pain and suffering that had been inflicted on so many people, and how disgusting and awful it was.

I met this woman there. I sat next to this woman who I had never seen before ... She didn't seem to know anybody ... she was crying and I put out my hand and she just grabbed onto my hand, and said, 'Thank you.' I said, 'That's okay', and I introduced myself. She was a woman's daughter; her mother had been raped by Malcolm Rewa. So we kind of cried together and I walked out with her and she still had my hand when we were walking out. I asked her if she wanted to have a cup of coffee afterwards and she said that she had stayed out of all of the trial and that was the first thing that she came to and I said, 'Well shit, what a day to come!' (Gabriel)

Gabriel also commented about how validating she found the experience, saying:

> It is so easy to take it personally and blame yourself for having post-traumatic stress disorder, for thinking mad things, for lashing out, for maybe treating people badly in your recovery without meaning to because you were hurting yourself. It was a relief to hear someone else say it, to hear someone else summarise your case, to read all the things that happened to you, and to be acknowledged in a room full of people that it did happen and these were the effects and it's real. (Gabriel)

Karen also described feeling overcome by the extent of the damage caused by this one man:

> The judge totally turned it around from it being Rewa, to focusing on the effects it had on us ... The magnitude of it, of just how much carnage he created ... You realise that everyone's experience has been like yours. What it comes down to is this huge, huge well of tragedy. (Karen)

As well as being a highly emotional and moving experience, it was also very affirming for the women.

> When the judge read out the testimonies that we had written on our impact reports, he did it with a lot of feeling and a lot of depth ... [A]nd he did it with so much dignity which gave you back a bit more of yourself, that someone with such esteem like that can understand where you're coming from, it was really great. (Ann)

Several talked of how powerful it was seeing the judge addressing MR:

> This is when the Judge really showed his true colours. He said to him: 'Malcolm Rewa, I have been sitting here in this court for three months listening to you and all the things about you. I am sick and tired of listening to it and now the day belongs to the survivors' ... he looked over to Rewa... and said, 'Malcolm Rewa, stand up!'...I knew that something very heavy was going to go down. It was great! (Shelley)

Not all the women wanted to go to the sentencing. Several said they felt it was time to move on with their lives.

> I wasn't that interested. I had other things I wanted to do. I'd started these classes at 'varsity, I was pretty busy with that. It was bad having an unpleasant secret like this when I should have been getting into the classes and making friends with the other students ... So, I put the necessary wall between academic life and the court trial that was going

on. They [police] rung me up afterwards and told me what was the outcome, so that was good. (Isabel)

Because having been at the trial and seeing him, I'm now at the stage where I just want to get on with my life and I don't really care ... I just wasn't interested in being there really, I just sort of figured that I didn't need to be there. (Jennifer)

Raquel also opted not to go, saying MR had already pleaded guilty to the charges involving her and she felt no need to be there.

The funny thing was, I don't know whether I had a sixth sense about it or what, but he kept everyone waiting for an hour. He wouldn't come out of his cell for sentencing. Now all those women that had gone there and all the people that had gone for sentencing got kept waiting for an hour and I know it sounds awful, but I laughed. I just thought, yeah that's typical. I was not surprised. I thought he's still controlling everyone's lives yet again. (Raquel)

Sometimes the women regretted not having gone, with Kathleen saying she later understood her decision as being consistent with the way she minimised the impact of what MR did to her.

How did the women feel about the length of sentence itself? Predictably, comparisons were made with the 25-year minimum non-parole period previously given to Joseph Thompson, who had been convicted of rape charges against more victims and younger victims than those attacked by MR.

That 23-year period is ridiculous, but at the same time I understand why. Joseph Thompson got 25 years, and dad said to me, 'It's good that he got 23 years because it doesn't make him the best, the one with the longest sentence. It just makes him second and he wouldn't like that!' (Karen)

When Karen later went and heard MR receive a 14-year sentence for raping Susan Burdett, it no longer seemed just:

To actually hear the judge give him 14 years for Susan's rape made me think: he gets 14 years for that; he gets 1½ years each for the rest of us. It's just a fucking joke, it really is. It actually made me feel like there was so many of us, we were all lumped together. He gets this sentence, but actually it's nothing ...

The justice system itself sucks majorly, just that whole sentencing. If 14 years is the maximum that's what he should have got for every single woman, and it shouldn't be concurrent, it should be consecutive. (Karen)

Other women also commented how unfair it felt that MR was not sentenced for each count separately.

> One of the things that used to irk me a lot, and still does, is that, 'I rape once, I get 8 years; I rape 25 times, I get basically six months for each rape.' It's like 'the more the merrier' really, and I find that really hard to cope with. (Shelley)

There were also some for whom the length of sentence seemed of relatively little consequence:

> Everybody around me kept saying, 'Oh he deserves more, he deserves more,' but that was fine by me. I just felt really sorry for his kids and his wife, but you do, especially when you are a mother yourself and you know he has got little kids. I just felt sorry that they had a father like that and they had to live like that, that they had to a) be without their father for that length of time, and b) know that their father had done those things. How's that going to affect you? (Kathleen)

Several of the women took consolation from the fact that even if he was released on parole as soon as he became eligible for consideration, MR would be in his sixties:

> [Police] said, 'Don't worry, he's away for 22 years.' I said, 'Oh good, he won't be able to walk by the time he gets out and by then I hope he's dead.' (Ann)

> He's not going to be able to harm anybody when he comes out at that age, is he? One would hope that he's not likely to be a rapist at 63. If he can't get an erection at 40, he's not going to get one at 63! (Suzanne)

For some of the women it was clear that the length of the sentence meant little after having been through all that they had. Gabriel's comments reflected the sense of powerlessness that was still pervasive, despite the efforts of the police and prosecutors to put a human face on the process.

> I said, 'Wow, 22 years!' and it didn't seem like anything. Not after listening to all of that. So what, big deal! The thing is, it didn't seem to affect him either. They read it out and he kind of went 'Umph!' and that was it ... I thought we should have all had a chance to spit on him before we left. It's only a small thing compared to what we were subjected to. I didn't think it would be too traumatising but I just wanted a chance to take some power back. (Gabriel)

Others still struggled to understand why he had done what he did and whether he could ever change:

> From watching him in court, he thinks he's had many injustices done to him, from when he was such a young boy. Lots of people go through what he's gone through and they haven't turned out to go and rape helpless women and break into people's places and rob them, but you can't tie yourself up worrying why the man is like he is. I don't want to call him, like I say, all the names under the sun because he's a sorry piece of a human being, but he is a human being. You can call him any names but it's not going to stop him from being a human being. His functionality is very similar to what ours is but there's obviously something in his brain and one day he's going to realise – well, hopefully! Maybe, maybe not, don't hold your breath! (Ann)

Ann was one of several of the women who considered MR should never be released from prison:

> I hope he dies in there, I never want him out again in my life. I'd be happy if he was in there for the rest of his life and then died, that would make me very happy, that's if he never got out. People say things can never really happen twice, but because it's happened once, there's a fear that it's going to happen again. (Ann)

Lorna also expressed this view forcefully in commenting:

> On the justice side, I think that he should never be allowed out ... He could have done something to help himself and he didn't. He chose to hurt so many people as well as his own family, his kids and stuff. What's it going to do to them to have a little Malcolm Rewa Junior wandering around in a few years time? (Lorna)

Rewa's televised apology

Shortly after the verdict one of the defence lawyers went on national television, appearing on a current affairs slot to read out what he said was an 'apology' from MR. The only women whom he was 'apologising' to were those whose cases he had actually pleaded guilty to because of DNA-linkage, a point which raised the ire of many of the others whom he had just been convicted of attacking.

Even those who were included in the apology felt angered at his audacity, and at least one of these women agreed to express her outrage by herself appearing on a television news program. The women's responses reflected the findings of other research showing that victims are often highly sceptical of apologies from offenders [1].

> You can't apologise for something like that ... It was a big PR stunt. It was all done by his lawyer, to get some sympathy. 'He's sorry for what he did.' Bullshit, he's not sorry. (Raquel)

Raquel said one of the hardest aspects for her, which a contrite MR could have remedied, was not knowing where she had been taken to and raped by him. Most of the women knew the location of their attack, since typically he broke into their homes, but Raquel had no such knowledge:

> I've got two hours of my life missing. I don't know where I was. It would be kind of nice to actually know where my body was, like where I was physically in that timeframe. If he was really sorry, I'd know, he'd tell me. He never has. (Raquel)

Karen also voiced her disgust at the apology:

> I was so angry. I could not believe that they could put that garbage on television! For whose benefit? For the lucky six that he admitted it to? And the rest of us? Well, we just didn't count at all. I couldn't believe that they could play something like that, I just thought it was sick, I thought it was really, really sick. (Karen)

Going to the Burdett retrial

While MR was convicted on most charges at the trial, the jury was undecided regarding the allegations involving the rape and murder of Susan Burdett. He returned to court for a retrial several months later. Most of the women felt their own days in court were over, but a few did go to at least part of this trial and were there waiting for the jury to reach their verdict – guilty of the rape but still unable to decide if he was also guilty of her murder.

Gabriel said she met up with Karen and enjoyed exchanging stories with her about how each of them was moving on with their lives. She was also aware of how positive it felt to be back in the court-room in a different capacity, still a bit anxious but not needing the connections and support she had at the earlier trial.

> My flatmate said to me, 'What are you going back to the murder verdict for, what are you doing?' And I'm like, 'Oh I don't know, go back in, take some power back.' And he was like, 'How can you even look at him, how

can you even go back in there?' But, you know, it's a reward to go back in there and feel better about yourself. It shows how much I've grown. (Gabriel)

Connie, even though she had felt a particularly strong connection to Susan Burdett, decided not go to this trial, and commented that she did not feel like speaking with her family:

I didn't want to talk to them. I guess I felt that I'm really nobody in their lives. I would like to think that I remember her in my own way. (Connie)

Only one of the women went back for his sentencing and commented how final it seemed, knowing there would be no further trials or court appearances. She described the incredible anger she felt towards MR as well as the relief that it was all finally over:

I was just totally overcome with emotion. I guess it was because I knew that it was really the end … I was just totally overcome, cried like I hadn't cried in the courtroom really. As they went to take him [MR] out, [another victim's partner], who was sitting right up the front, he stood up and started abusing him. By that stage Rewa was actually right in front of me, and I yelled out something like, 'Rot in hell!' (Karen)

Conclusion

The trial of MR was a long and protracted affair. As rape trials go, it was relatively straightforward in that he was already linked to six women's cases by DNA evidence and to the others by his distinctive modus operandi. The fact that these were attacks committed by a stranger on multiple victims while many of them were sleeping meant there was little scope for the savage assaults on a victim's credibility that feature in most rape trials [4, 9, 13]. What is salutary to observe is how difficult a process it was for many of the women to manage and survive. Their experiences provide further evidence of the ways in which the justice system, in being oriented towards the processing of the accused, fails to provide victims with what they feel they need. One woman described it this way:

When I did an interview with TV3 afterwards, one of the guys said to me, 'It's almost like he has more rights than you do throughout that trial.' [The trial is] not there to make you feel comfortable and relaxed and good about your experiences. It is not an opportunity for you to say how you are really feeling, it's not a place for you to make some kind of resolution from what happened and say stuff and let stuff go and move on with your life.

It's the same as being interviewed in a police room. It's a procedure set in place by legislation in order to have enough to put someone away. (Gabriel)

Her feelings reflect the views of many commentators who have criticised the ways in which trial processes impact negatively on victims, particularly in countries with adversarial justice systems where the state brings the case against the accused and the victims are called as witnesses [1, 23, 24].

By the time a trial occurs, the victims/survivors have moved on with their lives, and are often wanting to forget the details of their victimisation. In front of a courtroom full of people, including their assailant, they are forced to relive the rape. Gabriel described the horror and powerlessness of that moment:

[B]ecause all of a sudden I saw myself as being tied up, naked, gagged and being left on the bed by this man, and that was why court was so traumatic, because all of a sudden you saw what had really happened. That this person got off on seeing you that way and that was really horrible, that was really damaging to see that perspective. (Gabriel)

The women had to find their own ways of managing these processes. Some coped by staying somewhat removed from the trial, going in only when required to, and keeping its interference with the rest of their lives minimal. Others chose to survive by immersing themselves in the case, following its every turn.

I was quite obsessive about the case. That was my way of dealing with it. I had to know everything that was going on – and all the rest! I think I overdosed on it in the end, it was just too much … It doesn't matter what you do or what's been done to you, or what's been done to all these people, there's still this system in place that has to be followed. I think that's something that becomes really apparent in going through the court process. It's really out of your control. (Karen).

The women in this trial benefited from the special measures introduced to provide additional contact, information and support for them, measures that one could argue all victims should be entitled to receive. In addition, the women often determined for themselves what they needed to help them manage this part of their survival journey. Whether it was finding the most appropriate person to support them or sprinkling glitter around the box, these measures were designed to provide at least some sense of personal empowerment in the midst of a highly controlled and controlling system.

I am a little bit angry because at the end of the case, what happened, they got their man, they put him away but you have to carry on. It's not like a death but it's a pain like a death and it's something you never forget. (Ann)

5

Surviving others; others surviving

When one woman is raped, those around her are also affected. Their reactions to what happened to her are critical to her recovery and survival. While some will be highly compassionate and supportive, others may struggle not to blame or judge the victim/survivor. The responses of partners, families and friends of victims/survivors will be affected by their own reactions, including feelings of anger, anxiety, guilt and depression [1-4]

This chapter considers firstly how the women survived others' responses to the attack. In addition to her informal supports, what kinds of interactions did she have with support agencies and counsellors? Did she find their interventions useful and beneficial? And how was she affected by media coverage of this case?

The second part examines some of these issues from the opposite perspective, asking how the friends, partners and family members of the women were themselves affected by what she went through. How did her being attacked affect them, and how safe they felt? How did others survive?

Surviving others

Support agencies

Victims of rape and sexual assault are typically referred to a support agency to assist in their recovery. In many areas internationally a support worker or advocate is called in to support the victim through the medical examination and sometimes also the statement-taking process [5-8]. Such a practice arose largely from feminist concerns regarding both the vulnerability of victims/survivors and the risk of secondary victimisation [9, 10]. Having a support worker or advocate present provided a way for the victim's needs to be met as she underwent the arduous reporting and examination processes. While some studies have shown demonstrable benefits from having advocates present [6, 11] the potential has also been recognised for these agencies themselves to contribute to secondary victimisation [9, 10, 12]. This may arise as an unintended consequence of agencies being under-resourced and unable to sustain on-going staff training and supervisory practices. Moreover, any organisation (police, legal, medical, or support) needs to be aware of the danger of becoming more focused around its own organisational imperatives rather than the needs and priorities of its client groups [13]. Recent studies indicate that even within therapeutic organisations, the attitudes and behaviours of individuals can impact in either harmful or beneficial ways [5, 12, 14]. Thus concerns have been voiced about the negative impacts arising from contact with those who blame and are unable to listen or show empathy, in contrast to those who display acceptance and respect for the victim/survivor's needs and wishes. This has prompted some researchers to conclude: 'The service per se does not matter as much as the means of delivery and the characteristics of those offering the service' ([12] at p 1164).

Most of the women interviewed had been in contact with at least one support agency and/or therapist, and recounted vastly different experiences. They were divided between those who found the contact useful and a great aid in their recovery, and those who felt frustrated with the attitudes and counselling styles employed by some. The women attacked by MR were mostly highly-educated, professional women who were very articulate – their preference was often to research for themselves information that might assist with their recovery. A second major influence on their reactions to the support agencies may have derived from most of them already feeling supported by family, partners, or friends. As several said, they did not feel they needed to have someone listen – there were already others around them doing that. For this particular group of women, the need for agency support may have been felt less acutely than it is by victims from other backgrounds and contexts, or whose immediate family and friends are less available and supportive.

The things the women talked about which they did not find helpful included anti-male attitudes being expressed and counsellors seeking to impose a particular way of working on their clients. Some felt they needed specific advice and information rather than just a friendly, listening ear.

I think probably then I was waiting for someone to say, 'Well, this is what you need to do.' I probably wanted some answers about how I was going to feel in another one week, two weeks and how you were going to get on with your life. All she did was sit there and say, 'Tell me what happened and tell me all about it,' and then I left. I thought, 'Well actually I've done that, I've spoken to a few friends, I could have done that without coming to see you!' I felt like she offered me nothing. I think she felt that she was there to sit and listen to my story so that I'd feel better because I'd talked about it. She said, 'It's all right to cry, you know.' I said, 'I don't want to cry!' (laughs) (Jennifer)

The police recommended another counsellor whom Jennifer went to a couple of days later:

She was just light years better. She said, 'Okay, what are you hoping to get from me and how do you feel and what are your problems now?' At the time I think I probably identified my worst one as 'how do you get over the fear of it?' She said, 'Right, these are the things you need to think about doing.' She had practical suggestions and ideas on things that you can do.

Also I couldn't go to sleep with the light off, and she'd say, 'That's all right, you don't have to go to sleep with the light off. One day you will ... but right now you don't have to. Do all those things that you need to do to get some sleep at night and if it means looking in every cupboard and walking all the way around your house... if that's what it takes, you do that.'

Whilst you know that they're going to say, 'Well, everyone's different, you'll react in different ways ...' she'd go on and say, 'But you could probably expect that this might be the next thing for you ...' (Jennifer)

Some of the women felt uncomfortable with the stance taken right from the initial contact. Shelley had a worker from a support agency meet her at the hospital:

Her first words to me were, 'Aren't men bastards!' And I thought, 'Well no, they're not, because I've got a very nice father, and I've got a very nice brother and I've got some very nice male friends ...' I didn't agree with that statement. (Shelley)

She also found it difficult trying to manage this woman touching her and expecting her to talk, and asked for her brother to be there instead. It was great having him present while she gave her statement, she said:

He could actually relay it back to my family and in a more sanitised way. That was important to me, that someone actually understood or had heard first hand, and that I didn't have to keep repeating it again. (Shelley)

Later she felt she drew much of her support from her male partner, as well as from good friends whom she could ring whenever she wanted.

Marie, on the other hand, felt she benefited greatly from having a supportive counsellor, saying:

> I think going to counselling, that just helped me put everything in perspective and sort out my own feelings really. It just helped to be able to talk to someone who wasn't going to be judgmental, who wasn't going to be upset with what I said, or be shocked by anything I said. That's why I think the counselling was good. She didn't put across her point of view about men, she was very neutral. Initially I really needed someone just to be there. (Marie)

Several women described their initial reluctance to talk with a counsellor or therapist, and how for some that changed later as they recognised the possible benefits.

> I was in denial for quite some time that I needed [therapy]. When I was attacked, I was, 'No, I'm fine. I don't need counselling.' [Policewoman] was like, 'What! What are you talking about? You've just been through an incredibly traumatic experience.' I was like, 'No I'm fine.' I didn't trust anyone enough to think that they could possibly help me. I just reckoned I could do it all myself. (Gabriel)

She was one of several women who struggled with the image and names of the support organisations.

> Just because of the name, I think. 'Just ring the Rape Crisis number.' There was just something about it that made me feel like I had to be fucked up to ring it. Rape Crisis. There are two things that you need: you needed to be raped and you needed to be having a crisis! (Gabriel)

Gabriel said she was also anxious that she would be processed as a rape victim:

> I had this terrible concern that they would put it into boxes and do a big study. They would try to psychoanalyse me and tell me I needed to break down, or tell me that I should be angry when I wasn't feeling that way. So I was really scared about contacting them ... I never ever wanted to be called a rape victim or a sexual abuse victim. I refuse to be associated with a label and I was very clear about that to the police too ... I just didn't want to be another woman to add to the list. (Gabriel)

The presence of a support person was greatly appreciated by some of the women, even if they did not feel particularly connected to the individual. For example, Karen appreciated the initial agency worker suggesting to the detective when it was time to take a break. However, she felt uncomfortable with the worker's attitude towards the police in other respects, thinking she was *'waiting for him to make a mistake in some way'*. She said her experiences with counsellors later were much more positive.

> It has been crucial to have someone I could offload my stuff to that isn't my family or friends. I didn't want them to have to hear what I was going through. (Karen)

Helen had a support agency worker accompany her to the medical examination:

> I really wish she hadn't been there. I just remember I was still in shock, going 'Why me? I don't know why it happened to me because I'm really good,' and she said something stupid like, 'Are you sure you haven't done anything bad?' Something really weird like this ... You don't instil that sort of stuff into a woman when she's just been attacked, because you blame yourself anyway. I felt really degraded having her in there, because she obviously thought that I was a tart or something. It wasn't good. (Helen)

One aspect of counselling referred to by several women involved the way they felt counsellors assumed they wanted or needed to do certain things, rather than hearing where each individual was at and what she wanted for herself. Some felt pressured to go along with particular techniques, often feeling they had limited choice about participating. Raquel said of the counsellor she saw:

> She was getting me to imagine he [MR] was sitting there, 'What do you want to say to him?' It's like you're trying to talk to someone that you've never met, don't know, and it's somebody who kind of doesn't exist ... It just felt all very foreign to me. I didn't want to talk to him, I really didn't! (Raquel)

Suzanne went to one counsellor who insisted on focusing on the sexual side of the attack rather than the aspects Suzanne felt she was actually struggling with. She was persuaded to try again with a different therapist, whom she found even harder to relate to:

> It was a completely different kind of wavelength that she was on! She was telling me to, 'Close your eyes and see yourself floating over a situation'; to leave my body and pretend that I was an angel and look down and see the situation and tell her what I saw. I'm just not into that! I thought, 'Wow, this is really weird! ... So I just didn't bother, I just dealt with it myself after that. (Suzanne)

Ann also struggled with what one counsellor suggested she do:

> Before they caught Rewa, you think: 'Is he ever going to do it again, is he watching me, where is he, who is he?' I went to someone who said, 'Put him in a box and throw it away.' I said, 'You can't tell me to put someone in a box and throw him away when I don't know who he is!' I needed a face to put in the box before I could ever think of chucking him away, because what am I chucking away, an empty box? (Ann)

Some felt pressured by others to go to counselling, and did not always find it useful. Kathleen commented:

> I only went because everyone kept on and on at me and it just did more harm than good. During the course of the conversation it just got round to all sorts of silly things and she ended up telling me that she thought my father had molested me as a child ... I know for certain that nothing like that ever happened. That was like, 'I'm out of here! I'm trying to deal with this and you dump that shit on me!' It was hopeless, absolutely hopeless. It absolutely did more harm than good for me. You just cope with it in your own way and get on with it. (Kathleen)

Entrusting oneself to a therapist is difficult, and several women commented how they had to persevere with this process.

> At first, I didn't open up to her at all. For six months I looked out the window, turned my back completely to her and then one day, I turned around and she said, 'My goodness, I forgot what you looked like!' Because for months and months I just turned my back, put my fear out the window and talked to her and that was fine, painless. It was quite hard talking about things that I felt were dirty and that were in here and about my feelings to someone I didn't really know and I wasn't sure I trusted. (Ann)

Ann had a limited number of funded counselling sessions provided, and was amazed when the counsellor offered to keep seeing her once these had finished:

> She was prepared to give me her own time, which really made me feel that she thought my therapy was really important to me. I just wasn't a case number, I was a real person to her, with a real issue. At times, when I first went, it was like I don't want to live anymore and that was really important to her ... To me, in cases like this, if you get the wrong person, it could tip you exactly the other way. (Ann)

For Marie, her return to the courtroom so many years after the initial rape was aided by her return to counselling. She discovered that:

The feelings are still there. I thought it was in the past for me, but it just showed me how that there were still things going on. You deal with things as they come up and you deal with things to a point and then something will happen and then you might have to go through them again and deal with them again. That's when I found counselling quite a help because it made me realise that what I was going through was okay; where I was at and what I was doing was all right. (Marie)

Surviving media exposure

One very difficult aspect relating to this case was how public it was. MR had been front-page news for a long time, and there was huge media interest in his arrest and trial. Once the hunt for a serial rapist was on, every next woman attacked made headlines, and although names were not published, often sufficient identifying details were included that made them recognisable to those who knew them.

I actually had a guy who used to work, with me say, 'Oh, we walked by your house to see which house it was that you were raped in.' I just remember thinking, 'How dare you!' ... I was just amazed that there is this sort of, 'Let's all drive past the house where the rape was' thing. A lot of people identified me because my street had been identified. (Shelley)

It was also difficult for women to feel their cases were being added to a list of descriptions and areas where this man had attacked, so that at any time they could find themselves suddenly profiled again in the newspaper. Karen went away on holiday after she had been raped and noticed how much safer she felt:

Whereas in Auckland I felt totally paranoid and couldn't go out, in Welling-ton I felt, 'He doesn't know where I am, I'm okay here.' It was a really strong sense of safety that I just had totally lost in Auckland. I was walking down the main street [in Wellington], I got to a newsagent's and they had these huge headlines: 'Serial Rapist Strikes Again.' I picked up this paper and there's a list of attacks, and mine was in there. I was just devastated. I thought, 'For fuck's sake, I just can't get away from this. It's followed me to Wellington!' (Karen)

At the same time as she felt affronted by all the coverage, she felt compelled to know everything that was happening with the case.

I was obsessed! Despite my not wanting to read about it in the media, I was obsessed with reading the newspaper, listening to the radio. I never missed the news. I had to know what was going on the whole time. (Karen)

While the trial was on, there was coverage virtually every day in the newspapers. Some of the women talked about how hard it was hearing people in the street and in their workplaces discussing case developments.

The fact that all this stuff is going on in the media and it is about you, and somehow everybody else had access to that information and they were all talking about it but you couldn't control that. It's all out there and there is no hiding from it. (Gabriel)

The press were constrained by what could be published until the jury convicted MR. Then, as Karen described it, there was 'this explosion of media'. She explained how it impacted on her and others of the women who had been in the court when the verdict was announced:

We were all a mess for a wee while after that evening, just the shock of being involved in something so huge. And then the whole weekend of media, two page, three page spreads with photographs of Malcolm Rewa and his husky dogs which he used to train ... It was just horrible, horrible seeing that on the front pages of the newspaper. I had only been in the courtroom with him a few hours beforehand, because he had to stand up for the verdict. Just horrible. (Karen)

Many of the women were approached repeatedly for news interviews. Some tried to remove the media spotlight as much as possible, despite the persuasive powers of the journalists.

I felt pressured by the media and it was [partner] who was a lot more objective about it. He said, 'Do you really want to be identified for the rest of your life as the woman that was raped? Do you really want to have that?' So that's where he was really good. He said, 'I'll support you if you want to do it, but these are some of the things that you need to look at.' (Shelley)

Some of the women reacted against the way so much detail was presented on MR's upbringing, and the attention was taken away from the women:

It annoyed me, after he'd been convicted and they were doing all their spiel about him, about his background and his family history, and it was almost like they were really paying a lot of attention to him. The case wasn't really about him, it was really about the women who had been attacked by him. I feel they really sensationalised him too much. It was almost like they were saying because he had this background, it was okay to do what he did. (Marie)

The day after the conclusion of the trial, a much-publicised documentary about MR, including graphic re-enactments, was screened at prime time on national television. 'It was shown at 6.30 pm, in the time slot usually taken by Our World wildlife documentaries' [15]. This raised questions for the women regarding whether they would watch it, and how they felt about their children and others close to them seeing it. For Frances, the situation was further complicated by her mother also being in her house that night.

She [mother] was fluffing around trying to get them [her children] out of the room and they wouldn't go. They knew what it was about and who it was, so I think I was a bit distracted ... She said, 'Oh, I don't think they should be watching this. Why don't you girls come and read me a story?' trying to get them out of the room. 'No, we don't want to read a story', their eyes glued on the television. (Frances)

Exposure to such material might prompt questions from children, and sometimes the need for reassurance but, as Frances discovered, a simple, straight answer was usually enough.

They asked very simple questions. My younger one said, 'That man can't come back and attack you again, can he?' I said, 'No, he's in jail now.' Fine, that's it, that's all she wanted to know. There'd be that type of question. I might sit there and think, 'Right, here we go', and I'd get ready to leap into this big discussion and they'd just want a simple yes or no and off they'd go. That's all they wanted ... It would be very easy to bog them down with a lot of detail that perhaps they don't want. (Frances)

Some of the women felt angry at how MR was portrayed in this documentary. Gabriel felt annoyed at the way his arrest was depicted, acknowledging little of the profiling and investigative work and instead emphasising dramatic displays of the police hunting down their man:

He ran into a house and the police ran after him and the dog bit him and he said all these macho things and all the rest of it, and I just wondered why they had to put that on. Why did they have to do that? Why did they have to show the police with the dogs chasing him like an animal into the house, making him feel disempowered? Does it seem to satisfy all our sick needs out there for this guy to be an animal? To treat him like an animal, that whole punishment, lock him up and throw away the key kind of bullshit. It just made me feel sick ... (Gabriel)

How the responses of family/partners/ friends affected the victim

Many of the women referred to the various ways they were affected by how those close to them responded. One aspect some had to deal with was others sending them flowers, a gesture that could produce mixed reactions:

> *A lot of people knew and so I had this house full of flowers. I joked to someone the other day, I said, 'God, you send flowers when someone dies!' It's like everyone's in sympathy, it's like they're feeling sorry for you so they send you flowers. You can look at it two ways, though, because flowers are really beautiful and it's almost like a celebration – flowers are like a celebration of life because they're beautiful things. You could say that it's celebrating that I'm still here and I'm okay. (Raquel)*

Several women struggled with the way their partners seemed initially more emotionally expressive than they were. Such a disjunction may have arisen in situations where the woman was still using dissociation to survive, and found it difficult to cope with the ways those close to her were emoting. Kathleen said her husband arrived while the police were interviewing her, and it felt to her that:

> *He just walked in the room and cried and carried on like a twit. I was like, 'I just don't need this', so I just asked them [police] to take him away. I just couldn't deal with all his crying and carrying on. I mean, I hadn't even cried at that stage [laughs]. (Kathleen)*

Lorna said she felt anxious going out and leaving the children in the house while her husband was in his office, a shed down the garden. She felt he did not understand why she was so concerned that he check that all the windows in the house were shut first.

> *He thinks I'm being over-protective and over-reacting but it's not that. If he's out there and someone came in through the window, he wouldn't know about it. He's thinking along the lines, 'What are the odds of that happening?' but however low the odds, there is always that chance. So from that point of view I think he gets annoyed sometimes. (Lorna)*

Several of the women spoke of the support they received from siblings:

> *Me and my sister have actually talked about it quite a few times. It's almost like she got raped because she felt everything that I did, she sat with me through everything, my examination, everything. She also sat with me through my statement, through my court case ... The hurt and the*

hatred she felt actually scared me more than he did. She bloody wanted to get him. My sister, I saw more hate in her than I saw in myself. (Ann)

For some reason she just understands. We're very close in age... she could feel what I was feeling, so she knew if things weren't right straight off ... She was very strong for me, very supportive. (Helen)

Some of the women knew their families were supportive even though few questions were asked or comments made. While a traumatic event may prompt some family members into more expressive verbal communication, others were more comfortable saying little. Connie went to her parents' as soon as she had finished giving her statement to the police after the rape.

My mum knew what had happened. I sat down, she said, 'Are you all right, bub?' – that's my pet name. She comes up to me and touches my knee, looks at me and says, 'He didn't have sex with you, did he?' And I said to her, 'Mum, what do you think rape is?' 'Oh my God!' she said. My mum and dad, we don't talk about it. I thought, 'Mum, you've had seven kids!' (Connie)

She also described her parents' interactions with her the day she gave evidence in the trial:

In the morning, Mum woke me up and said, 'I've got your breakfast on, don't forget your shower.' and 'Will you be all right?' And then when I came home, they were both waiting and obviously they had a stressful day, waiting and waiting. I got home and Dad just said, 'Did it go okay?' I said, Yeah, I think so.' Dad said, 'Glass of wine?' I said, 'That would be nice.' It's the silent communication again when you know your family care but they can't put that into words for you. It's the silence that says, 'We do care but we're not going to say anything. What do we say?' (Connie)

Other women spoke of how it could sometimes be difficult to manage the ways in which well-meaning family members tried to take control of the situation.

[Mum] sent me to stay with some friends of hers on Waiheke Island. They're actually really lovely. They were an older couple and they were wonderful to me, they looked after me and pampered me. I was still bruised and battered around the face, so I wasn't really wanting to be in too much company. I was really shunted around at that stage. (Marie)

It was three days before Christmas when Gabriel was attacked and she struggled to manage her family's reactions.

I went over to spend Christmas with my father and I told my father and my grandparents briefly what had happened, with my brother there, and my father said, 'So you don't like being touched by men anymore then?' You just go, 'Oh God!' (Gabriel)

The Christmas Day plans were not adjusted in the aftermath of the attack, and it felt to Gabriel that she was expected to adapt to suit the rest of the family. This involved her picking up another family member and driving an hour or more out of the city.

I would have liked for somebody to ask me what I would have liked to have done on Christmas Day. What can we do to make you feel good on Christmas Day? Bearing in mind that you probably feel like shit right now, what can we do? Instead of having to drive out [there], I would have liked it if someone had come and picked me up and taken me somewhere ... I felt like I needed to be looked after. (Gabriel)

Instead she felt as if those around her were making assumptions about what she needed without asking her.

I just didn't feel like my wishes were respected. Everybody was talking for me or over me or around me or telling me how I should feel, or not so much how I should feel but what I should be doing. And that really frustrated me. I suppose that's why I felt quite isolated as well. I didn't feel heard. (Gabriel)

She struggled with feeling she had to move on and display what others would interpret as signs of recovery before she felt ready.

Family couldn't understand it. Different generation. We're talking post-war here, we're talking, 'Shush, get on with it, you'll be all right, don't let it ruin your life.' ... So I think they thought I had really gone off the rails and that really pressured me as well. I was living with my mother and she was constantly cutting out jobs from the newspaper and bloody forms for courses and it just really pissed me off. I just felt really pressured. I knew that I had to not do anything, I knew that I just had to be still and feel safe. (Gabriel)

Sensing how deeply some of those close to them were suffering could be heartbreaking in its own way. Raquel also struggled to manage her parents struggling to cope.

The woman from [support agency] told my mother to treat me as normal as possible. Now if you take that too literally, it's not necessarily a good thing for a rape victim. I think my parents took it too literally unfortunately. I don't think that was necessarily the best advice. You've got to do things

> *as normal as possible, but you can't forget that your daughter has just been raped! It was almost like it didn't happen. (Raquel)*

One incident that she found particularly difficult to manage involved a cousin from England who was visiting the country. He had been invited for a family dinner, scheduled to happen just a few days after she was raped.

> *My mother wasn't quite sure what to do after what happened to me. Do we still get him to come to dinner or not? She asked me how I felt. I wasn't really capable of making a decision. I was totally incapable of knowing whether he should come or not and whether I'd be okay or not. She didn't want to tell him what had happened to me because she figured he's only here for two weeks and she was worried about spoiling his trip and upsetting him and everything. When I look back, to me cancelling dinner was the most logical thing, or else getting me to go and do something with [boyfriend] and having him come to dinner and me just not being here ... I can sit here quite calmly now and think it through and go, okay those are the best options. At the time I couldn't – I had no idea of what was the best option ... What actually happened is he did come to dinner, but they didn't tell him what had happened. So I'm sitting there having dinner, pretending everything is great, and that was just terrible, just terrible. (Raquel)*

What Raquel said she became aware of was how much those around her needed their own reassurance after she was raped.

> *I did feel like I was on show that week. I got taken around – everyone wanted to see me. It was like they wanted to know that I was okay and when they saw me it was like, 'Oh, she's fine', and they felt better. I wonder if that's why I was so strong for such a long time because I knew that everybody was so worried about me? (Raquel)*

While it was difficult managing her parents' reactions at the time, Raquel came to appreciate how hard they were finding the situation also.

> *I knew I'd eventually have to forgive them for it, but before I forgave them I had to understand, and for a long time I couldn't. It took me a while to heal first before I could understand. (Raquel)*

Helen also described feeling the need to look after those around her:

> *You hope that your family is going to be quite supportive, or you have an expectation of how people would react and give you support and be there*

for you. Then you find out in the end that you're actually having to be there for them – they're just not strong enough to deal with it. (Helen)

Later Helen's mother arranged counselling support for herself, a positive move although it is often little recognised how useful it may be for those close to victims/survivors to obtain their own support.

Connie was concerned that her family would not manage seeing the extent to which the rape had impacted on her. Her solution was to move away, out of Auckland, partly for her own sense of safety and partly to protect them.

Because I had been destroyed, did I have the right to destroy the people around me by not picking myself up, being down in the dumps all the time, not coping, blah, blah, blah? ... If I had died, they would have been absolutely bowled out and then probably got over it and I would have been good memories, but a slow death would have destroyed my family. And hence, going away, they didn't have to see what I was like. Even today, my Dad rings twice a week, Wednesday nights and Sundays. We talk about nothing but he rings, twice a week. That's his silent way of saying, 'We care.' (Connie)

Shelley also said she came to realise how much her parents had been affected, even though little was said.

My parents were the ones that suffered the most. I actually believe that Mum and Dad suffered more than me, because I knew I was okay. I knew that I was all right ... I wasn't physically terribly injured and I knew that I would survive. Whereas my mother had often said to me for years, her worst nightmare was rape and here it was happening to her daughter. She suffered terribly. She was very emotional over it. ... Dad had to do something and I had this garage that needed to be demolished, so he demolished it and that was good for him to do that. (Shelley)

She found it difficult that so little was spoken about, and so few questions asked.

I think the other thing for Mum and Dad was that they'd been brought up in a generation where rape was never talked about ... My father certainly, being a typical male, you only talk about the gross domestic deficit and what the Prime Minister's doing ... I'd say to Mum, 'No-one ever asked me how I am.' I used to feel really upset by that. If I'd had a crushed pelvis and my head half caved-in from a car accident, and people saw me, they'd say, 'How are you?' Because I had this rape, no one would ever ask me how I was and it was the people that were closest to me that never referred to it. And she said, 'Oh yes, but all my friends always ask how you are.' So that told me that there was discussion happening around it and there was some support happening for her. And that was what it was, it was that people were supporting her and my children and yet I was not getting anything. (Shelley)

Despite her frustration, Shelley also recognised how well meaning her parents were and valued the ways they did show their support.

I think I appreciate them a lot more too, because it was so hard for them and they just really were so supportive and showed a lot of strength ... So I've kind of found a new respect for them really. (Shelley)

Other women also appreciated that their families felt more comfortable providing practical rather than emotional support. Jennifer, for instance, was very grateful for the times her parents offered to look after her children.

Basically they were just, 'What do you want us to do? We'll do it.' They were amazing. (Jennifer)

Although they never said so to her, she sensed that the impact on them was extensive, and felt in many ways it drew them closer together as a family.

Frances said she was attacked while her mother was away overseas, leaving her father to deal with it.

He needed to really minimise it in his own head, so I felt that I had to do that too, for him ... I had to just think, 'It's okay, it didn't matter, it's nothing.' (Frances)

She had others she could rely on for support, but also valued the things he did that showed he was concerned for her.

He had electricians at my house the day it happened, putting up security lights outside and that sort of thing. So, he did take it seriously. He's like, 'I'll do what I can but don't talk to me about it.' Maybe he thought that it wasn't good for me to talk about it, I don't know. By the time mum came back, it was eight weeks later. (Frances)

In some cases the women observed that parents or family members became more open and expressive afterwards. Karen described the positive changes in her father:

I think my father has changed quite a bit, showing emotions that I've never, ever seen him show before, which is really interesting ... It's quite amazing, but it's a horrible way for him to discover that he is capable of showing emotions like that. After the sentencing, when we came out, there were heaps of people there, everyone's running around hugging each other and all the rest. When I went to hug dad, he just broke down in tears and he held me for about five minutes and he just sobbed. [Prosecutor] says that the thing that sticks in her mind most about the trial was seeing my father hold me. (Karen)

Marie did not feel her being raped impacted on her relationship with her mother at the time, but long-term it did:

It didn't really change our relationship, we didn't become closer. We did later though. She had to work through a lot of her feelings. Probably about 10 years later we talked about it. (Marie)

What some of the women noticed was that, paradoxically, it was those whom they did not know as well who seemed more willing and able to ask how they were and acknowledge what had happened. In trying to understand this reaction, Shelley said:

I think it was two things. I think it was, 'Shelley's such a strong person she'll cope anyway.' And there was also, 'I don't want to make Shelley cry.' As adults we're terrified of someone crying in front of us ... I've asked a couple of people, 'Why didn't you do this?' and it was because, 'I don't want to remind you of it.' And so, what I noticed was that people on the periphery asked me – the lady down the road or [boss's] wife. People that weren't close to me ... They were the ones that would say, 'How are you?' meaning, 'How are you?' and I would always say to them first of all, 'Thank you very much for asking. I really appreciate you asking because you're the only one that is.' (Shelley)

Having friends or family not acknowledge openly what had happened could be a source of hurt and frustration:

I would have liked that validation because what happened to me wasn't an every day event and it wasn't something that happened to everybody. I didn't want sympathy. I didn't want, 'Oh, you poor thing!' I just wanted an acknowledgement that, 'I know this happened to you.' A lot of friends have actually never said anything to me. I might have got a card in the beginning, 'Thinking of you, love you, blah, blah' and that's been it. Yet had I had a baby, or lost a baby or whatever, it would be different. And I think my frustration is about the hoodedness of rape ... I found it like a kick in the guts. I accept it now. I can accept that's human nature. At the time I was angry about it ... But it's taught me something really valuable. I am a lot more sensitive to people who have had something disastrous or something critical happen in their lives. It actually taught me that most people do want to voice it. They want to say something about it. It's really been helpful for me because I really understand where they're at. (Shelley)

Some women were surprised when those they expected to be empathic were not, and others were:

Who you think your closest friends are are not necessarily the ones that are going to support you ... [they] can't actually cope with stuff because they've got other stuff going on, or they just have no understanding or compassion or no whatever it is you need to deal with someone who's going through a trauma. Some of the ones who you wouldn't have thought have been there for you have just been superb. But I've changed a lot of friends, friends who I thought were my really good friends, I don't see or deal with now ... Maybe I changed anyway and I wanted more or different things out of friendships. I was pretty devastated about some of the ways some friends dealt with things or some of the things they said or their beliefs or whatever. Some people just make the most insane remarks! In this case one of them was, 'Oh, you were attacked? I wouldn't have been attacked because I wasn't pretty and sexy.' Mmmm. Okay! And then it was the middle of summer, I put on a pair of shorts and a little bra top and [my flatmate] goes, 'Do you think you should be wearing that?' I was like, 'Hang on, you got yourself into trouble because you were obviously wearing what you shouldn't have been wearing?' I took her up on it and she did mean that. (Helen)

Helen said that among those affected by her being attacked was:

[T]he boss who made me redundant! She happened to tell me she got raped when she was younger and I think this is where half of her reaction came from. She hadn't really dealt with it. I had her up on it later saying, 'If you'd dealt with this, I wouldn't need to deal with it.' A friend of mine whose partner had dropped down dead which she never dealt with, that started to come up, so it does have a knock on effect. The dead and the wounded are lying around me, and what about me in the middle of it! (laughs) (Helen)

Helen's experience illustrates the capacity for one woman's rape to trigger traumatic memories and reactions in those around her. What both she and the other women often had to manage was others' reactions, for as researchers elsewhere have noted:

Victimization has a ripple effect, spreading the damage in waves out from victims to all those with whom they have intimate contact ([16] p 407).

142

How others react may also be affected by whether they have had their own experiences of sexual assault, and how these were responded to. Sometimes the victim/survivor may find herself having to manage an increased awareness of the prevalence of sexual violence, knowledge which can be simultaneously comforting and frightening:

> *Within two weeks of me being attacked, five women that I knew told me that something had happened to them. It's almost like they felt that they could tell me, because I'd understand – not that they needed to talk about it, but they were trying to say, 'Look, we understand what you're going through.' … I felt like I joined this club, this unspoken invisible club of women, and the scary thing is, it's a lot bigger than people realise – and that's the really frightening thing. (Raquel)*

Others surviving

The ripple effects of rape may result in many people beyond the initial victim being affected and potentially harmed by its occurrence. Thus while MR stood trial on charges involving 27 women, his actions impacted far more widely.

General impacts

> *He hurt a lot of people, not just us but our families and just women in general. I drive down the streets at nighttime and I see all these houses with windows open and I think, 'You're crazy,' but then, why shouldn't you go to sleep with your windows open? (Lorna)*

Lorna felt it was difficult for others to appreciate how far the ripple effects from one man's actions impacted into families and communities.

> *I don't think you've got any idea how far reaching it goes. My sister, my dad, my mum – my parents' marriage split up, which had other things as well but that helped to a point. And just for people in general. Guys even can't really go anywhere without being looked at twice – 'Are you safe?' … I think it has long-term consequences for most people. There is the odd person who is happy to walk down the street at night and not be worried but generally you get that sense that it's not safe and it shouldn't be that way and he's contributed to that. (Lorna)*

In a curious paradox, as the previous section showed, the people closest to the rape victim are not necessarily the most able to support her and be there for her. They are typically struggling with their own feelings and responses, and may also need information and support at this time. One of the women expressed this well:

> When you're a victim, you forget that there's a lot of other victims too. You're the victim of the actual crime, but there's a lot of other victims emotionally and it's hard when you're the victim/survivor to relate to that. You don't actually completely understand what they're going through. They're busy trying to cope with it and understand what you're going through, which is hard enough, and you're not really capable of understanding what they're going through. (Raquel)

The women all recounted ways in which their children, partners, families and friends had been affected.

Impacts on children

Three of the women had their daughters asleep in the house at the time they were raped. The girls ranged in age from 18 months to 15 years of age, and all experienced the shock of what had happened, its impact on their mother, and the immediate disruption to their homes. For some it meant sudden upheaval in the middle of the night, police invading their home and arrangements hurriedly being made for others to care for them while their mother was taken for a medical examination and questioning. The older girls in particular often feared MR would return, so were also very relieved when he was finally caught.

In Karen's case, not only had she unknowingly entertained MR in her house before he returned to rape her, but one of her daughters had seen him on an earlier occasion prowling around the property. This meant she was asked to give evidence at MR's trial, a further stressful experience.

> I just saw such a difference in her after that. It was like a huge weight lifted off her shoulders, it was just unbelievable. I hadn't realised how affected she was by it until afterwards. (Karen)

She felt her own behaviour following the rape strained her relationship with her daughters:

> I had severe mood swings and still can, it doesn't happen much these days. You think you're really angry about something but in fact, that's not what you're really angry about at all. In the first couple of years, all the time I was like that, so the kids had quite a bit to put up with. (Karen)

She also wondered how much her eldest daughter's behaviour was a result of the rape:

> I certainly think that [daughter] acted out more in the year afterwards than perhaps a normal, teenage, 15-year-old year. Things were really difficult between us. It's really hard to tell because of their ages. It's like that with a lot of stuff, having to actually separate what was caused by the rape and what was caused by normal life. That's been the same for me too. Would this have been different if it hadn't have been for the rape? (Karen)

She said the first year after the rape was the hardest, the time when Karen and her daughter were both the most vulnerable:

> I just wasn't there for her. I wished I had been there for her. We had a really difficult year. I think I could have lost her in a way. (Karen)

Frances had been attacked turning into her property after an early morning run and found it difficult having to respond to her children's reactions at the same time as she was trying to do what she needed to for herself. She felt both positive and negative effects had resulted from the incident.

> It probably was a negative thing with my kids. They were very frightened and became very insecure ... [Son] became really clingy. He wouldn't go to school, he'd have to go everywhere with me ... He was really worried that something was going to happen to me. Eventually he was seen by the school psychologist. (Frances)

On the other hand, her being attacked enabled issues of safety to be discussed with her children and nieces in ways that may not have happened otherwise:

> We ended up getting the local policeman to come and he spoke to them about keeping themselves safe ... He said, 'I can't say nothing is going to happen to you, but I can tell you how to keep yourself safe.' So that was actually really good. It was almost a positive thing with my kids. We spoke about a lot of things that they need to know about, but I probably wouldn't have done that otherwise. (Frances)

Shelley's children had also been in the house when she was raped, early one Sunday morning. She had been separated from their father for many years and had a new partner whom she was not yet living with. The children were scared and shocked and wanted to see their father.

They had spoken to him on the phone and he said, 'I'll come round and see you' and they really, really wanted to see their father. I believe they wanted normality; they wanted to see their father and see their mother and know that everything was all right. He said he'd be round at five o'clock or six o'clock that night and he didn't turn up till ten o'clock and the children kept saying, 'Where's Dad? We want to see Dad.' ... When he did come round he had some 'hello' type conversation with the children, that was all. (Shelley)

Some time later the children were staying with their father when he went out, leaving them alone in the house. The eldest was 13 and he felt they should have been fine, even though they told their mother they were frightened. She tried to explain it to him this way:

'I think you need to look back a few years when their mother was attacked in their home. You are their protector and you're leaving them and it makes them feel vulnerable and they can't articulate that to you. So the poor things have got the notion that what happened to their mother, it can very well happen to them. It will happen to them when their father goes out.' (Shelley)

She felt she struggled to help him understand and felt torn about how best to support her children:

I find that really frustrating and the thing is for me that I've got no control over what happened in the past, other than to say to the children that if they're really frightened they can ring me and I'll go and pick them up. But they're frightened to do that because of the outcome, the consequence of doing that with their father, that he'll be really angry. It's just a perfect nightmare. So it's those sorts of issues that are really ongoing. (Shelley)

Shelley felt he let both her and the children down, while she also acknowledged it was a difficult role for an ex-husband to be in.

He didn't quite know where he belonged in it. Where does the ex-husband fit? Should he be comforting and loving? Should he not talk about it? Should he ignore it? Should he offer some sort of companionship and acknowledgement to me? He chose to ignore it. (Shelley)

Suzanne said that within three months of the attack she had married and become pregnant. She thought her son had been affected by the stress she was under while carrying him:

When he was a baby, any little noise he would cry. Very, very sensitive. I believe that the initial thing was because when I was carrying him I was really nervous, I still am at nighttime. I think that has something to do with it. When I went to court he wondered why I was doing all this. When Rewa was on TV, I said to him, 'That was the man that hurt mum. He hurt me and he made my ear not work properly and he's gone into jail for a long time.' He was pleased with that. He said, 'If I see him, I'm going to get him and I'm going to hit him.' He was four. (Suzanne)

Another woman felt acutely aware that her daughters were living in South Auckland, where a serial rapist was active, but felt powerless to do anything:

I really should have been more afraid for them, but I actually reacted the other way. I got less inclined to try to influence their lives. I don't know, maybe I felt less in control. (Isabel)

Some found their older children very supportive. This was Marie's experience with her son when he knew she was returning to the courtroom:

My oldest son was wonderful. He'd come up and give me cuddles, ask how I was. I was quite surprised how he reacted. He was very angry, he wanted to come to court with me, he wanted to see him, he wanted to go up and punch him, I was quite surprised with his reaction. (Marie)

Kathleen's experiences with her family prompted her to consider how she hoped she would be if her daughter were ever raped:

I know that if it ever happened to her, I wouldn't be like mum was with me. You see, it's never happened to mum so she didn't understand how it feels ... How would I like to be? I would just be there. I would shut up, I wouldn't say anything. I would let her come to me, but I would let her know that I was there and that I understood what she was going through and that it was okay. And for her to let me know what she needs and I would give it to her. I'm not going to dump it all on her, [like my mother wailing] 'Why wasn't I there?' and 'The bond between us can't be that great or I would have known it was happening,' and all this cosmic crap! (Kathleen)

Impact on partners

Being the partner of a woman who is raped is a difficult position to manage. MR deliberately attacked women when they were home alone or with only their children in the house. Several women were separated from their partners, or their partners were away at the time. For the men involved this often prompted feelings of guilt and anger, strong reactions with the potential to disrupt their capacity for being emotionally available.

Telling their partners what had happened was the first hurdle. Raquel, whom MR had abducted off the street, went to see her boyfriend at his restaurant immediately after she was raped. She suddenly felt overwhelmed with the impact not only of what she had undergone, but what he was now to face.

> *I had to actually say to him. 'I've been raped.' Suddenly I realised, 'Wow, I've got to completely devastate somebody I love by just having to tell them that.' I realised instantly in that second: 'God, his nightmare is just beginning.' As far as I was concerned, mine had ended, but I had to start his, and I'll never forget, never forget that. (Raquel)*

He went to call the police and saw three people walk by the restaurant:

> *One of them was carrying a helmet, and he [boyfriend] got really defensive because he was thinking of people in the area [who might have done it]. He went outside and ended up in an argument with one of the guys and punched him. Obviously his anger came out. The fact that somebody had just done what they had done to me – he just needed to take it out on somebody, needed to punch a wall. I think that is a typical male thing to do. (Raquel)*

Raquel also observed other ways in which her boyfriend's reactions indicated he was struggling to manage what had happened.

> *I think [his] drinking was exacerbated by what happened to me, his inability to deal with it. It did distance us, it really did destroy the relationship … He had problems dealing with it. Six months later, I remember getting upset one day and talking to him about it and him saying, 'Come on, don't cry. Be strong.' He just couldn't handle seeing me upset because it would upset him. He wasn't capable of dealing with it. If I said the word 'rape', he couldn't handle hearing the word, and that's upsetting when your partner can't even deal with it, because you can't talk to them. It's the one person you want to lean on and you can't. He broke down at Christmas, which was nine months later, and actually was able to say, 'When Raquel was raped…' I remember hearing him saying that and me thinking, 'My God!' He could say it, and he was admitting that he was still upset about it, but he would never come to counselling with me. (Raquel)*

She had been raped in her car, and said afterwards it was her boyfriend who seemed to be more disturbed about what the vehicle represented than she was:

I sold it. It didn't bother me, it bothered my boyfriend. He didn't want me to ever get in and drive it again ... He didn't come out and say, 'Look, the thought of you driving the car and seeing the car really upsets me.'... I'm a very strong person. It's like, 'Well, if I want to drive my car, I'll drive my car.' It didn't occur to me that maybe I should be sensitive to him because he didn't come out and say that. (Raquel)

Several of the women spoke of the guilt their husbands and partners felt in the aftermath of the rape. Shelley had been apart from her husband for many years and was in a reasonably new relationship when she was raped by MR. She had met her new partner while he was living away from home, and he had decided to end his marriage:

The weekend he went down to tell his wife was the weekend I got raped. So there's a lot of guilt at that; he carries that. He said to me, 'I should have been in Auckland with you,' and he would have been. Had he been in Auckland with me it would never have happened, well, in theory. So I think there's a lot of guilt around that. (Shelley)

Shelley's partner felt that while support was being offered to her, nothing was available to help him to manage his own feelings at the time.

His comment about the whole situation was that there's nothing for the husband, for partners of rape victims. He felt there was just nothing out there for him and he felt really, really isolated as well in that situation ... As a male, his terms of reference were shifted as well. I think there was that sense of, 'I represent the race of rapists. I'm a male. All rapists are male. I represent them. I'm one of them.' (Shelley)

Even though she believed intellectually he was able to make the distinction, emotionally it was difficult to make the separation.

Helen also recognised how hard it was for partners to know how to respond:

I think it must be very hard for a partner actually, to know what the hell to do. Yeah, comfort, support, understanding it's not you, and they'll understand over time that it's not men as a race that are at fault – there's one particular person who's done it. It doesn't mean it's all men, but it might take them a weeny bit of time to get over that. (Helen)

Some of the responses made in the name of support or protection reflected more accurately what these men were feeling for themselves than what their partners actually needed from them:

It's almost like, 'Hey, let me do what I need to do because I'm the one who suffered all this.' It's a male being selfish and saying, 'I want to do this because it's affected me.' They're not really doing it to protect you ... I'm not inside a man's brain but just remember who the person is who's going through the trauma. That's all I would say to someone: 'Leave your own stuff out of it.' And if you can't explain to that person how it's affecting you, apologise and say that you will be there for them as much as you can, that you feel bad that it's affecting you this way. (Helen)

Research in this area has indicated how some men will assume the protector role after their partner has been raped. One way this may be evident is in their becoming fixated on trying to 'get the guy' [17]. In Connie's case, she and her husband were living apart when she was raped, and she felt he blamed himself for not being there. His reaction was one of rage towards MR, to the point that he became quite obsessive about the man. He went to court more often than she did during the trial.

He just used to wander in. It was like he had to get rid of his ghosts. Even when the sentencing was due he was there. I said to him, 'Keep away, don't go.'

JJ: *Did part of him want to go to court to see Rewa?*

No, part of him wanted to go to court to make sure Rewa was dead. If Rewa hadn't been guarded, he would have been dead. [Husband] would have killed him ... When they used to take Rewa from the cells back to the prison, [husband] used to get on his bike and follow the prison vehicle back ... I guess he was suffering in his own way because he wasn't there and feels so guilty about that. I guess he thinks others think that as well – 'If you'd been home, she wouldn't have got raped. You're to blame,' so to speak ... Personally, if Rewa hadn't been protected by police, [husband] would have killed him. He would have gone and got a gun off someone and he would have killed him. And he would have been quite willing to sit in jail for the rest of his life. (Connie)

The police knew Connie's husband was following the prison van, so that if MR made a break for freedom, he would be there, ready for action.

I didn't know what he wanted. Other than Rewa dead, possibly he thought he might have been the knight in shining armour for everyone ... He said to me, 'You could get Rewa while you're in court.' I said, 'No, you can't.' He said. 'You could if you wanted to.' I honestly think if it had come out not guilty, Rewa would not be breathing now.

I think [police] realised that [husband] had suffered more than me mentally, because [he] couldn't communicate what he was feeling. As time went on it was [him] that should have gone to counselling. It should have been him. (Connie)

When MR was convicted of raping Connie, she felt her husband was more relieved at the verdict than she was. He was in court that night, and phoned her at home. She found it difficult managing the strength of his feelings and her fears that he would act on his hatred for MR:

It was hard. Because I was trying to forget about something and to me, it was like he was saying, 'Me, me, me. I am number one again. What about me?' I was thinking, 'This is not about you! This is not your day in court!' It was like he had been raped and after all these years, it was him that had been violated. (Connie)

Even though their partners felt angry and sometimes became focused on MR during the trial, the women appreciated their support. As Connie said:

I guess I can be thankful that [husband] was there, but it frightened me. (Connie)

Feeling backed and reassured by their partners was important to the women. Karen said of her partner at the time:

He coped with it really well, I'm very grateful that he was there because I certainly would have found it a million times harder without him. (Karen)

Ann described how dependent she became on her partner and recognised the potential strain that her continuing anxiety could place on their relationship:

The hard thing on [him] is that he can't have a life without me after dark. He can't go out with his friends and drink if he wanted to, he can't go out and watch a football game at someone's house – we have to go, and it's not because I want to tag him ... He's fine with it now, he's used to it. He used to say, 'I wish I could have a night out with the boys,' so twice I've given him a night out – I've gone to stay at my mother's. (Ann)

In Jennifer's case, she was in the process of separating from her husband – in fact, the night she was attacked brought confirmation that her husband was seeing someone else.

Initially he just felt awesomely guilty because he wasn't there, and also because at the time he was bonking someone else – that's why I couldn't get him that night. (Jennifer)

She felt it complicated and prolonged their separation process, since her anxiety about being on her own now, combined with his guilt, resulted in his moving back in to the house.

The impact at the end of the day is that he stayed around longer ... I kept saying to him, 'You make a decision about what's happening with us because I don't want to carry on mucking around,' and he just wouldn't make that decision. I think that was part of why he wouldn't make it, because the guilt factor was still hanging in there. (Jennifer)

Frances felt shocked and angry that, when MR attacked her as she turned into her property, her husband did not come to her aid immediately.

I think I still feel really angry with him that he didn't come out. He heard the scream but he thought it was up the road. I actually think I lost a lot of respect for him that he could hear that someone was in distress, and it didn't matter. (Frances)

The partners/husbands of women who have been raped sometimes find it difficult to resume sexual intimacy. One factor that has been identified in relation to this derives from historical attitudes representing wives as the property of men. Rape was initially the means of securing a marriage partner, and raping another's man wife or daughter was a crime, not against the woman, but against her rightful 'owner' [18-20]. Burgess and Hazelwood [17] have documented ways in which the partners of rape victims may struggle to manage the stigma of rape, and even view the woman as having betrayed them sexually by 'having sex' with another man.

While most of the women with partners felt supported by them in resuming sexual intimacy, a couple referred to difficulties in this area. Kathleen said her boyfriend, whom she married the year after she was raped, was affected sexually more than she was.

He [MR] didn't put me off sex or anything. Put my husband off sex of course! Badly. I don't know if that's how he was dealing with it. He's said to me when we are having fights, 'Well, I've never had sex with anyone else!' ... It blows you away, it really does. I think, 'You really are on a different planet!'... I don't know whether he thinks I have betrayed him. I don't know if he thinks I might have enjoyed it ... I don't know whether he thinks it was his fault because he went to work early that morning, and we had been fighting the night before. (Kathleen)

One woman talked of fears others held about sexual health:

The man that I was going out with, he was quite supportive, he kept me at arms length for a while to make sure I hadn't caught anything nasty! (Isabel)

One major way some partners reacted was to become overly protective. At times this was experienced by the women as blame, that the men felt they were not capable of looking after themselves and this was why they had been raped.

Some of the women felt strongly about the needs their partners had for their own support, and were keen to offer advice from their own experiences.

If you've got a problem in your relationship and you're not getting support from your partner, this is what advice I'd give to a rape victim: Go and have counselling together. If your partner is not willing to go to counselling with you then he's not supportive and you shouldn't be with him. If somebody really loves you, no matter how hard it is to open up, if you ask them to go to counselling with you, to be there for you, they'll be there ... And that's what you deserve. You deserve someone that's going to be there for you. If they can't handle what happened to you, then you shouldn't be with them. I know that's a really hard reality, being on your own. Look to your parents, look to someone else, but don't be with somebody that can't be there for you because it is so damaging ... If you've been raped you need to be able to talk to your partner about it ... If you can't talk to them about it, who are you going to be able to talk to about it? ... It's a hard call though. (Raquel)

Many of the women commented how strongly they felt impacted on by how others around them were reacting. One likened the impacts of the rape to a wave from which the effects kept rippling out. Some felt bitterly disappointed with the ways in which others seemed to go into their own victim-space. Kathleen said of her mother and husband:

I know they had to deal with it, but I would have preferred mum to have been a bit more supportive – just quietly supportive. Not crying and carrying on ... And I would have preferred [husband] not to have gotten into this, 'Well, I have never had sex with anyone else' thing. He doesn't come right out and say, 'Well, you did!' but he might as well have because I know what he's saying ... I feel sad for him and I feel sad that I am probably going to have to put up with it for the rest of my life. (Kathleen)

Suzanne found it difficult when those around her reacted by rushing to protect her, in ways that felt almost smothering. Her fiancée was away for work when she was raped and he felt guilty for not being there. He came back immediately:

> He rang all his family and told them what had happened. His dad said she shouldn't stay in the house – she should come to my house. [Fiancée] agreed and they tried to push me to do it, and I didn't want to do it. I said, 'No, I want to stay here.' I had to dig my toes in to what I wanted to do. (Suzanne)

A major reason why she wanted to stay in her flat was so Suzanne could show her fiancée how dark it was at the time of morning MR raped her, since she felt he was struggling to accept that she could provide no description of her attacker.

> I wanted to show [him] especially the next morning, at the same time, how dark it was so he could see for himself how dark it was in that room. (Suzanne)

What she and some of the other women felt was that those around them often tried to take over, in ways that may have been well-intentioned but were experienced as controlling.

> I guess he felt bad in himself that he wasn't there. He was basically trying to make decisions for me and I didn't like that. Even some people here [at work], they assumed that they knew how I felt and they didn't know at all, and so they were trying to steer me into doing things that I didn't want to do. (Suzanne)

Marie found it hard to convince her husband that she wanted to go to court and testify against MR so many years after he had been convicted of raping her.

> It hasn't made us closer, it hasn't drawn us apart either ... I reached the stage where I didn't talk to him about it because I knew it was upsetting him and he didn't talk to me about it in the end either, so it just sort of happened ...
>
> He really didn't understand how I felt about the whole thing. It wouldn't matter how much I tried to tell him, he didn't really understand. He just felt it all happened that many years ago, and it should have been left in the past where it was. That was his attitude – why bring it all up again? He couldn't understand that because it had been brought up, I then had to deal with it ... But once I had made a decision that I was going to do it, he supported me through that. (Marie)

Raquel gave the example of how upset she became with her boyfriend when, at a Christmas party in her flat, she walked into her bedroom and found a friend of his sitting on her bed.

> She was sitting on the bed, on my side of the bed. I'd never actually met her, but she was a very, very close friend of [boyfriend]. It was our bedroom and I got so upset. There were people in my room, in my bedroom, that I hadn't said it was okay for them to be there. When you're flatting, the only private room in the house is your bedroom, everything else is shared. I went off at him. He never understood, he didn't even try and understand. When I talked to him about the woman that was sitting on the bed, he said, 'But she's like my sister!' I said, 'But I've never met her.' The fact that he didn't understand, he would only look at it his way. (Raquel)

This experience prompted Raquel to advise:

> When you're a rape victim and you get upset with something, if you're the person around them, for God's sake listen! Don't just say, 'But you shouldn't feel like that.' Guys are really good at that. 'You shouldn't feel like that.' 'Well, I do feel like that! Accept the way I feel.' (Raquel)

She also struggled to manage her parents' reactions, and said it was only later that she could appreciate the extent to which they also were finding things difficult:

> Mum said to me, 'Don't you think that we may have needed counselling too?' I remember thinking at the time it didn't occur to me that my parents might have needed counselling. (Raquel)

Ann, who experienced times of feeling suicidal, spoke of one friend who provided her with validation and positive feedback when she most needed it.

> I've still got cards that she wrote to me like, 'Believe in yourself. Look in the mirror – there's a beautiful woman there. Maybe you can't see her today, but you will see her again.' Things like that ... I look back and I think about those little notes that she wrote: 'Believe in yourself. Don't be a victim – you're only a victim if you let yourself be a victim.' Just lots of positive things. I was really, really lucky that I had people around that really, really cared about me. (Ann)

Impact on friends and neighbours

The friends of a victim/survivor may be able to provide positive and validating responses in the aftermath of an attack, but may sometimes struggle to manage their own reactions. As Ahrens and Campbell note: 'it is unlikely that friends of rape survivors ware any more prepared for this event than survivors' ([1] at p 959). The women observed that some friends were strongly affected by the news of their attack. Some noticed that they became more anxious and took more precautions.

> It was amazing how many of my friends said to me afterwards, 'Oh my God, I've changed my security', and how many of them didn't sleep. It just brought home to a lot of your friends how it could just happen to anyone. I bet I did a lot for the security business! (Jennifer)

Not all reacted the same way, with other women commenting how surprised they felt about how blasé some of their friends seemed:

> In fact, two of my closest friends still go out and leave all their doors and windows open, even at night. My girlfriend, who lives right next door to me, she's on her own and she goes to bed at night with her windows open, so it hasn't really made any difference or impacted on her. (Frances)

The women's friendships were variably affected by what had happened to them.

> They say in tough times you find out who your really good friends are. People weren't mean, they just didn't know what to say. (Ann)

> People's reactions are so different. It makes or breaks friendships in a way. Some of my friendships have become a lot stronger and some a lot less so. (Karen)

Some felt particular bonds were strengthened:

> My friends overall were just wonderful. I've been really lucky, I've had huge support and ongoing support. They've put up with me and all my different moods and faces and all the rest ... Certainly in some cases, my friendships have got far stronger. (Karen)

Others felt they moved away from friends who seemed less able to cope with or acknowledge what had happened. Isabel said initially she felt somewhat indignant at her flatmate's reaction after the attack:

My flatmate came back from her holiday and said that if she'd been there it wouldn't have happened and she wasn't going to go away again ... I didn't want to believe that I was making myself vulnerable by living alone. I'd like to feel that I had the right to live alone if it was my choice. I would like to feel that I live in a society where it's possible for a person to choose to live alone without putting themselves at risk. However, be that as it may, by the end of the following year I was living with [partner]. (Isabel)

She was one of several women who commented how surprised they were when so many others around them responded by disclosing that they also had been victims of rape or abuse.

My female flatmate had been a victim herself in the past, so she had an extra level of sympathy and also of anger against the attacker. A lot of people, in the weeks after that, came out of the woodwork and told they had been raped. It's like a door had been opened for them to talk about it. It was a bit of a shock to find it was such a common experience. I think it had marked these people's lives. If you looked at the way they were and found out that they had been attacked, you can say, that's why she's a bit funny. So maybe I'm a bit funny. I hope not. (Isabel)

There was pressure on some women not to tell family members what had happened, or to spare them the details. Others were clear it was their choice not to disclose to others. Patricia had just been staying with family and was attacked the night she returned to her own home. She commented:

I didn't tell any of them. I just figured then they didn't have anything to worry about. My sister actually talked to me that day and she didn't pick it up at all. I managed to deal with what she wanted to know, because I had been with her the night before. I had had holidays with her and had travelled up and all I could say was, 'Oh, I have unpacking to do.' (Patricia)

Neighbours were also often affected, given their proximity to where the attacks occurred. Several of the women felt they developed closer relationships with their neighbours afterwards. Jennifer talked about neighbourly responsiveness increasing:

The neighbours all knew what had happened, so as soon as the alarm made the merest squeak, there were about ten people standing on the front door step going, 'Right, what can I do? What's happened?' (Jennifer)

Frances described a similar reaction from her neighbours when they heard the smoke alarm sounding and came rushing over – only to discover it was because her mother-in-law had burned the chops!

One of Shelley's neighbours organised a victim support meeting after she was raped.

I live around quite a lot of elderly women and we all got together just to talk about our own personal safety and how all my neighbours were feeling about this. It was actually held at my place and that was really good. It was really comforting, because these women were all in a state of shock as you can imagine, probably more in a state of shock than me at that time. And I think that they needed to see me to make sure that I was okay and the victim support woman kind of facilitated that little meeting, and it was really helpful. Really helpful. It was fantastic. (Shelley)

In commenting how the reactions of others affected her, Helen said:

It's like devastation, it's disbelief about how people react really. Some of them I just cannot forgive for the way they reacted. Six weeks later, 'Well, you should be over it by now!' 'Yeah, you're probably right – I should be!' Now I've learned to say, 'Well, I've not been through this before – have you been through this? How do you know whether I should be over it or not?' But at the time, you don't know what you're supposed to do … I actually ended up just cutting everyone out, I just had enough. My flatmate fell to pieces. She basically fell to pieces. I still can't forgive her for the way she was. It was like it could have happened to her. She sold her place and said that there was no way that she was going to move in with me because the way I was, I was going to ruin her life! (Helen)

Conclusion

No victim/survivor of rape lives in isolation from others, and an attack on any one individual ripples out far and wide in its effects. Partners and family members are often profoundly affected, and may struggle to manage their own reactions while also wanting to support the victim/survivor. Some experience secondary traumatisation [3], becoming adversely affected themselves through their proximity to the victim/survivor of rape. Their reactions may also reflect adherence to dominant rape myths, prompting blaming and negative responses. How those close at hand react affects the victim/survivor also, and has the capacity to both aid and impede her own survival journey. This may mean that she has to manage not only the direct impacts of the sexual assault itself, but also the diverse ways it has impacted on those around her.

As Raquel observed:

While I was dealing with it really well, it hadn't really occurred to me how upset everyone else was at the time, because I was still in my own little world, in survival mode ... It's hard because they [family and friends] can't always do the best thing for you because they're really messed up themselves. (Raquel)

6

Surviving and moving on

To be raped is to be violated in ways that may affect victims/survivors physically, psychologically and socially.

> Experiencing violence transforms people into victims and changes their lives forever. Once victimized one can never again feel quite as invulnerable ([1] p 374)

Research indicates that while some women may experience relatively short-term effects, others will have chronic, long-lasting symptoms [2-9]. These differences appear to relate more to factors concerning the victim than the offender, with the severity of symptoms evident in victims of stranger rapists being similar to many of those apparent in victims of marital or acquaintance rape [3, 4, 6, 10]. Factors that seem more influential include victims having already experienced forms of sexual or violent victimisation, their state of mind at the time of the attack, and the extent to which they subsequently receive support and positive intervention. The most frequently experienced effects include fear, anxiety, depression, and loss of self-esteem, with the clustering of symptoms often resulting in the diagnosis of post-traumatic stress disorder [1, 5, 9-13].

> Overall, a pattern of reactions has emerged in the research that indicates that rape is a life event that causes considerable upheaval in a victim's psychological functioning for a considerable period of time, perhaps the rest of her life. ([9] pp 234-235)

The law recognises the potential impact of rape by providing sentencing guidelines indicating that it is the most serious criminal offence from which a victim emerges alive – the only penalties that are more severe are for murder. As we saw earlier, some of the women attacked by MR felt at the time that they might die during the incident. Obviously the women interviewed all lived to testify against their attacker, and this chapter aims to explore the ways in which their victimisation affected them and, more significantly, the diverse strategies and ways by which they choose to survive and move on.

Overall impacts

MR chose as his means of attack a style designed to overpower and subdue his victims, quickly inducing high levels of fear in the women – his was a form of sexual terrorism [14]. The women all referred to multiple ways in which their lives had been impacted upon. Some had been badly beaten – one sustained serious hearing loss from blows to the head, another could not walk for a week from a back injury, and several had severe bruising and strangulation marks. Many experienced sleep disturbance, nightmares, anxiety attacks, weight loss or gain, increased use of cigarettes or alcohol, loss of confidence and overall loss of self-esteem. Some lost their jobs, others had to move house, all had their lives and relationships affected in ways that were ongoing for years.

The rapes and sexual assaults perpetrated by MR initially dest-royed for many their sense of safety in the world. A faceless person whom they could not identify had attacked most in their own homes. The fear that gripped them was palpable in the room even as they discussed it with me, years after the attack.

> I had no idea who it was that had attacked me. Out there, there was an unknown person who had broken into my house and raped me. I was terrified. I could not move for fear. I couldn't go out of the house, I couldn't do anything, I couldn't be alone. I was totally paralysed. (Karen)

Some said it was difficult to know what they felt afterwards:

> I didn't feel anything really ... I felt that the worst that could have ever have happened to me had happened to me, and you couldn't really get any worse than that. (Shelley)

Others feared they were responsible in some way, that they were to blame:

> There was this feeling: I have done something wrong, this proves it, I am not a nice person. (Patricia)

The impacts extended deep to the very core of their being, in ways that felt almost unsurvivable:

> It's not like a death but it's a pain like a death and it's something you never forget. (Ann)

> *Broken bones, bruises ... can heal and they disappear or mend. It's the inner you that's affected. I guess it's your soul that's basically been destroyed. (Connie)*

The fact that most of these women had been attacked in their homes added to their sense of insecurity. Their safe space no longer felt safe. Frances had been attacked by MR as she came home after having been out for a morning run:

> *The immediate effect was just that feeling of being violated on my own property. It wasn't like I was out in the street somewhere else and I could think, 'It's okay, I'm at home now, I feel safe, I'm safe here.' I've lost that feeling of safety in my own environment. (Frances)*

What many described was how overnight they were transformed from feeling strong, independent and capable into a state of anxiety and vulnerability:

> *It took me from a confident at-home-alone type person who really was at ease and comfortable in my own home environment, on my own, to a person who was incredibly nervous and frightened at being home alone. That was the main impact that it had on me. (Shelley)*

> *If I had thought about the possibility of me being raped by an intruder, I would probably never have realised the impact that it would have had on my life. I certainly remember in the weeks afterwards, or the days afterwards, people saying to me, 'This isn't going to be something you are going to get over in a few weeks, this is going to take you a long time.' It's only now, after three years, that I can look back and see how much my attitude has changed. In the beginning, I was just an absolute mess, I just didn't have any control over that. (Karen)*

A couple of the women said they were initially reluctant to recognise the impact, in part because they were minimising it or trying to keep it manageable:

> *It really turned my life upside down. At the time I wouldn't have thought that but now I think I've come to a point of actually acknowledging just how horrific something like that is. It is quite easy when it happens to downplay it while you're in the midst of it ... You never expect something like that to happen to you. (Gabriel)*

For many it felt as if every aspect of their lives was affected in some way:

> *It's so weird, and it's not just the impact of the actual thing, it's just everything that knocks on. The way friends and family deal with it and*

finance and the job, and it all adds to it and it changes your whole life pattern.

I think people just see it for what it is. Like if you get hit on your thumb, that hurts, your thumb hurts, that's all, and then it stops. It's like a physical thing. Being raped, okay, that's a physical thing, but it's everything else that goes with it. It just hits every corner of your life. (Helen)

Five key questions arose in the minds of many of the women as they struggled to come to terms with what had happened to them.

Why? Why me?

Many survivors struggle to make sense of what has happened to them. For some of the women this was apparent in their desire to understand both why this man raped, and why he raped them. Raquel said she was *very analytical* in the week immediately following the rape:

I was trying to get inside his head because I was thinking about what he did and why … It was like I wanted to know why it happened, why he did it, why he treated me the way he did? It was like I was in the third person … I think when you're in survival mode, you pull a part of yourself out of yourself, or you shut a part of yourself away and you're working on a different level. I didn't cry all week; in fact, I tried to cry a little bit the next night. I really just could not cry, because maybe I was suffering post-traumatic stress syndrome or shock. I just felt so pleased to be alive. (Raquel)

Connie also wondered how someone could do this given how colossal the impacts are:

I don't think he realises that he actually takes the inner you away from you, that you're only a shell, someone that's just fluffed the whole being out of you. Everyone struggles to get themselves back again. (Connie)

Ann described how difficult it still was to comprehend why this man had done this to her:

There is a major impact on people's lives with things like this. Even though mine's been eight years, just the different things that you've been through alone – who you are, what you are, why you're here, do you want to be here? Obviously, after that happened, I could have suicided – it's like, 'What's in store for me?' I don't ever want to go through this again … You're wondering: why this man has followed you, why he did this to you?

It's taken me years, but I've worked out it wasn't me, it wasn't my fault. But when it happens, of course you blame yourself. What did I do wrong, have I done something somewhere, have I really slacked someone off so much? Why did he pick me? Why didn't it happen to Mary Smith next door, why did it have to be me? (Ann)

Is that him?

One aspect many of the women talked about finding difficult was the fact that they had no idea who their attacker was or what he looked like. Several referred to the added vulnerability they felt, fearing that the next man they passed on the street could be their attacker – but how would they know?

I expected to see this person who raped me, everywhere. So, I had a few real paranoid attacks. I had a particular fear of traffic lights for some reason, of sitting at traffic lights and thinking, 'What if I look over there and he's in the car next to me?' (Karen)

When I'd be driving around the streets, I'd be looking at anyone and thinking, 'Is that him, is that him?' That happened for quite a long time. In fact, my husband and my brother-in-law were getting up in the morning and driving around in cars too, trying to find someone. They did that for a couple of weeks too. It was always that awareness that maybe he's somewhere ... I would worry that maybe they'd come across him and he'd have a gun. (Frances)

Not knowing who had raped them led some women to fear that the attacker mixed in their social circles. For Kathleen this was a very real anxiety given comments MR made about her partner during the attack:

It still wasn't clear that it wasn't one of [partner's] friends or one of [partner's] associates. Because of the band, he would go out playing at parties and things and I wouldn't go because any of them could have been him, could have been there. I just didn't go and [partner] would have to make up excuses why I wasn't there. (Kathleen)

Others were afraid they would unknowingly pass their attacker on the street:

I didn't know who it was and he could have walked past me everyday and that was quite hard as [suburb] has all these dark faces – it could have been anyone of them. (Lorna)

Could it happen again?

Many of the women said that, having been raped once, they feared being raped again.

> *I knew that I could not survive it again … My fear was that I'd actually have to kill myself, because I couldn't go through it again. That was scary. (Shelley)*

For some there was the fear that this particular attacker could return, while many spoke of now having a generalised sense of their own vulnerability.

> *I'll never be in that stage again when I think it won't happen to me. Once it does happen to you, you know better. So, the odds of something happening again are really low but the odds of that happening in the first place were pretty low. You realise you are not invincible, you realise that bad things do happen. (Lorna)*

Having others try to reassure them that 'lightning never strikes twice' provided no comfort:

> *A friend of mine said to me one day, 'Oh well, don't you feel relaxed that the random chance of it happening once to you, the chances are it will just never happen to you again?' I said, 'No, the whole fear that you deal with is not that rational. It's happened once, it could definitely happen again.' If anything it just makes it more real – if it happened once, it could happen again. (Jennifer)*

Even knowing MR was in prison did not remove the anxiety that one day he might still return:

> *You tend to put what's happened over here because he's out of range, he's 99.9 per cent safe and away from you, but there's always that 1 per cent that he can get out and will he come after you? Will he wake you up? Will he try retribution on all these women? It's always there in your head. (Ann)*

Connie said she wondered what might happen when MR was released from prison.

> *I hope to God he won't come looking for me (laughter). I doubt whether there will be any chance of that, but who knows? They tend to want criminals to go home now and be re-thingied in society, don't they? Even the fact that he was found guilty does not mean that it could not happen*

again. I guess that's a disturbing factor but it's life, isn't it? You can only protect yourself so far. (Connie)

A difficult time for many of the women to manage was the anniversary of the attack, especially the first anniversary:

I know the first year was really hard, getting through the first anniversary was really hard. I remember going to bed that night thinking, 'This time exactly one year ago I was piling into bed and my whole life was going to change within two hours.' I was thinking about it in that way.

JJ: Do you have a sense of that now on the anniversary?

A little bit, although it doesn't knock me in the face any more. (Shelley)

Who do I tell?

A difficult question for many to resolve arose in relation to whom they would tell about the attack. Rape victims/survivors often struggle with decisions about disclosure, anxious both about how others might view them as well as how those they tell will cope [15].

I'm sure a lot of women, their family might know but they wouldn't want everyone else to know. That's another issue ... who to tell and who not to tell and who knows and who doesn't? It didn't bother me if people knew or not, but I wouldn't have gone and told a whole lot of people. (Raquel)

Some of the women described having no hesitancy in telling others what had happened, although they were not always sure why or what they wanted:

At the start, I was very chatty and telling everybody what had happened and making sure that everybody knew to lock their windows at night. But I think inside I was just desperately terrified and quite alone. I think it took quite a while for that to go ... I felt really desperate to talk about it and to let everybody know so that they knew why I was acting strangely, because I was aware that I was ... You're hyper-vigilant, you're not sleeping and you talk fast because you're all over the place, looking out of the side of your eyes kind of thing. For me I made sure that I told everybody but I don't know what I expected in return from people ... I wasn't able to know what kind of support I wanted because I was just in the middle of my trauma, coping. (Gabriel)

Gabriel later felt pressured by family members not to say too much about what had happened to her when they gathered to celebrate Christmas, three days after she was attacked.

I've got elderly grandparents. A shock can kill them (laughs) … And very conscious of the fact that I didn't want to mention that I had been sexually assaulted. I implied it, without having to explain it, knowing that that would cut but not being able to lie because I had to acknowledge it myself. (Gabriel)

Some of the women were anxious about how those close to them would react, and how they would manage.

I can remember being at Auckland hospital with the doctor for the examination, I can remember saying to this doctor, I don't know how I'm going to tell my parents, they're just going to be so upset. I remember her saying to me, don't worry about your parents, they'll cope with it. She didn't know my parents, but she was absolutely spot on. Unfortunately, my parents found out about it because my ex-husband found out about it and he rang them up, so they found out in the worst possible way. They must have been so shocked. (Karen)

Deciding who to tell will be an issue facing the women for the rest of their lives. Several entered into relationships within a year or so of the rape, and had to determine whether, and when, to disclose this to their new partner.

I pretty much told him basically once we were getting serious. We got married within several months of meeting … He needed to know me and that was a profoundly impacting part of my life and quite new at the time we met … If he could handle that I could know if he was worth marrying. (Lorna)

The issue of who is the one to tell is also important. Some of the women felt fine about family members telling others what had happened, while several experienced this as another invasion of their privacy. Raquel described how upset and angry she felt shortly after she was raped and had told her mother a little of what MR had done to her.

I told her what happened, not in detail – just an outline. I didn't expect her to go repeating it to everybody else. I walked in and heard her on the phone one day … I heard her say, 'He hit her over the head and blah blah …' She was talking about the event and what happened. I got quite a shock … I didn't know who she was talking to. It's that control thing again – I didn't want anyone to be told what had happened unless I said it was okay. It's like hang on, this happened to me, a very private, very personal thing. I make the decision to tell you, I don't want them to know unless I say so. She was telling someone else without my consent what happened to me. (Raquel)

Will I ever be the same again?

In the wake of trauma, survivors may fear that their world has been so abruptly changed that they will never feel the same again. The terror that gripped the women from the time they knew MR was present felt consuming, and many struggled to imagine how they would ever feel safe again. Jennifer feared the fear would never leave:

> At the time when it first all happened, you think, 'Oh my God, am I always going to feel like this, am I always going to be this scared?' I could never go to bed at night without checking every single door was shut, looking into every room and making sure someone wasn't in that room, despite the fact you know that there's no one there, but you can't do it, and then one night you just think, 'I didn't check every room tonight, I've just gone to bed,' and it's just time that takes you there. And then being able to accept some nights you still will go and check everything, and some nights I still even do it, opening that stupid closet that no one will fit in, if that's what it takes. (Jennifer)

She acknowledged that while the impact of the fear, and its control of her life, had eased over time, nevertheless this felt like an aspect of her life that would never revert to how it was before the night she was raped.

> Even in the middle of summer I still wouldn't go to sleep and leave the kids' bedroom window open when I went to bed at night. Those are the things that are still in the long-term effect of your life. It just makes you so much more aware that it could just so easily happen, whereas before I wouldn't have even thought about it, before you always thought it couldn't happen to you. (Jennifer)

Specific areas of impact

It felt to many of the women that every aspect of their lives was affected in some way – every waking and sleeping moment, every deed and activity, every relationship and interaction. One of the areas most impacted upon was their ability to be in the dark and to sleep, understandably given the predominantly nighttime attacks and their loss of safety.

Sleep patterns

Sleep disturbance has been widely recognised among rape survivors, with disrupted sleep patterns and frequent nightmares often reported

[16, 17]. All of the women spoke of ways in which their sleep patterns had been impacted upon. Some went to friends or family the night after they were raped and never slept again in their home. Karen went to a friend's:

> I won't say I slept because I couldn't close my eyes. [Friend] and I slept in one of her kid's rooms, in twin beds … I was so scared I couldn't close my eyes. It was horrible. For weeks, and months afterwards, I could actually feel fear in my fingers and my toes. It took me such a long time to get over that, just sheer terror. (Karen)

Gabriel left her flat and went to her mother's, and described the fear that gripped her each night:

> Constantly looking out the window because he hadn't been caught yet and I was sure he was going to come up the driveway, track my car down, just paranoia. Pushing furniture up against my bedroom door every night, I would have a chest of drawers and a washing basket and just, oh God, just for ages … and it shattered my belief that the world was a safe place and I had always believed that it was. I had never believed that anything like that would happen to me, ever, and it did and that just turned everything upside down. I could no longer trust anything that I thought before then because I was wrong, because someone had invaded my space and I thought that would never happen. But it had and all of a sudden, it wasn't that the world was an unsafe place; it was that my world was. (Gabriel)

Gabriel found it easier to sleep in the daytime, so she could immediately see the source of any noise and not feel as vulnerable as she did in the dark. Kathleen could not sleep in the bedroom after the rape and opted for the lounge floor instead, or went to her mother's. Several women said that, years later, they still felt too fearful to sleep alone in the house at night and made comments suggesting they felt almost childlike in their responses.

Ann described what a long, hard process it was for her trying to feel safe enough to sleep in the dark again:

> For years, I'd wake up, I'd have my eyes closed and think someone's here and your heart would be beating so hard that you'd want to vomit and you're too scared to open up your eyes and look. But, having [partner] here everyday, I don't go through those things like I would have … Every place I lived in I had a TV going all night and a lamp on at night in my room, every night. Then I started, after a year or so down the track, I'd put a timer on and make sure I was asleep before the TV went off, but then I'd

wake up at 3 o'clock in the morning and the room was totally black and I'd panic. Panic, looking for my remote to turn it on to give me some light. Never able to sleep with the window open, hot as. Always put my bed in position where I could see the door and where I could make an exit. When I met [partner], it was the first time in years I've ever slept with a male, but he had to hold my hand when I went to sleep. You know when you sleep you slowly drop your hand? I'd wake up and he'd say, 'It's okay, I'm here', and I'd go back to sleep ... The first night that I slept without a television and a light, I was like 'Wow, guess what I did!' and people would be like, 'Huh?' but to me it was like, not as exhilarating as winning Lotto or something like that, but it was like, I did it! (Ann)

In the first two years I couldn't get up to go to the toilet. So I'd stay awake longer, and my partner would have to come and take me. I'd have to wake him up and say, 'I need to go to the toilet – can you come with me?' Now I can get up, I'm a big girl now, I can get up and go to the toilet, but like last night when I got up I noticed that a light was on. I find it really hard to go and investigate the light. So I left it on and went quickly back to bed again. I'm a real wuss at times and I never used to be. (Shelley)

Shelley also described the dramatic change in her sleeping habits from being a 'wonderful' sleeper to being unable to sleep. As she explained it:

It's not a cognitive thing: 'Oh, I can't go to sleep in case I get attacked.' My brain often doesn't let me go to sleep ... (Shelley)

Others said they realised they intentionally delayed going to sleep:

Quite often I'd stay up late at night, which is partly because when your kids go to bed, you go, 'Oh yes, my time', but other times I wonder: is it because you still have that reluctance to go to sleep at night? Sometimes it's almost 2 o'clock in the morning and I'm still reading my book and I think, 'Why am I doing this, why aren't I going to sleep?' (Jennifer)

Several described finally getting to sleep, then being disturbed by terrifying nightmares:

Oh God, I'd have really physical nightmares. They weren't just dreams about things, they were like feeling hands here and things crawling out of your chest. Like a beast crawled out of my chest – what do I do with it? I mean, I can't take that to a counsellor. I didn't feel like I could talk to anybody about that. That was my own personal process. It was like opening a jar of demons. I felt like I was face to face with the most hideous creature. It was like all your nightmares rolled into one, everything that you can possibly be scared of when you are a child. It was like you had conjured it up and there it is. But how do you expel it from your life? How do you expel that image, that dragon that you have conjured up – or that you haven't conjured up, that's just appeared on your doorstep? How do you expel it and banish it and get it out of your thoughts and stop seeing the blackness that you saw? How do you do that? (Gabriel)

Marie commented on the change in her sleeping after she was raped in 1975:

I was a very heavy sleeper before it happened but now I wake at anything. I still wake at quite a lot of things, still haven't gone back to what I was … I remember as a kid I'd always be scared of the dark, but you get over that and then I had gone right back as I was when I was a child initially. (Marie)

She also noticed in the lead-up to the trial, more than 20 years later, that her sleep again became disturbed in ways that echoed the initial impacts:

I couldn't sleep again, I had more disturbed sleep. The fear actually came back, but not anything like it was. (Marie)

Recreation

The loss of safety affected the women's ability to participate in the social and recreational activities they previously enjoyed. Some who had been highly physical and athletic before they were raped described feeling as if their energy was channelled elsewhere:

Before all this happened, I used to be bouncing around the whole place. I do triathlon, and over the years, before it happened, I was a very fast runner and now I just don't have the energy. Recently I did do the Half Iron Man because it was something I wanted to do three years ago, but it was real hard work. I still feel that I'm stuck inside with all this energy, trying to deal with this anger and this pain and when that's released … it's almost like a cloud lifted off my head and concrete lifted from me. (Helen)

The women's heightened concerns about safety and security affected their social and recreational options.

You've got to think about your security at all times. Even now, three years later, it's always on your mind to know that if you're going to go to a party that you have someone to get you back from a party. You lose your freedom, you've always got to think ahead, you can't be as spur of the moment as you'd like. (Helen)

For some women their anxieties were exacerbated by crowd situations heightening their sense of exposure and vulnerability.

> I went to Opera in the Park, and it was only two months after the attack. I'd gone with the kids. It was a really stupid thing to do, I was actually meant to meet a friend there and you know what it's like, perhaps you don't, but there's 200,000 people there! I arranged to meet [friend] somewhere and it had got mucked up, she wasn't there. So, we found somewhere where it was easy for the kids to find me, [daughter] went off to find her friends and left me, it was still light at this stage. Well, I sat there, panicked about being amongst all these people, thinking, 'God, what if I see him?' I just sat there and I just cried – here I was sitting there all by myself with 200,000 people and I just cried. I literally couldn't stop crying. [Daughter] came back and I made her stay with me. So, I didn't go to the next one. (Karen)

Work

How the women's working lives were affected differed greatly. Some felt they needed to take a period of time off work in order to concentrate on their healing and enable themselves to move on, while others felt that the very structure of going to work aided their recovery, and insisted on returning as soon as possible.

> For the first year I was absolutely fine, but that's because I now know I had a lot of mechanisms for dealing with it, and I worked my butt off – I was the best, I got promoted about three times because I was so good at work, but that's all I used to do. (Helen)

Raquel felt she was able to keep her work life completely separate, and even though her job entailed high public exposure, she was determined it would not be affected:

> I never lost my confidence, no, no way. Because he [MR] had nothing to do with it. Why would something in my personal life? Lots of high-profile people have problems with their relationships in their personal lives. It's not going to affect their ability to work. (Raquel)

Employers also differed in their responses. In Kathleen's case her employer wanted her to stay away from work while her bruises healed so the elderly folk she worked with would not find out she had been raped. When she returned, she said:

> I wasn't allowed to talk about it at work, in case some of the old people overheard. It was a bit hard. It was like, 'It's not my fault. I didn't want this

to happen and hello, this does happen in real life.' They knew. They were not stupid, they read newspapers and they knew, I'm sure they all knew. But you know it's a very Victorian attitude – you don't talk about these things. (Kathleen)

Other women felt those they worked with wanted to know more about it than they felt comfortable disclosing. Suzanne went back as soon as she could:

Although they were extremely supportive ... a lot of people didn't know what had happened, or how far Rewa had gone. So a lot of people snooped around and they'd ask questions like, 'Exactly what did he do to you?' That ticked me off a bit because I didn't really want to talk about that with anybody. (Suzanne)

Several women spoke of how difficult it was needing time off work, first, in the aftermath of the attack and again when the case went to trial. Some faced redundancy; others felt forced to resign. Gabriel went back to work a couple of weeks after the attack, and had the police ringing her there and arranging follow-up meetings, which annoyed her boss.

She called me into her office and told me that I was affecting the work place and that she really thought I should have some time off. She was really almost pissed off at me. It was not like she was saying, 'How are you feeling? Is there anything I can do? Would you like to take some time off?' I had no acknowledgement from her that anything had happened ... I just pretty much lost it. I was so angry! I walked out of her office and thought, 'Fuck this! I'm not going to work in this shitty hole!' So I resigned ... That was quite devastating for me, having to leave that place, because I was only 18, it was my first job since leaving school, and I had worked really hard there, moved up the business. I felt like I had lost that as well. I was quite devastated. (Gabriel)

Gabriel then had five months of not working and having counselling. It was a difficult time:

I couldn't work and I was blaming myself for it. I should be working and I'm not, I'm just watching videos all day. Although part of me said that I needed to do that because that was my healing time, there was another voice saying, 'You should be getting back to work, you should be enrolling in courses, you should be, I don't know, getting on with it.' (Gabriel).

Helen had moved to a new position about a year before the trial, and described her boss's attitude as *horrendous*:

> *She was totally unsympathetic. She knew what had been going on, but she said, 'Well, if you're going to go to court, then you'll have to take it as unpaid holiday'. (Helen)*

She was made redundant, which compounded the other financial losses incurred in the aftermath of the rape. These included needing to sell a house she had only bought recently, buying another, flying overseas to see her family, and paying for counselling – twice a week during some of the hardest times.

Other women were more fortunate in having understanding and supportive employers. For example, one woman said:

> *I had to let them know because I was going off every now and then and not coping and they were excellent. They were wonderful. If I had an employer who wasn't understanding, I would have had to leave work. I took sick leave for all my court appearances. Anything I did, I just took sick leave and there was no problem. They were very supportive. (Marie)*

Karen also felt very supported in the workplace:

> *They paid me for any time that I had off. They didn't even use my sick pay. They were just really wonderful. I was very lucky in that respect. (Karen)*

Some women described the ways in which they had tried to organise their work in order to make it more manageable. Karen, for instance, spoke of how three years on she still had a heightened startle response:

> *I still have post-traumatic stress symptoms, I still jump. My office at work, I've got my computer where I can see out the door, but if I sit at my desk, I've got my back to the door. Of course people knock on the door and I jump every time and all these poor people – they say, 'I'm really sorry' and I have to say, 'Don't worry, I startle really easily.' (Karen)*

Being in meeting spaces with men could be difficult.

> *I used to suffer really badly afterwards from panic attacks, which isn't good. And again it affects your work – I'm sitting in a meeting with about six men who I would never have had problems with before and basically having to say, 'Look I'm feeling rather sick, I'm going to have to leave the meeting,' and just because of my breathing basically. I was frightened to death! (laughter) (Helen)*

Employment that involved night work presented additional difficulties. Ann had to devise a plan to manage when her boss asked her to do a shift finishing at 9.30 pm one night:

I said to [boss], 'You know I'm going to use your cell-phone all the way home?' and she said, 'Yep that's fine.' As soon as I got in my car, I always check before I get in anyway – our car is also alarmed and has got a wheel-brace on it – I dialled [partner] and I talked to him. He has to talk to me even if he's watching TV and doesn't say anything, he has to be on that phone from the time I drove over the harbour bridge and onto the motorway and out here. He'll talk to me all the way until I get to the driveway and I'll go, 'Here now,' and he'll have the door ready for me. (Ann)

Travelling out of town for work was also a challenge. Shelley devised what she described as *a ritual around her own safety,* pushing furniture against the door and keying the emergency number into her phone so she could press 'Send' if need be. She decided to move from staying in ground-level units to high-rise hotels in order to feel safer. Despite her precautions, she described two relatively recent incidents that unsettled her. One involved a man knocking on her hotel room door at around 3 am, then opening it while she was getting out of bed. He had not identified himself and turned out to be the night security man investigating complaints that there was a party in one of the rooms.

It just completely threw me and I couldn't sleep for the rest of the night. I was really upset – all that kind of 'strangers in the night' sort of thing – and I did make a complaint and he made an apology ... When he apologised to me he said, 'I'm sorry, but ...' and then went on to say there was a party, and I just said to him, 'I don't give a shit about you or what you thought – I'm just telling you what I thought at the time and how it impacted on me.' (Shelley)

A few months later, in another city, she checked in with the same hotel chain:

I was allocated a room and I went up into the room and it was dark when I walked in and there was a man asleep in the bed. And it was again someone on night duty who had just chosen a bed to sleep in ... I said to them, 'I choose your hotels because it's safe and now you've com-promised my safety twice and I'll never go back.'... The other thing that made me upset is that when I went down and said, 'There's someone in the room,' they laughed. They thought it was hilarious. I said, 'I don't think it's funny. There's a man in my room that you've allocated to me. I expect that room to be free when I walk in.' I felt very angry at that. Whereas a lot of people might laugh and think it's quite hilarious, I lose my sense of humour when it comes to that sort of thing. So that's how it does impinge on me ... As my work mates said, 'Of all the people he came into your room!' (Shelley)

Relationships

All of the women described the different ways they felt their relationships with other people had been impacted on by MR attacking and/or raping them. Isabel spoke of how profoundly she felt a loss of confidence and self-esteem:

> *There's times in your life when you feel quite empowered and you feel that you've got something to offer to people and if you lose that feeling, if people just treat you like you're just a thing, you might feel you don't have much to offer to people. (Isabel)*

Rape erodes a sense of trust and safety in relationships, prompting some victims/survivors to withdraw from others.

> *I was very quiet with everyone. Quiet to the degree that I really was empty. I was struggling with myself and I just didn't know what to do ... I didn't want to say to anyone, what do you think I should do, or should I do this? I was very quiet. Just let me be. (Connie)*

> *[After the rape] I seemed to be more remote from people, I don't know if it's a consequence. I was very shy as a young child and maybe I closed back into my shell. (Isabel)*

Suzanne was attacked by MR one month before she was due to be married. It was difficult deciding whether or not to go ahead with the wedding:

> *I should have stuck to my guns on the wedding. I wasn't ready. I'm always the big, strong person, I don't get emotional, but it was too soon – I didn't enjoy it as much as I could have ... I would have liked to have put it back a couple of months but it didn't happen, never mind. I would have put it back if I had my way but my fiancée wanted to go ahead with it – the old protection thing. We'd made all the plans anyway ... It's basically one of the special days in your life and it wasn't so special because of that. (Suzanne)*

At the reception, reference was made in the speeches to her strength following the attack, alerting all those present to what she had undergone a month earlier.

A lot of my friends, particularly my girlfriends that I went to school with, didn't know anything about it, so they were all flabbergasted about it all. (Suzanne)

Helen said she spent the first year keeping herself busy working and training and avoiding intense relationships:

Then I found a new boyfriend who was also very shallow, who didn't talk about things on a deep level, so we just went out and went wild and had fun. And all of a sudden, I think it was the anniversary, something triggered and I just started to get really angry ... I really cared for him an awful lot and I was actually trying to try to speak to him, but he wasn't the right person to speak to. He couldn't handle it, so it started going downhill and I just about killed the relationship, nearly killing him in the process, like thumping and being not really violent but more verbally violent and then by July the relationship was downhill, the job was going downhill, the whole of my life went straight through to rock bottom, and Jesus, that was the end of my life – I had to be dragged out of that hole; it took a long time. (Helen)

Raquel felt that she may have stayed in an unhealthy relationship because of the rape:

I am really quite sure that if I hadn't been raped I would have left a lot earlier, in fact I know that. The other thing is maybe the problems wouldn't have been so great if I hadn't been raped – who knows, the relationship might have worked a lot better? I'll never know. I ended up a victim in my relationship. Even though you think you're really strong and you are really strong, you still need someone to lean on for quite a while. The thought of not having that person to lean on or trying to leave that person that you want to lean on, that's really difficult ... I didn't feel strong enough to just be me and be on my own. (Raquel)

I used to get these fears that my relationship was just me being with somebody to help me get through court, that I had transposed something on to that relationship. That I had created it somehow out of my wants and needs to have someone with me to get through it and that at the end of it all I wouldn't need him and I'd spit him out. And he felt like that too, we talked about it. Do I really love him or am I just co-dependent? Do I just need somebody right now and if so, so what? I need somebody right now and he's there. We have had a lot of problems. (Gabriel)

Some women felt they may have entered into relationships as a way of helping them manage feelings of insecurity:

Looking back now, I probably threw myself into a relationship fairly quickly because I didn't want to feel that I had been affected in any way ... I met [husband] quite soon afterwards. He was actually really supportive and knew everything that had happened ... I kind of did things that I wouldn't have done otherwise either. Wild things like sex before marriage and those sorts of things that I wasn't going to get into ... Our first year of marriage was a terrible year because I was still really afraid of being alone in the dark and afraid of being alone. (Marie)

Other women found it difficult initially to conceive of being in a heterosexual relationship again:

Every man, except my dad, was a suspect. I was really worried at one stage because I hated men and I felt comfortable with women and I thought that I was going to be gay and they [counsellor] said, 'No, truly this is something you do go through.' The thought of being intimate with a man – it was like no way, no way in hell! But obviously as life goes on, the side of you being a woman accepts and changes. And [partner] is really understanding and he's a really good guy. (Ann)

It is often assumed that one of the most difficult recovery aspects for women who have been raped will be resuming sexual intimacy, and other research in this area shows that for many women it is [3, 9]. Some of the women said they were impacted on negatively.

What has happened in sex is I get flashes of the rape, of the attack. It's a bit freaky ... you just get fearful and you can't actually go along with it. (Patricia)

Most said that the impacts on their sexual lives were relatively minor, compared with other effects, and several spoke of how determined they were to resume sexual intimacy with their partners soon after the rape.

I think it was quite important for me to know that I could have a good experience and I was quite relieved next time I did have a good sexual experience. (Isabel)

I wanted to know I was still a woman, that I was still sexually appealing ... I need to know that somewhere out there someone will want to touch me in that way, not, 'Wham, bam, thank you ma'am, see you later.' (Connie)

One way some said they managed sex was by compartmentalising, maintaining a clear distinction between shared intimacy with their partners as opposed to what MR did to them.

I'm the sort of person that makes a clear distinction between making love/sex and rape ... I'm not going to associate or connect the two things as being remotely alike. I came home and made love with my boyfriend on the Monday afternoon, it was something I wanted to do. We were two-and-a-half months into our relationship and we were still in the honeymoon phase and we were having sex all the time, it's like why should what happened ... ? .That had nothing to do with my sex life, absolutely nothing. It doesn't change how I feel about my boyfriend, it doesn't change the way I feel about sex ... It was an invasion of my body and it was an act of violence. (Raquel)

Several women commented that the actual rape was not the worst part of the experience for them, and wondered in part if their age and sexual experience helped them in this respect:

The rape part of the event was the least frightening part of it. Being tied up with my face down, not being able to breathe with him circling around the room, going through all my drawers and my wardrobe – that was the most frightening thing. Because I didn't know what he was doing. At least when he was raping me I knew what he was doing and he had such a little weenie anyway it didn't matter. That was not fearful at all. I can understand it would have been fearful for a young child who'd never experienced sex. But certainly I've always thought, I'm a good age, if you like, for that to happen because I could actually rationalise it. (Shelley)

Ann said she felt aware of the girls raped by Joseph Thompson for whom this would be their first experience of sex:

These young girls were just starting to be women, not even to the point of being women yet, and they got stripped and made to feel like dirt ... I knew what it was like to make love and to love someone before someone come along and did really undignified things to me. I knew what it was like to be with a man and make love and to feel like a woman before I went with someone that made me feel like shit. (Ann)

Some women were surprised to find themselves going through a stage of being more sexual than they had been previously:

I actually got into quite a period of wanting to have a lot of sex, which [partner] was quite happy about! But it was an abnormal amount, I thought, once or twice a day for weeks on end. I really didn't think about it at the time, but afterwards, I thought maybe that's actually a response to some kind of grief or whatever that I didn't know about. (Karen)

It's almost like I was promiscuous, but I wasn't. I didn't act out a lot of my promiscuity but I felt quite promiscuous, if that makes sense. I was really aware of attractions to lots of different men and wanting to be attractive myself. Do you know what I mean? Making time to initiate friendships with attractive men, just in order to feel good about myself or something like that. So I had a lot of different experiences with different men that weren't necessarily sexual, but kind of had that element to them for me somehow. I was quite desperate about it too. I always had to have a crush on somebody and rejection would be absolutely devastating. I think I was searching for a boyfriend to help me feel better about men. (Gabriel)

What Shelley found difficult was the lack of guidance and acknowledgement that she might want to be sexually intimate with her partner.

No one said anything! I was given all these tablets: a morning after pill and a Chlamydia thing and all these antibiotics in case you had these terrible bugs and HIV and all that jazz. And no one ever said to me, 'Well, this will last you three weeks and actually you can have sex after ...'. After you've had a baby or had a hysterectomy, people are really willing to tell you when you can have sex. But after I was raped, it was like there were no clear guidelines on when I could, and actually I did want to have sex ... I wanted to get back on the horse again to see: was I normal, was I still normal? (Shelley)

Issues of power and control

Early commentators often spoke of rape as 'unwanted sex', presenting it from the offender's perspective as a crime of passion. More recent theorising, by feminist writers in particular, has emphasised that rape has more to do with violence than sex, and is typically motivated by the desire for power and control [18-21]. In the act of rape the rapist seizes control of the victim's body, violating the victim's sense of autonomy. The sense of disempowerment experienced is immense. Another person has taken charge of one's body, manipulating it like a puppet, reducing the victim to an object, a prop in that man's world.

In the aftermath of rape many victims describe a heightened sensitivity to controlling or bullying behaviour. This can be apparent in sometimes contradictory ways, resulting in both avoidant and confronting responses. Some women spoke of how their levels of anxiety around bullying behaviour increased after the attack:

One of the biggest bullies in my life was my ex husband and after the attack I was terrified of being anywhere near him on my own. (Shelley)

Raquel also described initially being less assertive in relationships with men, then moving to the other end of the spectrum:

> For a long time I wasn't able to stand up for myself as well as I should have been. I wasn't able to say, 'This is what I want; this is what I don't want; I'm not happy with this.' I accepted a lot of things in my life that I wasn't happy with, just to keep the peace or because I didn't feel like I had a right to say … After being in a situation with someone being in complete control over me physically like that, I continued to allow other people to have control over things … I was letting them abuse me. And it took a long time. Gradually I got stronger and stronger and I stood up for myself a lot more. It took a while; eventually I actually became a lot more assertive than I used to be. What happened was I went from being a victim and coping, just in survival mode, to going to the extreme. I went to the extreme of being very controlling of my life and trying to control everything around me, and then being very upset if I couldn't. That's why I had problems in my relationships. (Raquel)

She described going through a stage where she enjoyed the power she had through being able to taunt and control men sexually:

> My ex-boyfriend said to me, 'You're the kind of girl that guys look at and want to sleep with but are not interested in having a relationship with.' He found it difficult having a relationship with me because of the attention I got. We were going to lots of dance place things and I'd get loads and loads of attention. I think part of it, it sounds terrible, but I was getting off on the fact that I had lots and lots of guys looking at me, wanting me. It was like, 'You can't have me!' It was like a power trip for me. It's like me getting my own back. 'You can look but you can't have. Sorry!' It was like, 'Ha, ha, ha I'm in control!' I did get very controlling. (Raquel)

Several reflected on the ways they felt their opinion of men diminished after the rape, and observed how difficult it was managing their feelings of anger towards men, and how strongly they reacted against any form of control:

> I can't stand to be controlled by men at all now. I've never liked that, but any sign of control of any type, trust is gone completely. I don't trust men. It's getting better. The anger! I lost a boyfriend or I'd leave him because I was so angry at men that he was getting it all. (Helen)

Some struggled to manage the fears and concerns of those around them regarding their safety. For example, Raquel initially rebelled against her boyfriend's efforts to ensure she had someone to walk her down the road.

I thought he was being paranoid, he was pathetic. I was like, 'I'm fine, I'm fine. Don't smother me,' sort of thing. And he was only looking after my safety but I sometimes felt it was a bit overboard. I didn't want to deal with the fact that I had to do that ... And I certainly didn't want someone to be controlling me either. So I used to rebel occasionally and walk down to my car. It was the feeling that because of being raped I had to do this ... You're supposed to do it because it's sensible. (Raquel)

Although she reacted against what felt like 'smothering' at the time, Raquel also described later incidents where she became aware of feeling vulnerable on her own in social situations. Seven years after she was raped she was overseas with her partner at a club when he left her on her own briefly:

Suddenly I was standing there and I looked around and I saw a few guys looking at me, and I thought, 'I'm in Sydney, I don't know anyone here and I'm standing here by myself. Oh my God!' (Raquel)

Gabriel described an increased sense of needing her own space to feel safe, particularly her own physical space.

I hated people touching me or bumping into me. If someone grabbed my hand to check the time or something, spasms would rush through me. I was my own person. I didn't want anyone touching me apart from people I knew and loved. Any stranger that tried to chat me up I would cut down like a knife, or anybody who bumped me I would be angry. (Gabriel)

One time she saw a strange guy she knew from working at a café walking up the footpath towards her.

He and I were walking towards each other and I moved to get out of his way and he moved to get out of my way and I walked into him! I absolutely freaked out because he was big and he was wearing black clothes. I started to get these terrible phobias about dark skinned people which I am kind of embarrassed to talk about. Anyone with prison tattoos on their hands, not that I ever saw any tattoos [on MR], but just anybody who looked dodgy or gang related, I would find myself crossing roads ... just going out of my way to get away from them. (Gabriel)

What others described were times when they felt their own anger and need for control was expressed in hostility towards others.

At work one day, some girl was driving me totally up the wall, nothing to do with her, it just was anger. I snapped. I just threw a glass, didn't throw it at her, I threw it at the wall and it was aaarrghh! I thought, 'Oh my God, I never used to do these things.' I found out I was becoming more of the abuser so I wasn't the abused. I got out of that quickly when I started realising what I was doing, but yeah, it's frightening. You just think you're losing your marbles, and you do. (Helen)

Blame and guilt

A common reaction for many victims of rape is to blame themselves for what has happened, in part because so many societal beliefs about rape hold the woman responsible [2, 15, 22-24]. In the case of the women attacked by MR, there was little scope for victim-blaming since they could not be accused of flirting, drinking too much, or 'asking' to be raped. Despite this, some of the women still struggled not to blame themselves or feel blamed by others. One way this was apparent was in how some behaved after being raped.

I dress totally differently. Before I used to wear quite short skirts. I thought, maybe it's because I dress like that? I went through things – maybe he looked at me like a whore so I'll dress like one and I did that for a while, and my sister said, 'No, no, no!' And then I went the total opposite, became the nanny. (Ann)

Other women also referred to a heightened awareness of how people judged their appearance.

People are looking at you, knowing that that's what's happened to you. Like, 'Oh, she's been raped but look what she's wearing! Is it any wonder?' You know? I remember going to a fancy dress party afterwards and we had to dress up, and I remember a group of the women sniggering and carrying on. I won first prize. I had to get up there, feeling really uncomfortable with all these people thinking, 'Oh, look, she deserves it. Look at what she's got on!' Like, 'As long as we don't dress like that we'll be all right.' (Kathleen)

Shelley said it was important to her that she had not done anything she could be blamed for:

I hadn't done anything to provoke it. That's one of the reasons why I think that I have no self-blame. I didn't leave a door open. I didn't do anything wrong for it to happen and I think I probably wouldn't have coped as well had I actually made a mistake ... Female blame, always the guilty mother, guilty daughter or whatever, whereas I hadn't left a window open, I hadn't met him, I didn't know him – so I had no guilt about it. That was one of my coping mechanisms. (Shelley)

Others were also adamant that it was not their fault, even when those close to them implied a degree of responsibility.

> I never ever considered that I was responsible for it or held myself accountable for it. I've found out since that [husband] actually said to [friend] one day, 'She did leave that window open, I've told her not to leave that window open.' I think [friend] nearly turned around and thumped him! ... I never thought it was all my fault because I left this window open. I never dumped on myself why it happened. I always felt it was his [MR] fault because he was just an idiot, what was he doing in my house anyway? (Jennifer)

What the women said they needed to survive

Recovery from rape is an individual journey, as evidenced in personal accounts from survivors [25-28]. It is also a journey that, for many, passes through similar themes and issues, and the women attacked by MR described these fully. In the aftermath of rape, doing anything can feel difficult. The women spoke of the things they found hardest during this time. Many referred to the loss of safety, and their concern that the fear they now felt would rule their lives forever.

> Fear, the irrational fear. That will always be the predominant thing, just being able to cope with being scared. It's a really major irrational fear. (Jennifer)

> The thing that stayed the longest is the darkness, the nighttime stuff. The invasion of privacy, the noise and the darkness – that pitch black. I will never, ever forget how dark it was. (Suzanne)

> The effect that someone has come and violated you and there's nothing you can do and are you ever safe for the rest of your life if you are by yourself? It was so easy for a man to come and do that and have such an impact on your life. It's a whole scary scenario and are you ever really safe? You can lock yourself in your palace – someone can always get in. (Ann)

Several spoke of how hard it was having others know what had happened.

> Going back into a normal situation, going back to work, having to face people. If I could have hidden away I would have, and never come out of hiding again. (Marie)

Being raped resulted in multiple impacts on all the women, physically, emotionally and socially. It also took them into the strange new world of the criminal justice system with all its many demands and procedures. With so much to manage, what did they need to help them survive?

> I needed two things. I needed information about the attack. I know that sometimes police can't tell victims everything because it's unhelpful to the process but I needed as much information as I could get about it ... And I wanted a buddy, I wanted a rape buddy. I didn't want a counsellor ... I knew nobody who had been raped and there was nobody that I could identify with. Just to really understand what it feels like to get up in the night and not be able to go to the toilet because you're terrified there's going to be somebody there. (Shelley)

Some women used medication to help, such as anti-depressants or sleeping pills. Many had counselling, although their experiences varied greatly (see Chapter 5). Several of the women described how, years after the rape, they still felt too afraid to be on their own, something that could take a toll on their relationships. Ann talked about the impact of her ongoing fear of aloneness on her partner:

> We did go through a hard part where we fought about it to the point where I said, 'If you don't like it leave, go, because this is the way I am.' Even my boss said once said to me, 'Ann, that's something you're going to have to get over.' I said to her, 'Until the day you, your sister or someone close to you ever goes through an attack, don't ever mention that to me again.' That was about a month ago. Just the thought makes me 'aaahhh', and I start feeling sick ... You can't make someone overcome something, it comes in time. I've said to people, 'Do you think I like being like this?' I think I've overcome heaps, but the dark and the thought of being alone, just makes me crumble to pieces. I always hope that one day I will be over that, but now eight years on, I'm not holding my breath about it. (Ann)

All the women spoke of their fears of the dark, of managing arriving home at night or being in the house alone. Several commented that they were fortunate that financially they could afford to have lights, deadlocks and security alarms fitted, although some struggled with the decision to adopt this strategy:

> I thought if I have an alarm it's going to be reminding me all the time, but it actually hasn't worked like that. I'm not concerned about walking into the house like I was, that used to freak me out so much. (Karen)

The loss of trust experienced in a rape attack is huge. While some women withdrew from relationships for a while, others chose to go through part of the healing process in a relationship.

> *I had a boyfriend after I was attacked ... four or five months afterwards, and that was my first kind of real love as well and he had also been sexually assaulted by a woman, so that was quite an interesting situation for us to work through. So I was able to work through a lot of my sexual stuff with him and you know it was things like I couldn't have my wrists touched or different parts of your body, you would have to have the light on or a window open so that you could see the person's face. There are different types of physical positions that can be male dominated or sexually dominated by your partner which weren't okay. There is a whole process to overcoming that kind of stuff and I did quite a lot of that with him which was really good ... I felt very trusted and safe and that was really important. I think if I hadn't have had that positive sexual experience after being attacked, if I had entered a relationship that wasn't positive in that way, it could really have damaged me quite a lot more. But it hasn't as such so that is good. (Gabriel)*

Taking back control of one's life was important, and for some this meant establishing a clear separation between the attack and other parts of their lives. Several of the women spoke of how they resisted seeing MR as a person, finding it easier to imagine him as something else, something 'other'. Gabriel referred to a dream or premonition she had two weeks before she was attacked and linked this to the ways she tried to cope by not seeing MR as a real person – something that was hard to sustain when he was physically present in the courtroom.

> *I never let him be a person to me because my way of forming meaning was to associate extreme evil or extreme badness with that person, and because I won then I had conquered him. But he was still around, see, it didn't fit, you know? He was actually a person and he existed and he had to go to court. My way of forming meaning was fighting this bizarre made up force. It was like that for me. Fighting a beast. Slaying the dragon.*
>
> *And that really helped me too, but it sounded pretty mad to all my family and my friends. I think some of them got the general grasp of it, though. My mother was quite good, she said, 'Well, if you dreamt about it, why didn't you move out?' (laughs). It's not so much that I dreamt about it as such, but a sense that something strange was going to happen. Which is probably why I've been able to find meaning so well because I could easily look at it and say that it was meant to happen and this is what I've got out of it and now I'm up and off. Maybe that helped me to shift from victim to survivor mode as well. That instantaneous meaning. This is what it means, this is what it means. I've slayed the dragon, I've won, I'm off. (Gabriel)*

A similar strategy was employed by other women when they chose a different way of compartmentalising what had happened. Ann achieved this not by changing MR's identity but her own:

> My family call me Anna, but after I got raped, after I went through this with Rewa, I actually changed my name to Ann and that's how I live now. My family can't change but that happened to Anna, not Ann, and I had to play this little game with myself. That is how I coped. Just put it in a box – that happened to her but this is me. (Ann)

Connie decided her recovery depended on her moving out of the city where it had happened, and away from the concerned faces of her family:

> When I got raped, I couldn't mentally hack being in my own home. I had my home blessed, I did 'life things' but it was not living ... About a year later, I decided, that's it, I'm outta here because if I don't I will die ... I moved out of the area. I went away. I could face it by myself. It was the fact that to look at me was hurting them most ... I didn't go back to Auckland for maybe two, three, years, I still don't like going back ... I guess it's like anything, say if you're involved in a road accident and your passenger got killed, whenever you went down that road you would always remember that particular spot and I guess me going to Auckland is a reminder that I will always remember. I don't have fond memories of going back but I've started to go back ... They gave me the support – 'as long as you'll be all right.' I didn't want to say to them, 'I have no idea if I'm going to be all right.' (Connie)

Another way of achieving a sense of separation was through changing their appearance, which for Gabriel involved shaving off her hair shortly before going to the trial.

> When I went to court, it was two days before my birthday or something that I testified. My mother and I decided that she was going to give me a new bed for my birthday and I realised that I had kept my bed from when I was attacked – I was actually partly attacked on my bed. I realised that I had had my hair for almost that long as well and I thought about what that represented for me and the bed was nightmares and fear and it was a couple of years of putting my head on that pillow. [Shaving] the hair was an act of boldness on my part, stripping that away, letting that go, letting go of your vanity, leaving your vanity with your bed. Phew! See ya! (Gabriel)

A difficult aspect for some of the women to manage was a sense of expectation or pressure from others as to how they should be feeling or what they should be doing.

Shelley described how she felt annoyed when others told her she *needed to feel angry,* saying she found other ways of managing her feelings:

> He [MR] was like this black blob that did something really awful to me. It's the same relationship that I would have with the car that knocked me down ... I don't in any way say that you should treat it as an accident, but I have no relationship with the car either. There's too many other things in healing to get on with. That wasn't a conscious thing, that I'm not going to be angry. It's just that I've never found that space there. [He was] just a big black virus that did this to me. (Shelley)

She felt pressured by the way some people seemingly expected her to recover quickly, as if from the flu:

> It's a bit like after the funeral, we'll give you the flowers and we'll say nice things but a week later you're supposed to get on with it and act normal. I often felt anger at people's inability to ask me how I was. (Shelley)

Other women also said they felt those around them expected them to be angry and expressive:

> I actually find that it's other people that get into the, 'Oh that bastard, he should be strung up!' I think if they want to deal with it like that, that's okay. I can't go there really. I still have such a lot of anger that I actually have to remove myself of thinking of him, because I just know of the intense emotion that I feel being in a courtroom with him, it's just too huge to deal with. (Karen)

> It took me a long time to get angry and it wasn't until when he got caught, then I was able to. I was angry about how [ex-partner] treated me, I was really angry and really bitter about that and I took it out on [him]. After they caught Rewa, my anger started to come out gradually over a long, long period of time. I think it takes a long time of healing before you can get angry at Rewa. Maybe for other women the anger comes out earlier; for me the anger came out later. (Raquel)

What several of the women said they really valued was friends, partners, or family members who could let them say and do whatever they needed to for their own recovery. Gabriel valued the 'healing journey' she had been on with her partner, who supported her so fully through the trial:

He was really good at acknowledging and allowing me to just be what I was being and feel what I was feeling and not try and make it all better for me. Just sit with it. He would just sit with me when I cried, he wouldn't say a word and initially that frustrated me and then I realised that was really what I wanted, just someone to sit with what was going on with me. (Gabriel)

A couple of the women also referred to the role their faith in God played in helping them recover.

Knowing that God is with me is a great thing and knowing what he wants from me and knowing that he has it all in the Bible, how to deal with things too, a wee handbook for life there. So there is that side, and the other side is that you have your natural personality – I am determined, I'm stubborn. (Lorna)

Managing fear over time

Many of the women described how there seemed to be no magic answer to overcoming their fears, and often referred to the passage of time itself as a healer. Some felt they needed to remove pressures and expectations and give themselves time to recover before moving out of their comfort zones. What several stressed was the importance of recognising their own limits, and not expecting too much of themselves too soon.

I went flatting once. I thought I was cured. I was going to go by myself to prove to the world that this man, whatever he is, is not going to run my life anymore. I lasted three months in a flat – I came out looking like a total haggard mess! Never slept at night, slept with one foot in the bed and one foot out, with a butcher's knife at the side of my pillow, waiting ... (Ann)

The most important thing with recovery I've found is just time, and that's all it is – it's just taking each step when you're ready to take it, waiting until you're actually confident to spend a night by yourself in the house and things like that ... I think that was one of those things that the counsellor said to me, 'You do what you have to do, it doesn't matter how stupid it feels.' I think of the cupboards I used to always open and look at, some of the things I used to look at were ridiculous really, no one was going to fit in there! (laugh). If they were hiding in there they were seriously sick! But I remember saying to her, it was that irrational thing, it's doing those irrational things. She said to me, 'Do those things that it will make it work for you. It doesn't matter how you feel about it. It doesn't matter whether it's absolutely ridiculous, if that's what it takes to make you feel secure at night when you go to bed, you do them.' (Jennifer)

Karen described the progression over time, gradually extending her sense of safety and feelings of autonomy:

> *I couldn't go into the house at night. If I got home and it was dark and no one was home, I couldn't go into the house. Then I got to the stage where I could go into the lounge, but I couldn't go into my own bedroom, and that was awful, I just found that fear totally debilitating. I'd just never experienced anything like it. The rational part of me was thinking, 'Oh, this is really stupid, of course you can go into your bedroom,' but I was paralysed, I was literally paralysed with fear and I just couldn't do it ...*
>
> *It does just dissipate with time. I used to give myself a good talking to and all the rest, but really it just goes with time. For me the whole process is about time ... You just have to take little steps. That was hard for me, to take little steps. I wanted to be out there, I didn't want to have this fear – which made it even harder to admit that I did have it, but I couldn't do anything about it. There were lots of areas in my life where I curtailed what I did, I was very conscious about what I wore, I was very conscious of who I talked to. Whereas previously I would take anybody at face value, that just changed so much for me, it really did. (Karen)*

Alternatively, others felt they needed to make themselves do things early on in the recovery process, in order to minimise possible long-term impacts developing. Suzanne's fiancée and his family insisted that she should not sleep in her flat after she was raped there and that she move out:

> *They tried to push me to do it, and I didn't want to do it. I said, 'No, I want to stay here,' and I had to dig my toes in to what I wanted to do ... It's like falling off a bike – if you just run away from it straight away, how are you going to face it? I'd have to say it was pretty hard going but I had to do it. (Suzanne)*
>
> *I made myself stay there. My sister-in-law kept saying, 'Come and stay up here,' but I made myself stay there because I knew that this is what my life is going to be like now, I actually have to get used to this. So I always slept with radios on and I shut myself in the room with the alarm on out in the rest of the house. I don't do that now. (Frances)*

Lorna described staying at her parents on an isolated farm property:

> *The first time that I was in a situation, which was probably within a month, maybe even less [of the attack], where I had to be in the house alone, mum and dad said, 'Will you be all right? Do you want to come with us?*

Da de dah.' I was like, 'Well, I have to deal with this and if I don't deal with it now, it will be worse the next time.' So I stayed on my own. It was just during the daytime, but I decided I had to do it then ... I refused to be kept a prisoner ... Generally I just got on with life. (Lorna)

She noted that for her, everything became easier once she had done it the first time:

Having to face people who knew me and who knew what happened, because you don't know how they are going to react to you ... That would probably have been the worst thing. Going back to work the first time ... Then staying on my own for the first time. It's really the firsts of things. [What helped was] knowing there was only going to be one first time. Once you've done it, it's done. (Lorna)

What several observed was suddenly realising that they were doing things again that they had stopped doing in the immediate aftermath. Frances commented:

It's quite interesting – over the last three or four weeks, I've really in lots of ways almost claimed my property back again. I spent a lot of time out in the garden, getting it up to scratch, which I hadn't done before. I've just felt really happy just to be at home. I haven't wanted to go out and do anything or be anywhere else, I haven't been like that for years. (Frances)

Some of the women spoke of the changes others noticed in them over time also:

People who have known me for years have said, 'At least you've got life back in your eyes again, you're not like a zombie anymore, you're more confident in yourself.' And basically I don't take shit from men anymore ... No one can give me back me, only me if I choose to find me again. (Connie)

Ann reacted angrily, however, when she felt others were being glib in their references to the healing properties of time, experiencing this as pressure:

People say time will heal, and I heard that so many times and I thought, 'Yeah, well up you! You don't understand, I don't want to talk to you!' (Ann)

Awareness of the other women

One of the distinguishing features of this case was the number of women brought to court to testify against the same man. Being part of a large, highly-publicised serial rape case added another layer of experience for the women. Many said they took comfort from knowing there were others like them:

> It was quite comforting to know that I was just part of a group, that it wasn't a one-off, that there was actually a whole bunch of us that this had happened to. (Shelley)

> It probably sounds a bit weird but I was actually quite pleased that it wasn't just me. Not that I wanted it to happen to anyone else of course, but it made me feel a lot more comfortable. I wasn't the only one. There was some one else out there who understood how I was feeling. Even if I had never met them, they were there. (Kathleen)

Knowing that others existed was also frustrating when no contact was permissible. Some of the women recalled the aloneness they experienced after the rape:

> Initially we weren't allowed any contact at all and I felt incredibly isolated. I felt very alone and all I had was the female police officers telling me that, 'So and so said that too ...' She never gave the name. So I did feel incredibly isolated and I was actually quite desperate to connect with somebody who'd been through the same thing. Then I went to the sentencing and met a few ... it was wonderful to actually meet these people. (Shelley)

In the absence of tangible information, Helen said:

> You make up your own stories. 'Society says that all women are stupid and are asking for it. Does that mean the other 26 are like that?' That sounds really awful, but it almost is like that: Are they normal women? Are they all his girlfriends? You don't know. (Helen)

As the trial progressed, some of the women began noticing each other at court, particularly those who returned for the verdict and/or sentencing. Some felt it would be good to have a get-together and one of the women organised a lunch at her place. This was an informal gathering of as many of the women as wanted to come, along with the police and prosecutors, and including some partners and family members. It was an important occasion for many who attended. Shelley felt it was such a powerful experience that she commented:

> I didn't even want to go home! I just felt it was the most amazing experience I'd ever had. When I left I just wanted to shout to the streets that I'd just had this wonderful time and it was just so wonderful to meet them all and there was such a sisterhood there. (Shelley)

Karen also rated it very positively:

> *Certainly the lunch was one of the most healing things that happened for me. I would imagine we were all incredibly nervous about what it was going to be like in the same room ... A lot of women just went to court and gave their evidence, and they didn't go to the court again. Nearly all the women came to the lunch. It was an incredibly emotional experience. I would say that that's where my real healing came, to actually feel the strength of those women and to know how much we'd all been through ... There's a bond there that is indescribable but it's there: we had all suffered at his hands, we all had to rebuild our lives. I found it was just very empowering. (Karen)*

Patricia felt the contact with the other women was important for her not so much in terms of healing and recovery, but to bring things to more of a conclusion.

> *I like to think that I was pretty well healed by the time I got to meet them all ... But it was all part of the completion process ... It is just something else to say that everything else I went through wasn't for nothing, that some good is going to come out of it. (Patricia)*

One disconcerting feature for some of the women was noticing the physical similarities among MR's victims. The police had noted how he stalked a particular 'type', targeting in particular fair, attractive women. Karen described how this had fuelled her curiosity:

> *I had always wanted to meet the other women ... I had been told about all these similarities between us. I can remember the police saying to me that there were these similarities in us, about us. They included me in it, but I didn't actually think I fitted in the blonde, beautiful profile. There's quite a similar look, something about the cheekbones or just being fine featured. There's quite a similarity. When you take us individually, you can't see it, yet when we were all in a group together, it was like wow, this is really quite freaky! (Karen)*

Gabriel also said she initially found it weird walking into the lunch:

> *There have been some times where it has been just really bizarre. Coming here and drinking champagne with women who were raped by Malcolm Rewa! You walk into the room and eight of them are blonde and thin and pretty much the same height and 'Ohh!' It freaked me out! It was sick! I got over that and talked to everyone and they were really lovely and I really enjoyed them but it was freaky. He had a really specific type that he*

went for and I looked around this room and it was like oh my God. It felt like I was looking in a fishbowl! (Gabriel)

Some women said they had felt anxious beforehand about what would happen at the lunch and were relieved that it was not too intense or full of sad story swapping.

That was the one thing that put me off about going – I didn't want it to be a morbid thing. You have already been there and done that a few times. You go through the event, the statement, whatever else happens, the court process, the pre court process so I didn't really want that to happen. I didn't want to go into a situation with a whole lot of bitter women, but they weren't like that. (Lorna)

I was really concerned that when we first started to share our stories that it would be a competition as to who got beaten the most and who got raped four times and all that kind of sick stuff. I was quite scared about that because of what [another victim/survivor] had said to me: 'Oh, you're so lucky you weren't raped' ... I think I just undervalued my own experience because I wasn't raped. I wanted to acknowledge my own experience and not make light of it. (Gabriel)

Isabel had been keen to go but was unable to find the venue on the day. She was a little ambivalent regarding whether she thought it would have been good for her to meet the other women:

We wouldn't have had much in common really. The only thing we've got in common is having been a victim. But I guess it would have been interesting how they dealt with it. I don't know. I've got mixed feelings because I don't know whether I would enjoy it really. It's a funny way to make friends, isn't it, having been a common victim of the same thing? (Isabel)

Her concern was reflected in comments made by several others, who were clearly uncomfortable at the prospect of building relationships on the basis of a rape connection.

When they had this thing about wanting to get together, a part of me thought, 'How nice,' but another part thought, 'Well, the only thing I have in common with these other ladies is that we were all raped by the same man.' I had nothing else to say to those other women apart from if it just hadn't happened I would never know them. I thought, 'Somewhere it's got to stop, where this person has even a slight control on my life,' and I made it that day. I didn't want to celebrate with the other women because you celebrate to mean happiness, you don't celebrate a sadness, and that's what I believe he's left me, part of my life has been really sad. (Ann)

Suzanne went to the lunch but also described mixed feelings:

I remember one of the victims making reference to something like the brotherhood or the sisterhood of survivors, and I didn't like that – I didn't want to be a team. If they'd had another lunch or something afterwards, I wouldn't have gone ... Probably because we were only brought together by one circumstance so I didn't see the need to continue that 'team', if they call it that. There was really no real need for us to meet each other, although I think it helped everyone too, but once we met each other at that lunch, that was it. (Suzanne)

Jennifer, on the other hand, felt she may well have been able to establish good relationships with some of the women – but not in these circumstances.

There were some people there that I thought if I'd met them in a different situation, I might have stayed in contact with them and been good friends. But because that was the thing that you had in common, I think it would be hard to be friends with them and not at times harp back to it. (Jennifer)

The lunch was affirming for many because it enabled them to see the other women involved in their 'ordinariness'. Frances reflected:

When I met them here, I was amazed at how ordinary these people are. They're anyone's sister or wife. I don't know what I thought before that, I hadn't really consciously thought of anything, but I was surprised – these were just people going about their lives, trying to just do their own thing, or do whatever people do, when this happened to them.

To see so many all at one time was quite an eerie sort of feeling too – this is why we're all here. This is the common thread between all these women. We could have been a knitting group! It was quite a strange feeling that everyone was here because of Malcolm Rewa, it was quite weird. My sister-in-law came with me. We hardly said a word the whole way home and just as we were driving down our street she said, 'That was really bizarre!' and I said, 'Yeah, that's how I feel too.' It just felt really strange, not horrible, but we both came away with this 'wow' feeling. (Frances)

One factor that seemed to affect how the women felt about meeting each other involved the length of time since they had been attacked. In most cases it was the more recent victims who appeared to want, and appreciated, contact with each other. Raquel, whose attack had been one of the earlier ones, observed that meeting the other women may have been more beneficial for some of MR's later victims than for her, since they were at an earlier stage of the recovery process. Of the lunch, she said:

> I'm not interested in being around people that are still dealing with it, because for me that's draining my energy. I've put it behind me. For me, I don't want to keep contact with the women because I don't want to keep it in the present, I don't want a connection with Rewa ... It's too late for me. I've already been through my process. It would have been fantastic, absolutely fantastic to have some of those other women around three or four years ago. It would have been great. So for some of them it's going to be fantastic for them. For me, it's of absolutely no benefit. In fact it would be detrimental for me to continue ... I just felt really sad. I felt sad more than solidarity. I just thought, 'My God! Isn't it terrible – all these lives that had been ruined for a period of time' ... I just thought how sad it was. (Raquel)

From the women's comments it is clear that many gained from the opportunities to meet and connect with others involved in the case. This experience could be validating and comforting, and was an important step in some women's recovery. It is also apparent that not all the women wanted contact with others, however, and even many of those who did were aware that this would be a temporary connection. For, as some directly noted, the only thread linking these women's lives together was that they had all been sexually attacked by the same man – not the most positive of platforms on which to build a relationship.

Gabriel summed up how several felt when she asserted that, even if the only thread linking these women's lives was having been attacked by MR, their survival stories deserve recognition.

> I wanted to acknowledge all the women for their experiences. I acknowledged them for the pain that they went through, but I was more interested in acknowledging, like, 'Congratulations! You have survived the most horrific thing anyone could conjure up in their dreams, and you've done it! Do you realise what you have done?' Do they realise what an achievement it is just to survive this kind of thing?
>
> Do I realise that? Do I acknowledge that? You have to and you have to do it all the time and it is not just once. You have to keep looking back and going, 'Wow, I can't believe I got through that! Shit!' So that is what I try and do with people who have disclosed to me, whether it's a client or a friend, that they have been abused. To acknowledge the strength and the

journey that they have had from there and the journey that continues. That it is ongoing, yeah, the continuous journey. (Gabriel)

Moving on: Life after rape

The women's lives were all changed by the attack, and some of the many negative impacts have been described in this chapter. It would not be a complete account, however, without mention of the positive impacts also acknowledged by many of the women. Life was never the same again, and although initially this seemed for the worse, over time other effects became obvious.

Fearing they might die in the attack prompted several women to reassess what life meant to them. Suzanne, for instance, said:

Probably the biggest change that it made to my life is I said I never wanted children and after that happened, it made me change my views ... I could have quite easily just been gone, just like that, that's just how quick life can go and I really did think that that was quite a possibility at the time ... So when I got married the next month, I decided yes we will ... It just made me realise, maybe it would be quite nice to have a little mix of [husband] and me. (Suzanne)

Some of the women talked of a conscious process by which they sought to integrate this experience into their life.

I questioned why it happened and what do I want to change about my life, because your life is automatically changed and for me I had to think about, 'Okay, my life has changed. Now what do I want to do with that change? Where am I going to take that change? What am I going to get out of this?' (Gabriel)

Gabriel talked extensively about her own survival journey:

I think subconsciously I started that process as soon as it happened in the ways that I could to find meaning for myself in order to survive and cope. I think that now that I have studied a bit more about trauma, I understand the concept a bit better than I would have when I was in the middle of it. For me everything continued on but I felt really different and I felt like I needed to throw myself into things quite a lot, so I threw myself into my relationships with people and threw myself into everything else and it was only when I had worn myself out or exhausted myself from that that I started to think about what impact it had had on me.

I stopped working ... until I realised, after five months of stopping, that I needed to move forward and started to make plans to do that, because after five months of stopping it is quite hard to start again. So for me, I suppose, that's where that shift would have happened. I don't think there is a shift in what happens, I think there is a shift in consciousness. There is something that shifts and all of a sudden you stop going, 'Why did this happen to me? Why can't I get over this?' ... It's that self-blame kind of talk. But I do think, 'I was a victim of sexual abuse and I have survived it!' I don't think I can say any more. (Gabriel)

In terms of what they believed had helped the most, Connie was adamant that for her the best thing had been moving away to start a new life elsewhere:

Closing the door and starting again. Perhaps I could have done it in Auckland, but I don't think so. It all boils down to the individual. I had lost myself, the mentally strong individual had disappeared and that's what I struggling with. Where am I? I knew I was there, but where? God only knows where! And that's what I was trying to do was get myself back on track – not my physical self, my mental self. (Connie)

Some of the women reflected on how they felt their levels of awareness and understanding had increased in the aftermath of the attack, extending their abilities to empathise with others enduring pain and trauma. Helen explained this by referring to the way her reactions to news stories of disasters and tragedies had changed:

Not just reading that this happened but actually being really in it and understanding what people have been through. That there's real evil, and not just saying it's evil but understanding what that means. Before the attack happened, I'd read the newspaper and you'd read something like, 'Earthquake: man gets buried or woman gets buried and is found two days later', and I'd think, 'By gosh, that's terrible.' But now I can think, 'Oh my God, how would they feel inside that box?' I can understand the pure fear, pain, terror. (Helen)

One thing Patricia said she learned from the attack was the importance of people sitting up in bed as soon as they heard strange sounds at night. This helps to clarify the direction noises are coming from as well as reducing the fear.

During my attack there were two women who were lying in their beds awake hearing the attack and thinking it was coming from somewhere else. They weren't aware that I was in trouble ... so the thing is to sit up, sit up when you hear noises ... You will have to write that somewhere – that if they hear noises, sit up! (Patricia)

The stress of the trial also prompted the appearance of various physical and psychological symptoms.

I actually became ill when I went to court and I have been since then. I've got some kind of strange eczema right in my private parts, which is quite symbolic for me, and I've been to all kinds of different doctors and it hasn't actually healed. So I'm still dealing with my past in a sense ... Maybe that area of my body just shut down because it couldn't cope, it didn't really want to feel. (Gabriel)

A paradoxical aspect of trauma is that while at the time it may seem like the worst thing that has ever happened, later it can be experienced as a positive turning point in people's lives. Surviving what may be considered unsurvivable can prompt a new sense of confidence in one's own strengths as well as providing a different lens through which to view the world. Several of the women reflected that, despite it being such an ordeal at the time, afterwards they could recognise that it had also brought about positive outcomes.

I hope I would never have to go through it again and yeah it was probably the worse time in my life but out of it I have grown so much, I wouldn't chose to go through it again but I'd hate to think where I would be now if it hadn't happened. (Lorna)

Some of the women referred to practical strategies learned and implemented:

I have a phone right by my bed with numbers punched, so that I only have to push one thing if anything does, I always know that that's there too. (Frances)

Karen spoke of how she reduced the risks for herself:

If I know I'm going out at night, I'll close the curtains and turn the lights on before I go so I don't have to walk into a dark house. Just things like that, they're not major things, they're things that make a huge difference to my sense of safety. They're just tools that you use really. You just can't describe what it's actually like to have that powerlessness, that's what doesn't go away because it's already been taken, so you can't pretend that it didn't happen. It's always there. You integrate it into your life and you move on. Otherwise, it's far worse and he has really taken away yourself, and I won't let that happen. It's taken a long time for me to come to terms with that and to feel strong enough in myself to recognise it really. It's like a part of you isn't there – you learn to live with that missing part, and when you learn to live with it, you know that your healing is really beginning and you're on your way. (Karen)

Others talked about how they viewed themselves differently as a result of what they had been through. Marie said she felt like this after making herself go and testify in court against MR:

> I think it's made me a stronger person, it's made me meet the challenge of doing something I didn't want to do. I'm still wondering now what's going to happen next? I feel that I've been through that, been there done that, what's next. Because it was just such a major thing for me to do, and life has settled back down to a normal routine again. (Marie)

What several women referred to was the need to put this experience in perspective, use whatever help was available, and move on with their lives. As Ann acknowledged, this is both difficult and essential:

> To stop letting something eat you inside. There's no shortcuts. People who take shortcuts and say, 'I'm okay,' are only going to suffer in the end, because you're denying yourself the pain, the emotion, the hurt, the anger, the why, and you have to do that. My counsellor always said to me, 'Don't ever hide anything, if you want to talk about it.' At first I talked about how he [MR] was scum, he was shit, I wanted him to die, I wanted him to have a slow death and watch it. But talking, growing, has made me think – he's nothing. I don't even want to call him a name because I'm wasting my energy on him and I want to put my energy into good things that are going to turn around for me now. Gone are the days where I want to be sad and crying and trying to analyse, 'Why me?' (Ann)

Conclusion

The women's stories presented in this book provide compelling accounts of what it means to survive rape. They endured the attack itself, the ensuing police and court processes, and the various ways in which others around them responded. Their survival journeys will continue throughout the rest of their lives. Irrespective of how fully they may have recovered, the possibility always exists for the memories and feelings of that night to be triggered in other situations. Through-out their lives decisions will need to be made regarding when to tell others that they were among the women attacked by the serial rapist, Malcolm Rewa.

Their accounts provide a window into many different issues. First, as the victims of the same attacker, their stories illustrate how similar acts committed by the same offender can impact in such varied ways. While there has been academic discussion regarding the different impacts of attempted versus completed rapes, the women's stories suggest that an attempted rape can be equally injurious to a woman's sense of safety in the world. As some discovered, the legal determination of rape was not necessarily reflected in their experience. The victim impact reports completed by the women showed that all of them had experienced severe effects, and the variability in these was not necessarily linked to how complete the rape was. Knowing that MR was driven by the desire to rape and had broken in to their homes with that intention was disturbing in its own right. Whether they were raped or not, all the women suffered high levels of fear and other major impacts in the aftermath of the attack.

Secondly, the treatment of these women as 'real' rape victims resulted in the police and prosecutors providing considerably higher levels of information, preparation and support than that received by most victims of rape. The positive ways in which these measures impacted on the women clearly show the advantages of providing such high levels of care for victims of crime. Rape cases internationally have been attracting growing attention for the high levels of attrition – it is very difficult to get a case of rape into court, and even more difficult to secure a conviction [29-31]. There were women attacked by MR whose initial complaints were not initially well received by the police, and even some who were disbelieved at the outset. Positive support from the police later, and a commitment to preparing them for the trial, resulted in these women subsequently being willing to co-operate and appear in court. The women's stories show that a key way to reduce high attrition rates is to increase support for victims/survivors, and reinforce the importance for everyone interacting with them of listening empathically to each individual.

Thirdly, the women's accounts are valuable for the ways they challenge conventional, often limited, understandings of what it means to resist and survive a rape attack. They provide powerful examples of how psychological survival may be occurring concurrent with physical victimisation. The creative ways different women chose to limit the control and domination of their attacker attest to their inner strength, their resolve to fight back with their spirit even while their bodies were bound.

Several of the women said they were keen to be part of this book because they hoped it would not only help other victims/survivors, but also those close to them. Raquel stressed how important it was for those around to listen carefully to what the victim/survivor was saying – and sometimes also what she was not able to say:

> One of the things I would love to say to anybody that is in this situation
> [is], listen. Somebody that's been raped is not necessarily going to be

able to come out blatantly and say, 'I need help' or 'I need this' or 'I need that.' They're not going to know what they need. You've got to try and read between the lines, but you've got to keep your eyes and ears open for those tiny, little subtle cries for help or that something's not right or comfortable. (Raquel)

Likewise, Helen said she felt now she had a better understanding of what to say to those close to her who wanted to support her:

I think what I've learnt is to actually tell them what I need, and know that they're not going to solve it, but just be there. Because a lot of people try and solve it and understand, but giving them permission not to understand and not have to make things better but to be there to just either bring me a cuppa tea if I want it, be there to just sit with me if I want it, or give me a cuddle or go away. But, also for them to understand that none of this is personal and just try and be there and be strong for someone. I think then they'd find that they were being more useful. Don't get put off by the way someone is – you've got to understand that they've gone through something that they've not been through before, so how do you expect them to understand how they're going to be? And don't be too hard on yourself because you don't know how you'd expect yourself to be either. (Helen)

Other people would often feel they had to solve it, or take control of the situation and tell the victim/survivor what she needed to do:

They try and push you to be a certain way. For example, you should be talking about this. Talk about it. You're not going to get better unless you talk about it. And everyone's a shrink, everyone's a psychologist, and this is the way they think they'd react so this is how you must react. Just let someone get on with it and accept that that's where they're at. And even if they don't accept where they're at, just let them be and support them, however you can. And you'll not get it right (laughs) – understand you're not going to get it right! (Helen)

Ultimately, the women's stories demonstrate that surviving rape is not only the accomplishment of living beyond the attack, but a lifelong series of decisions and actions, a series of survivals. These women survived being attacked by one of the worst stranger serial rapists in New Zealand, and their experiences illustrate the complexity and richness of what it means to be 'serial survivors'.

Appendix 1

Writing this book

This book is about the processes involved in surviving rape. As with most life experiences, it is not the experience itself that is as crucial as the learning obtained from it. The process of surviving is ongoing – like life itself. Writing this book has also been a survival journey – negotiating access, conducting interviews, managing the ways the material triggered my own fears, the anxiety of finding a publisher, honouring my word to these women, struggling with how to do their stories justice.

Each stage of the journey presented its own challenges, external practicalities as well as inner fears and demons. There is growing recognition of the ways in which research involves the emotions, particularly among feminist social scientists [1-5]. Gathering data is not like picking daisies or collecting stamps – it is an interactive process impacting emotionally as well as intellectually on all participants. As Campbell and Wasco [6] articulate it:

> The overarching goal of feminist research is to capture women's lived experiences in a respectful manner that legitimates women's voices as sources of knowledge. In other words, the process of research is of as much importance as the outcome. ([6] p 783).

While the word 'research' sounds removed and distant, in the interview context itself I sensed I was not, could not be, merely a remote distant recorder of others' voices – my presence and participation were vital in encouraging these women to speak as fully as possible about events and emotions still palpably raw in some. It was a privilege to sit with them – and a responsibility.

In this appendix I outline the background to the book and my involvement with the women and share, from both my perspective and theirs, what it was like participating in the interview process.

How this book came about

I had interviewed rape survivors in the early 1990s as part of a criminological study researching complainants' experiences with the police, courts, doctors and support agencies [7, 8]. At a national conference in 1996, after presenting the results, I was talking with Detective Sergeant Dave Henwood, who had been a key player in the arrests and interviews of both Thompson and Rewa. He commented that he thought I would really value the opportunity to meet with the women he was involved in supporting during the lead-up to Rewa's trial. However, as he pointed out, these women would not be able to meet each other or be interviewed until the trial ended, so for the moment that was that.

Nearly two years later he rang to say the trial was over, the offender locked up, and some of the women at least were keen to tell their stories – was I interested? He gave me the name of one woman to telephone. After I spoke with her, she offered to host an afternoon meeting at her place where others could come to meet me and discuss the research. I flew up to Auckland and nervously made my way to her apartment, unsure what to expect. A small group of women arrived and I was immediately impressed with how reflective and articulate they were about their experiences. It was an amazing encounter as they quickly moved from discussing the possibility of my interviewing them to sharing with each other their own experiences and survival stories.

This book developed from that meeting. An important concern was determining whether these women wanted to have their experiences shared more widely – did they want to tell their stories? All of the women who came to that meeting agreed that they did, and one factor motivating them was the absence of good, real, and accessible books to read following sexual assault. If they could contribute to a book that others could use, this would be another way of turning their trauma into something positive.

A couple of the victims had left New Zealand, or been initially from overseas themselves. The women I met contacted those of the others still in the country to tell them about the interview project. It was explained to them that, since I was already undertaking doctoral research on rape victims' experiences of reporting to the police, I would have two main purposes in interviewing them: To obtain material on how the women experienced police processes, to incorporate into my thesis research; and to gain an overall understanding of how they were affected by the attack and the ways in which they survived.

Of the 27 women MR was charged with raping, I was able to interview 14, as well as another woman, Marie, whom he had attacked years earlier and who was called upon to give similar fact evidence in the current trial. All were interviewed after the trial was over, which meant the incidents were fresh in their minds even though the initial attacks may have happened many years earlier. The interviews were often long and intense, lasting up to four hours at a time, with most women interviewed on more than one occasion. While I wanted to ensure that each was asked similar questions in order to provide a good and reliable set of data, I was equally concerned to provide an arena within which they could tell their own stories in their own words.

Many of the women were keen to have their survival stories written up as a book and available for others. I felt a strong sense of responsibility to ensure this outcome. It has not been an easy goal to reach. My initial contacts with publishers received strong support for the idea of bringing out such a book but a reluctance from the marketing people to commit to such a venture. I was told that, 'books on rape don't sell'. One woman publisher admitted to feeling anxious about possible repercussions from the women's attacker if she was involved in such an enterprise, a sad admission but one which indicated how pervasive the fear wrought by this man had become.

I grew despondent of being able to fulfil my commitment to the women and transferred my concentration back to my doctoral research, completing it and then turning the text into a book [9], all the time continuing my teaching career at Victoria University of Wellington. Life events intruded, several years went by, and still the women haunted me. I imagined them perched on my shoulder, gently reminding me that their stories were still to be told. Meanwhile I shared some of their experiences with students in my lectures, in conference papers, and in public addresses. Each time the response was the same: People need to hear this material – when are these stories being published?

On New Year's Day 2006 I made a resolution to redo the initial book proposal and send it out for consideration, concentrating on international publishers following the initial rejections from those based in New Zealand. Within a month, two had expressed interest and I was pleased indeed to receive warm encouragement for the concept from Trisha Valliapan of Federation Press, and we signed an agreement to publish. The sense of relief I felt was huge, and I realised again how strongly I felt the responsibility of sharing these women's stories, not least because of how powerful and moving I found them.

Relief jostled with anxiety the more I went through the interview transcripts, trying to decide how best to organise the material, and what to include. Given what we know from rape prevalence studies, these women were not typical in that most of them did not know their attacker at all, while the majority of victims/survivors do know the men who rape them, often intimately. I worried about contributing to the fear of 'stranger-danger' by writing a book about stranger attacks, yet kept being drawn back to the powerfulness and intensity of these women's accounts. There was so much to learn from their experiences, so much inspiration to draw.

I needed little convincing that this book needed to be written. The women were so generous in providing such full accounts of how the attacks impacted on them – in itself an educative tool. They were able to document how they, as women attacked in circumstances they could never be blamed for, experienced police and court processes – did the fact that they were 'perfect victims' mean they received 'perfect policing'? What kinds of lessons could be gained from understanding what they valued in terms of information and procedures? Talking with these women also provides a sense of what difference it makes to be part of a group taking one, common attacker to court. What was it like knowing the other women existed? Hearing about their experiences? Finally meeting them? As far as I can tell, this study is the first to be conducted with multiple victims/survivors of the same attacker, and provides the opportunity to see how the offender's distinctive modus operandi impacted on different women, and how differently they reacted in essentially similar circumstances. Part of what makes their accounts so compelling is the cumulative sense of these women's skills and abilities in surviving such a traumatic episode in their lives.

Honouring these women's trust has been one of my biggest struggles. I wanted so much to tell their stories that I found it difficult writing myself in – how dare I write my words, when every word of mine meant one less of theirs. It was incredibly hard deciding which quotes to use, which examples to include, which anecdotes to share. I was reminded of how, whenever I go to a lake to feed the ducks, I desperately strive to ensure each duck gets it fair share of the bread; with these accounts I worried as to how to give each woman equal voice, till I realised I could not. This was neither my aim nor my responsibility – my aim was to take and craft the stories, experiences and examples they shared with me and weave them into the work that I feel most powerfully communicates the main ways in which they were impacted upon and survived. Nevertheless, I still fretted that no matter how much I tried to get it right, I always ran the risk that there would be somebody for whom I got it wrong.

I wanted to keep the authenticity of their voices and at the same time turn this into accessible writing for the reader. In speech we use many connectors and spacers – we take breaths with words like 'um' and 'yeah'. Reproducing those in full grated on the page. The same utterances that made verbal speech flow, punctuate written speech in ways that detract from its meaning. Accordingly, minor editing has been carefully undertaken throughout.

Questions of confidentiality were also paramount. For that reason I deliberately provide few details regarding specific characteristics, identities and locations in the book. The women either chose the names they wished to be called or left me to assign an alibi. Details such as specific dates have not been included; however, the introductory accounts of each woman's attack and survival are listed in the chronological order they occurred.

This book is about the women and based on their stories – for that reason I decided, after conferring with others, to refer to Malcolm Rewa in each chapter only by his initials (MR), other than when the women themselves refer to him. The background material about his life and sexual offending was also relegated to an appendix for the same reason – to reinforce that this book is not about him and what he did; it is about the women and how they survived.

What was the interview experience like for me?

Meeting with and interviewing these women has felt like a wonderful gift with its own obligations attached. As I struggled with my responsibilities to the women, I came to realise that I was in danger of ignoring my responsibilities to myself. I thought I had learned my lesson doing earlier rape research, when it became clear that I was being traumatised by what I was hearing. The terror from my own experiences of sexual assaults and a gang abduction resurfaced – experiences that helped me to be empathic but which themselves needed to be managed.

Doing the actual interviews often had a profound effect on me. One of the women had offered me her apartment to stay in while she was away, and it was a great venue in which to interview the women since it was safe and private, and most had been there before. The first night I stayed there, after doing an interview, I went upstairs to bed and could not sleep. I was tense, anxious, convinced I could hear footsteps creeping up the stairs. Next day I wrote of the night before:

> I felt the breath of fear on my neck again and knew I needed to be careful.

I had been so focused on looking after the women, having drinks and snacks on standby, paying attention to their emotional needs, that I had overlooked my own vulnerability. While I was physically with the women, I was focused on their words, their reactions, their needs, and often the impact of what they were saying did not really hit me until after they had left, or when I listened to the tapes and read the transcripts at home.

While I often checked if the women had support available following each interview, should they need it, I began to realise how I also needed my own supports. I am grateful for both the informal support of my partner and the professional support of a therapist in helping me through this time. I finally recognised the value of debriefing sessions, as well as the importance of giving myself breaks between interviews.

There were still hard moments. On one occasion, my own ambivalence about whether I had the right to interview the women collided headfirst with one woman's own ambivalence about being interviewed. We had talked at length on the phone and set up a time to meet, then she abruptly changed her mind. This incident disturbed me greatly, and I wrote in my journal:

> It's been really hard today and I've wondered if I should be doing this at all. When one woman screamed down the phone at me and said Rewa had taken over enough of her life and she didn't want to talk to me or have any more to do with it, I just felt shattered. I cried and felt guilty and felt like she was so angry with me, but then she can yell at me and make me disappear but she could never yell at Rewa and make him vanish, or yell at the police and get them to leave her alone. But that is how I make sense of it tonight.

The more women I met and interviewed, the more I was impressed by the power of their stories. It was the same man who attacked each of them, yet no two women reacted identically, nor were impacted upon the same. Not every woman had been raped, and penetration was often incomplete due to the attacker's sexual dysfunction, yet this made little difference – all of the women had been dramatically affected in so many diverse ways, with each finding her own ways to regain her sense of self and power in the world. My response after interviewing one woman was typical when I wrote:

> She's only just gone and I feel quite overwhelmed with emotion. There's a huge sadness for all Malcolm Rewa inflicted, for the vast pool of tears and heartache he's generated, for all the fear and terror he's given rise to. There's an anger and a fury for the sheer callousness and brutality of it all ... And there is a wonder, an amazement, at how so many of these women have survived and resurrected their lives, how they've not only salvaged what Rewa left behind but been able to transform the shattered fragments into lives of strength, courage and quiet (or, in some cases, wonderfully loud!) beauty. Rewa tried to reduce these women to dust but they are the ones standing tall and strong.

At least some of the anxieties I felt regarding what I was subjecting the women to were eased by the ways I came to appreciate how validating the interview process could be, a factor mentioned directly by many of the women themselves.

What was the interview experience like for the women?

Victims of crime generally often struggle with the way in which, in adversarial justice systems, they are treated as witnesses and seldom allowed to tell their own story in their own words. The responses of police agencies, for instance, may feel harsh in the way they reduce the victim's experiences to 'evidence', and how they react can convey suspicion and/or blame to the victim/survivor. Encountering cross-examination and social scepticism, survivors may falter in their recall and increasingly distrust themselves and their own testimonies [10-12]. Alternately, in some contexts, survivors' experiences of telling and retelling their stories may be empowering and transformative [13, 14]. The decision to participate in research that has the potential to trigger painful memories is a difficult one. So why did these women, after all they had been through, agree to talk it through again with a relative stranger?

What several said was that they hoped it would fill a gap in the material available for others struggling to survive their own victimisation.

> *I feel that I want what's happened to be able to help someone else. I want to be able to make a difference somehow. Maybe in years to come, it will help somebody, but that would probably help to close things for me too, to*

end everything – if I knew that what happened has been beneficial to someone. (Marie)

The women also hoped it would inform those working with rape survivors and give them a resource to use:

This book needs to be written and it needs to be given to all of the agencies so that every time they get a rape victim, they just give them this book! (Patricia)

What was uppermost in the minds of many was the opportunity to take what had happened and put it to a positive end – as one of the women said:

I'm really pleased that you're doing the research, it's quite unique and hopefully there can be stuff gained from it – we haven't all been through this just to put him in jail. (Karen)

Some were aware that they might feel vulnerable after being interviewed and arranged to be met by their partners afterwards. At least two of the women told their counsellors about the interview.

The counsellor I'm going to knows that I'm seeing you, so I've put those systems in place. She's great. She's like, 'Call me in the middle of the night if you need me'. She's that sort of person. I've got a really good support system there, so you'll feel safe about me and I feel secure about me as well. I'm fine, I don't know how I'm going to react – it might be nothing, it might be everything, but that's fine, I've got the support group there. (Helen)

Many of the women I interviewed spoke of how they found it a positive and affirming experience. What they said they appreciated was the time and space to reflect on all that had happened, and acknowledge how well they were doing. Several spoke of how those close to them did not always want to know the details, or felt uncomfortable talking about it.

I think what I've needed is time on the subject. I've needed having these interviews with you, I've found them incredibly healing. It's just been time to talk about it, and I know that's what counselling is as well, but I didn't need strategies for survival because I had them already so it's actually been really good for me to have some objective questions which I can answer, and do the debrief and look at the side issues. It's been excellent. (Shelley)

Gabriel also said, at the end of our second interview:

Now I feel a lot better than I expected to feel. I feel really heard and acknowledged and I feel really relieved that my personal story has come out from my personal perspective. That it wasn't me answering your guided questions – to a certain degree it was, but I feel really good about the way it all came out.

What some of us have experienced has been an hour with the counsellor or three hours in court or nine hours giving the statement. And for a specific reason – questioned for a specific reason with a specific purpose. Although you have that too, it has been good to be able to incorporate what is behind our answers ... It is all about acknowledging that your experience was important. It did happen, it is valued, you are valued, you are respected for your experience. It is not shut down, shoved away, and not talked about. (Gabriel)

The interviews illustrated how each stage of the process following the attack became an exercise in survival – surviving the assault, managing police interviewing, surviving and coping with going to court, surviving all the many impacts on their lives, and also managing how those close to them were affected. The picture that emerges demonstrates that surviving rape is not a one-off event but a continual process. The different procedures and aspects each pose their own challenges as the victims/survivors manage the various and on-going intrusions and encounters that follow in the aftermath of rape. This book has presented their stories – the losses and the triumphs, the battles and the victories. Their accounts make both their fear and courage palpable, and are a gift to us all as we survive our own traumas or support those around us, personally or professionally, in theirs.

This is unique material, moving, detailed, challenging. It demonstrates the many diverse ways in which a sexual attack can impact, not only on the woman herself but on her partner, parents, children, friends, neighbours – all of us. For when one woman is raped, a whole community hurts. That is why we need to understand so much more deeply the impacts of rape, and why we must do all we can to minimise its occurrence.

Postscript March 2008

As I read again the women's stories, years after first hearing them, I am surprised over and over again at how moving I still find them. As I slow down my typing and think about the woman behind the words, I repeatedly find my eyes welling up with tears. Each woman became so real to me in the interview situation. I felt so totally engaged with them, wanting to understand and appreciate not only what they had faced but what they had all so powerfully overcome. I felt honoured to have them share so openly with me such huge, personal experiences from their own lives. That sense of awe and privilege remains with me today.

Appendix 2

Malcolm Rewa, serial rapist

Malcolm Rewa was the name used later in life by Maurice Morgan Lewis, a Māori born in 1953 in a small settlement north of Auckland, New Zealand. His mother was killed in a car accident when he was one and, as the youngest of three children, his father sent him to the city to be raised by an aunt. He was caught stealing women's underwear at age 9, and shortly afterwards received the first of many convictions for burglary. He was made a state ward and moved around a succession of foster homes before joining the army in 1974. Eighteen months later he was discharged and shortly after committed his first known sexual attack. Rewa's wife thought their first baby was about to be born and he dropped her at Auckland Hospital, then headed for the nearby nurses' home where he sexually assaulted a young nurse. He panicked and ran off leaving his clothes and a friend's driving licence at the scene, as well as a palm print. He was caught, pleaded guilty to attempted rape, and was sentenced to four-and-a-half years' imprisonment [1].

In the 1980s he was heavily involved with the Highway 61 gang, where he earned a reputation for violence. A gang associate, who was later a secret witness at Rewa's trial, told the court: 'Everyone knew, you don't f--- with Hammer' [2]. The nickname was said by some to derive from the hammer he always carried on his motorcycle to use as a weapon when needed [1, 3], and by others to arise from an incident in prison where he used a hammer to attack another inmate [2]. Either way, those who knew him said he was a 'no nonsense' kind of guy, physically strong and macho in attitude: 'Rewa wears staunchness like a badge. "Fuck the police" is tattooed on a leg' [2].

As well as his motorbikes, he had a four-wheel drive vehicle that he used to transport the Malamute sled dogs he raced. On this vehicle were painted the words, 'Lone Wolf', a name that journalists consi-dered an apt description for the man himself ([3], "Lone Wolf: Career of a Rapist"; [2], "Lone Wolf: The Malcolm Rewa Story'). Similarly, a book profiling the *Who's Who of New Zealand Crime* highlighted this description: 'Malcolm Rewa was a successful Malamute dog sled racer. He was no more than an animal himself, preying on women and raping them'. ([1] p 219)

His first known rape following the nurses' home attack occurred on New Year's Eve, 1987. The woman was recovering at a friend's place two days later when she saw and identified Rewa visiting the house. She actually named him to police but Rewa had a mate provide him with an alibi and this, combined with police doubts regarding the complainant's credibility, meant that the case remained unsolved. By the time this woman finally saw her attacker appear in court, he had sexually assaulted or raped at least 26 other women. In describing Rewa as a serial sexual predator, a detective inspector observed: 'I liken them to mad dogs that attack sheep. They don't stop.' [4].

Rewa had a distinctive style to his attacks, most of which were committed in Auckland against women whom he had established either lived alone or were home alone, or with children sleeping, at the time. He was a skilled burglar and would break in to the house either in the middle of the night or early morning, surprise and overcome his victims, usually binding their arms and sometimes their legs, occasionally blindfolding and gagging them. He would typically remove their clothes from the waist down, drape them over the side of the bed, and shine a torch on their genital area. The problems Rewa had with erectile dysfunction meant he frequently masturbated, and digital penetration was accomplished more often than penile. Often he would leave the woman tied up while he searched the house for cash or ATM bank cards, returning to demand the PIN number and sometimes to rape or sexually assault her a second, and sometimes a third, time. Some of the women were severely physically beaten as well. Before he left, Rewa would often loosen the binds a little, and wrap the woman up in a duvet.

After the 1987 rape, Rewa was next identified in 1995 following his attack on an Auckland businesswoman in her flat. She saw him when his balaclava fell off and was later able to identify him from police photographs [5]. Detectives began visiting Rewa's home and questioning family members, whereupon he retaliated by laying a complaint alleging police harassment. His arrogance was also his undoing – during the reviewing of files prompted by his complaint, investigators observed similarities to other unsolved rapes [5].

The police were in the process of having forensic evidence linking him to these crimes examined when he committed his last attack, in May 1996. His youngest victim, a 15-year-old girl, was walking her dog near her home when he attacked and beat her round the head.

She screamed, alerting her parents who came running, and her father was able to note the car registration number as Rewa sped off. This latest evidence was all the police needed to go to his house later that night and arrest him. He was wearing only a towel when the officers burst in, and tried to make a run for it but was stopped in his tracks by a police dog. At the station, bleeding and bandaged, he refused to acknowledge or talk to detectives, and his attitude prompted Jan Corbett, who had written an earlier account of the hunt for Joseph Thompson, to observe: 'Rewa conceded nothing, neither guilt, shame nor feeling for his victims. Instead, in the manner of serial rapists, he wanted to talk about his unhappy childhood' ([3] p A11).

While he was being held on remand in Mt Eden Prison awaiting trial, he married his long-term partner [4, 6]. She had been with him for 18 years, and it was often her car that he used when he 'disappeared' at nights. She kept a low profile but described him as a good husband and father to their three children. During this time it emerged that Rewa had simultaneously sustained a two-year relationship with another woman, who was later to describe him in court as 'attentive and very loving' and the man she wanted to marry [6]. He also had three other children from his first marriage, including a daughter who attended parts of his trial and said 'she was still trying to come to terms with the enormity of what her father had done' ([7] p 3).

The trial was held in the Auckland High Court in 1998 and lasted three months. Rewa faced 45 charges, and on the first day he pleaded guilty to those involving women whose cases he was linked to by incontrovertible forensic evidence. While he became increasingly adept at ensuring he left no traces at the scene, the distinctive characteristics of his attacks and his obvious sexual dysfunctionality provided their own line of evidence. After more than three days deliberation the jury, comprising six men and six women, convicted him on most of the charges against him, apart from two involving women attacked while out running, and the charges involving Susan Burdett. (Rewa went to retrial for the charges involving her in December 1998, where the jury convicted him of her rape but could not agree that he was also responsible for her murder.)

Media coverage throughout the trial had been extensive, and there was now an explosion of articles describing the police investigation, the offender's tactics, and details of the women's horror. Most focused on the perpetrator, the attacks, and the investigation. Only a few referred to the ways these women survived, one example being an article that described how one of the women felt the power turn in the courtroom after she sprinkled glitter in the witness box to help her stay strong ('Angel dust helped victim through court ordeal', [8]).

Details emerged of connections between several of the women and the offender. For example, one woman had been a friend of Rewa's partner, and had visited and met him in his home before the night he came and raped her. Rewa was present when she later described to his partner the ordeal she had endured. When she later said she was terrified the rapist was still watching her house at night: 'The couple assured her she needed only to ring and Rewa would "come over to check the place over"' [9].

Three days after the guilty verdict was announced, Rewa's defence lawyers appeared on a national television show to read his apology to the women – but only to the six whose cases he had been forced to admit. The handwritten letter said Rewa would 'turn back the clock of time' if he could, adding: 'If it's any consolation to my victims I will continue to pay with shame and embarrassment, ridicule, and forever be persecuted by the police and the media for the rest of my life' [10]. His 'false "apology"' [11] was met with outrage from diverse quarters:

> The statement horrified police, politicians and rape counsellors who described it as tacky, appalling and without remorse. [10].

Rewa's lawyers were also 'slammed', and criticised by the New Zealand Bar Association president for the inappropriate behaviour they displayed in communicating to victims on behalf of their client via the media, rather than through the judge. '[This] could only be described as public relations purposes when the client still had to be sentenced by the court' [10].

A month later Malcolm Rewa returned to court for sentencing. Many of the victims/survivors were there, along with four of the women jury members and detectives involved with the investigation. While the prosecution described Rewa, 45, as 'every woman's worst nightmare', the defence presented him as the victim of a dysfunctional family, possibly with a history of sexual abuse, and devastated at 13 by the death of his dog [12]. Presiding over the court was Justice Anderson, who emphasised Rewa's brutality and the danger he posed, and took what was described as 'the unusual step of reading each victim impact report out loud' ([12] at p 3). The headlines next day described how victims hugged and celebrated the news that the judge had sentenced Rewa to preventive detention with a minimum non-parole period of 22 years [13]. By the time he can even be considered for possible release, he will, unless he is dead, be 67 years old.

Notes and bibliography

Chapter 2

1. Taylor, P (1995) 'Hunting an evil shadow', *The Dominion*, 22 February, p 13.
2. Panckhurst, P (1994) 'Streets of fear', *New Zealand Herald*, 30 April, p 1.
3. Welch, D (1994) 'The shadow that haunts South Auckland', *The Listener*, 23 July, pp 19-23.
4. Corbett, J (1996) *Caught By His Past: How They Got the South Auckland Serial Rapist*. Auckland: Tandem Press.
5. 'Rapists on prowl at same time' (1996) *The Sunday Star Times*, 28 January p A2.
6. Hazelwood, RR and Burgess, AW (1999) 'The behavioural-oriented interview of rape victims: The key to profiling', in RR Hazelwood and AW Burgess, (eds) *Practical Aspects of Rape Investigation: A Multidisciplinary Approach*. CRC Press: Boca Raton.
7. Bart, P and O'Brien, P (1985) *Stopping Rape, Successful Survival Strategies*. Oxford: Pergamon Press.
8. Heyden, SM, Anger, BF, Jackson T and Ellner, TDl (1999) 'Fighting back works: The case for advocating and teaching self-defence against rape', *Journal of Physical Education, Recreation and Dance*, 70(5): 31-35.
9. Ullman, S (1998) 'Does offender violence escalate when rape victims fight back?' *Journal of Interpersonal Violence*, 13(2): 179-192.
10. Ullman, S and Knight, R (1992) 'Fighting back: Women's resistance of rape', *Journal of Interpersonal Violence*, 7: 31-43.
11. Hazelwood, RR and Warren, JI (1999) 'The serial rapist', in RR Hazelwood and AW Burgess, (eds) *Practical Aspects of Rape Investigation*. CRC Press: Boca Raton.
12. Firth, A (1995) 'Interrogation', *Police Review*, 28 November, p 1507.
13. Brereton, D (1997) 'How different are rape trials? A comparison of the cross-examination of complainants in rape and sexual assault trials', *British Journal of Criminology*, 37(2): 242-261.
14. Gregory, J and Lees, S (1999) *Policing Sexual Assault*. Routledge: London.
15. Lees, S (ed) (1997) *Ruling Passions: Sexual Violence, Reputation and the Law*. Open University Press: Buckingham.
16. Mack, K (1998) '"You should scrutinise her evidence with great care": Corroboration of women's testimony about sexual assault', in P Easteal, (ed) *Balancing the Scales: Rape, Law Reform and Australian Culture*. The Federation Press: Sydney.

17. McSherry, B (1998) 'Constructing lack of consent', in P Easteal (ed), *Balancing the Scales: Law Reform and Australian Culture*. The Federation Press: Sydney.

18. Reekie, G and Wilson, P (1993) 'Rape, resistance and women's rights of self-defence', *Australian and New Zealand Journal of Criminology*, 26(2): 146-154.

19. Jordan, J (2004) *The Word of a Woman? Police, Rape and Belief*. Houndmills, Basingstoke: Palgrave Macmillan.

20. Griffin, S (1971) 'Rape the All-American crime', *Ramparts*, 10(3): 26-35.

21. Burgess, AW (1999) 'Public beliefs and attitudes toward rape', in RR Hazelwood and AW Burgess (eds) *Practical Aspects of Rape Investigation: A Multidisciplinary Approach*. CRC Press: Boca Raton.

22. Fossi, J, Clarke, DD, and Lawrence, C (2005) 'Bedroom rape: Sequences of sexual behaviour in stranger assaults', *Journal of Interpersonal Violence*, 20(11): 1444-1466.

23. Block, R and Skogan, W (1986) 'Resistance and non-fatal outcomes in stranger-to-stranger predatory crime', *Violence and Victims*, 1(4): 241-253.

24. Cohen, P (1984) 'Resistance during sexual assaults: Avoiding rape and injury', *Victimology*, 9(1): 120-129.

25. Burton, N (1998) 'Resistance to prevention: Reconsidering feminist anti-violence rhetoric', in S French, V Teays, and L Purdy (eds) *Violence Against Women, Philosophical Perspectives*, Cornell University Press: Ithaca.

26. Hollander, J (2005) 'Challenging despair: Teaching about women's resistance to violence', *Violence Against Women*, 11(6): 776-791.

27. Jordan, J (2005) 'What would MacGyver do? The meaning(s) of resistance and survival'. *Violence Against Women*, 11(4): 531-559.

28. Kelly, L (1988) *Surviving Sexual Violence*. Polity Press: Cambridge.

29. Kleck, G and Sayles, S (1990) 'Rape and resistance', *Social Problems*, 37(2): 149-162.

30. Brecklin, LR and Ullman, S (2005) 'Self-defense or assertiveness training and women's responses to sexual attacks', *Journal of Interpersonal Violence*, 20(6): 738-762.

31. Jordan, J (1998) *Reporting Rape: Women's Experiences with the Police, Doctors and Support Agencies*. Institute of Criminology: Wellington.

32. Scully, D (1990) *Understanding Sexual Violence: A Study of Convicted Rapists*. Unwin Hyman: Boston.

Chapter 3

1. Gregory, J and Lees S (1999) *Policing Sexual Assault*. Routledge: London.

2. Kelly, L (2002) *A Research Review on the Reporting, Investigation and Prosecution of Rape Cases*. Her Majesty's Crown Prosecution Service Inspectorate: London.

3. Walby, S and Allen, J (2004) *Domestic Violence, Sexual Assault and Stalking: Findings from the British Crime Survey*, Home Office Research Study 276. Home Office: London.

4. Walby, S and Myhill, A (2001) 'New survey methodologies in researching violence against women', *British Journal of Criminology*, 41(3): 502-522.

5. Gilmore, K and Pittman, L (1993) *To Report or Not to Report: A Study of Victim/Survivors of Sexual Assault and Their Experience of Making an Initial Report to the Police*. Centre Against Sexual Assault (CASA House) and Royal Women's Hospital: Melbourne.

6. Koss, MP, Gidycz, C and Wisniewski, N (1987) 'The scope of rape: Incidence and prevalence of sexual aggression and victimization in a national sample of higher education students', *Journal of Consulting and Clinical Psychology*, 55(2): 162-170.

7. Campbell, R and Raja, S (1999) 'Secondary victimization of rape victims: Insights from mental health professionals who treat survivors of violence', *Violence and Victims*, 14(3): 261-275.

8. Chambers, G and Millar, A (1983) *Investigating Sexual Assault*. Scottish Office Central Research Unit: Edinburgh.

9. Hall, R (1985) *Ask Any Woman: A London Inquiry into Rape and Sexual Assault*. Falling Wall Press: Bristol.

10. Heenan, M and Murray, S (2007) *Study of Reported Rapes in Victoria 2000-2003*. Office of Women's Policy: Melbourne.

11. Lea, S, Lanvers, U and Shaw, S (2003) 'Attrition in rape cases: Developing a profile and identifying relevant factors', *British Journal of Criminology*, 43(3): 583-599.

12. London Rape Crisis Centre (1984) *Sexual Violence: The Reality for Women*. The Women's Press: London.

13. Rose, V (1977) 'Rape as a social problem: A by-product of the feminist movement', *Social Problems*, 25: 75-89.

14. Wright, R (1984) 'A note on attrition of rape cases', *British Journal of Criminology*, 24(4): 399-400.

15. Adler, Z (1987) *Rape on Trial*. Routledge and Kegan Paul: London.

16. Temkin, J (1987) *Rape and the Legal Process*. Sweet & Maxwell: London.

17. Estrich, S (1987) *Real Rape*. Harvard University Press: Cambridge, Massachusetts.

18. Holmstrom, LL and Burgess, AW (1978) *The Victim of Rape: Institutional Reactions*. Wiley: New York

19. Medea, A and Thompson, K (1974) *Against Rape*. Farrar, Straus & Giroux: New York.

20. Smith, L (1989) *Concerns About Rape*. HMSO: London.

21. Young, W (1983) *Rape Study: A Discussion of Law and Practice. Volume 1.* Institute of Criminology and The Department of Justice: Wellington.

22. Jordan, J (1998) *Reporting Rape: Women's Experiences with the Police, Doctors and Support Agencies*. Institute of Criminology: Wellington.

23. Jordan, J (2001) 'Worlds Apart? Women, rape and the police reporting process', *British Journal of Criminology*, 41(4): 679-706.

24. Jordan, J (2004) *The Word of a Woman? Police, Rape and Belief*. Palgrave MacMillan: Houndmills, Basingstoke.

25. Lievore, D (2005) *No Longer Silent: A study of women's help-seeking decisions and service responses to sexual assault*. A report prepared by the Australian Institute of Criminology. Australian Government's Office for Women: Canberra.

26. Temkin, J (1997) 'Plus ça change: Reporting rape in the 1990s', *British Journal of Criminology*, 37(4): 507-528.

27. Epstein, J and Langenbahn, S (1994) *The Criminal Justice and Community Response to Rape*. Issues and Practices in Criminal Justice series, National Institute of Justice. US Department of Justice: Washington DC.

28. Herman, J (2005) 'Justice from the victim's perspective', *Violence Against Women*, 11(5): 571-602.

29. Du Mont, J, Miller, K and Myhr, T (2003) 'The role of "real rape" and "real victim" stereotypes in the police reporting practices of sexually assaulted women', *Violence Against Women*, 9(4): 466-86.

30. Harris, J and Grace, S (1999) *A Question of Evidence? Investigating and Prosecuting Rape in the 1990s*. Home Office: London.

31. Kelly, L, Lovett, J and Regan, L (2005) *A Gap or a Chasm? Attrition in Reported Rape Cases*, Home Office Research Study No 293. Home Office: London.

32. Krahe, B (1991) 'Police officers definitions of rape: A prototype study', *Journal of Community and Applied Social Psychology*, 1: 223-244.

33. Young, A (1998) *'Violence as seduction: Enduring genres of rape'*, in A Howe (ed) *Sexed Crime in the News*. The Federation Press: Sydney.

34. Feldman-Summers, S and Norris, H (1984) 'Differences between rape victims who report and those who do not report to a public agency', *Journal of Applied Social Psychology*, 14: 562-573.

35. Koss, MP, Dineri, TE, Seibel CA and Cox, SL (1988) 'Stranger and acquaintance rape: Are there differences in the victim's experience?', *Psychology of Women Quarterly*, 12: 1-24.

36. Williams, JE (1984) 'Secondary victimization: Confronting public attitudes about rape', *Victimology: An International Journal*, 9(1): 66-81.

37. Edwards, A and Heenan, M (1994) 'Rape trials in Victoria: Gender, sociocultural factors and justice' *Australian and New Zealand Journal of Criminology*, 27(3): 213-236.

38. Kennedy, H (1992) *Eve Was Framed: Women and British Justice*. London: Vintage.

39. Burgess, AW (1999) 'Public beliefs and attitudes toward rape', in RR Hazelwood and AW Burgess (eds) *Practical Aspects of Rape Investigation: A Multidisciplinary Approach*. CRC Press: Boca Raton.

40. Christie, N (1986) 'The ideal victim', in E Fattah (ed) *From Crime Policy to Victim Policy: Reorienting the Justice System*. St Martin's Press: New York.

41. Fisher, BS, Daigle, LE, Cullen, FT and Turner, MG (2003) 'Reporting sexual victimization to the police and others: Results from a national-level study of college women', *Criminal Justice and Behavior*, 30(1): 6-38.

42. Kelly, L (1988) *Surviving Sexual Violence*. Polity Press: Cambridge.

43. Myhill, A and Allen, J (2002) *Rape and Sexual Assault of Women: Findings from the British Crime Survey*. Home Office: London.

44. Campbell, R (2006) 'Rape survivors' experiences with the legal and medical systems: Do rape victim advocates make a difference?' *Violence Against Women*, 12(1): 30-45.

45. Campbell, R and Raja, S (2005) 'The sexual assault and secondary victimization of female veterans: Help-seeking experiences in military and civilian social systems', *Psychology of Women Quarterly*, 29: 97-106.

46. Martin, P and Powell, R (1994) 'Accounting for the second assault: Legal organizations' framing of rape victims', *Law and Social Inquiry*, 19: 853-890.

47. Olle, L (2005) *Mapping Health Sector and Inter-Agency Protocols on Sexual Assault*. ACSSA Issues No 2. Australian Centre for the Study of Sexual Assault: Melbourne.

48. Stenius, VM and Veysey, BM (2005) '"It's the Little Things": Women, trauma and strategies for healing', *Journal of Interpersonal Violence*, 20(10): 1155-1174.

49. Kassin, SM and Fong, CT (1999)'"I'm innocent!": Effects of training on judgments of truth and deception in the interrogation room', *Law and Human Behavior*, 23(5): 499-516.

50. Ahrens, CE (2006) 'Being silenced: The impact of negative social reactions on the disclosure of rape', *American Journal of Community Psychology*, 38(3-4): 263-274.

51. Burgess, AW and Hazelwood, RR (1999) 'The victim's perspective', in AW Burgess and RR Hazelwood (eds) *Practical Aspects of Rape Investigation: A Multidisciplinary Approach*. CRC Press: Boca Raton.

52. Nixon, C (1992) 'A climate of change: Police responses to rape', in J Breckenridge and M Carmody (eds) *Crimes of Violence: Australian Responses to Rape and Child Sexual Assault*. Allen & Unwin: Sydney.

53. Fleming, D (1998) 'Police wouldn't believe me', *New Zealand Woman's Weekly*, 15 June, pp 20-23.

54. Adler, Z (1991) 'Picking up the pieces', *Police Review*, 31 May, pp 1114-1115.

55. Goodstein, L and Lutze, F (1992) 'Rape and criminal justice system responses', in I Moyer (ed) *The Changing Roles of Women in the Criminal Justice System: Offenders, Victims, and Professionals*. Waveland Press: Illinois.

56. Jordan, J (2002) 'Will any woman do? Police, gender and rape victims', *Policing: An International Journal of Police Strategies and Management*, 25(2): 319-344.

57. Toner, B (1982) *The Facts of Rape*. Arrow Books: London.

58. Gavey, N (2005) *Just Sex? The Cultural Scaffolding of Rape*. Routledge: Hove.

59. Campbell, A (1996) *Bernardo Investigation Review*. Ministry of the Solicitor-General and Correctional Services: Toronto.
60. Corbett, J (1996) *Caught By His Past: How They Got the South Auckland Serial Rapist*. Tandem Press: Auckland.

Chapter 4

1. Herman, J (2005) 'Justice from the victim's perspective', *Violence Against Women*, 11(5): 571-602.
2. Freckelton, I (1998) 'Sexual offence prosecutions: A barrister's perspective', in P Easteal (ed). *Balancing the Scales: Law Reform and Australian Culture*. The Federation Press: Sydney.
3. Koss, MP (2000) 'Blame, shame and community', *American Psychologist*, 55(11): 1332-43.
4. Lees, S (ed) (1997) *Ruling Passions: Sexual Violence, Reputation and the Law*. Open University Press: Buckingham.
5. Martin, P and Powell R (1995) 'Accounting for the second assault: Legal organizations' framing of rape victims', *Law and Social Inquiry*, 19: 853-890.
6. Orth, U (2002) 'Secondary victimization of crime victims by criminal proceedings'. *Social Justice Research*, 15(4): 313-325.
7. Scutt, J (1997) *The Incredible Woman: Power and Sexual Politics,* Vol 1. Artemis: Melbourne.
8. Taslitz, AE (1999) *Rape and the Culture of the Courtroom*. New York University Press: New York.
9. van de Zandt, P (1998) 'Heroines of fortitude', in P Easteal (ed) *Balancing the Scales: Rape, Law Reform and Australian Culture*, The Federation Press: Sydney.
10. Jordan, J (1998) *Reporting Rape: Women's Experiences with the Police, Doctors and Support Agencies*. Institute of Criminology: Wellington.
11. Gregory, J and Lees, S (1999) *Policing Sexual Assault*. London: Routledge.
12. Orth, U and Maercker, A (2004) 'Do trials of perpetrators retraumatize crime victims?' *Journal of Interpersonal Violence*, 19(2): 212-227.
13. Scutt, J (1998) 'Character, credit, context: Women's lives and judicial "reality"', in P Easteal (ed) *Balancing the Scales: Rape, Law Reform and Australian Culture*. The Federation Press: Sydney.
14. Jordan, J (2004) *The Word of a Woman? Police, Rape and Belief*. Palgrave Macmillan: Houndmills, Basingstoke.
15. Easteal, P (1998) 'The cultural context of rape and reform', in P Easteal (ed) *Balancing the Scales: Rape, Law Reform and Australian Culture*. The Federation Press: Sydney.
16. Mack, K. (1998) '"You should scrutinise her evidence with great care": Corroboration of women's testimony about sexual assault', in P Easteal (ed) *Balancing the Scales: Rape, Law Reform and Australian Culture*. The Federation Press: Sydney.

17. Madigan, L and Gamble, NC (1991) *The Second Rape: Society's Continued Betrayal of the Victim*. New York: Lexington Books.
18. Winkel, FW and Koppelaar, L (1991) 'Rape victims' style of self-presentation and secondary victimization by the environment: An experiment', *Journal of Interpersonal Violence*, 6(1): 29-40.
19. Adler, Z (1987) *Rape on Trial*. Routledge and Kegan Paul: London.
20. Kennedy, H (1992) *Eve Was Framed: Women and British Justice*. Vintage: London.
21. Hopkins, CQ, Bachar, K and Koss, M (2004) 'Expanding a community's justice response to sex crimes through advocacy, prosecutorial, and public health collaboration: Introducing the RESTORE program', *Journal of Interpersonal Violence*, 19(12): 1435-1463.
22. Anderson, Justice NC (1998) Sentencing Notes of Anderson J: *R v Rewa (aka Michael Lewis)*. T322/96 High Court: Auckland
23. Daly, K (2006) 'Restorative justice and sexual assault: An archival study of court and conference cases', *British Journal of Criminology*, 46: 334-356.
24. Hopkins, CQ and Koss, MP (2005) 'Incorporating feminist theory and insights into a restorative justice response to sex offenses', *Violence Against Women*, 11(5): 693-723.

Chapter 5

1. Ahrens, CE and Campbell, R (2000) 'Assisting rape victims as they recover from rape: The impact on friends', *Journal of Interpersonal Violence*, 15: 959-986.
2. Riggs, D, Kilpatrick, D and Resnick, H (1992) 'Long-term psychological distress associated with marital rape and aggravated assault: A comparison to other crimes', *Journal of Family Violence*, 7(4): 283-296.
3. Morrison, Z, Quadra, A and Boyd, C (2007) *'Ripple effects' of sexual assault*. ACSSA Issues No 7. Australian Centre for the Study of Sexual Assault: Melbourne.
4. Ullman, S (1996) 'Social reactions, coping strategies, and self-blame attributions in adjustment to sexual assault', *Psychology of Women Quarterly*, 20: 502-526.
5. Astbury, J (2006) *Services for Victim/Survivors of Sexual Assault: Identifying needs, interventions and provision of services in Australia*. ACSSA Issues No 6. Australian Centre for the Study of Sexual Assault: Melbourne.
6. Campbell, R (2006) 'Rape survivors' experiences with the legal and medical systems: Do rape victim advocates make a difference?' *Violence Against Women*, 12(1): 30-45.
7. Lievore, D (2005) *No Longer Silent: A study of women's help-seeking decisions and service responses to sexual assault*. A report prepared by the Australian Institute of Criminology. Australian Government's Office for Women: Canberra.

8. Lovett, J, Regan, L and Kelly, L (2004) *Sexual Assault Referral Centres: Developing good practice and maximising potentials.* Home Office Research Study No 285. Home Office: London.
9. Campbell, R (1998) 'The community response to rape: Victims' experiences with the legal, medical, and mental health systems', *American Journal of Community Psychology*, 26: 355-379.
10. Madigan, L and Gamble, NC (1991) *The Second Rape: Society's Continued Betrayal of the Victim.* Lexington Books: New York
11. Wasco, SM Campbell, R, Howard, A, Mason, GE, Staggs, SL, Schewe, PA and Riger, S (2004) 'A statewide evaluation of services provided to rape survivors'. *Journal of Interpersonal Violence*, 19(2): 252-263.
12. Stenius, VM and Veysey, BM (2005) '"It's the Little Things": Women, trauma and strategies for healing', *Journal of Interpersonal Violence*, 20(10): 1155-1174.
13. Martin, P and Powell, R (1995) 'Accounting for the second assault: Legal organizations' framing of rape victims', *Law and Social Inquiry*, 19: 853-890.
14. Campbell, R and Raja, S (1999) 'Secondary victimization of rape victims: Insights from mental health professionals who treat survivors of violence', *Violence and Victims*, 14(3): 261-275.
15. The Dominion (1998) 'Graphic documentary "too early"', *The Dominion*, 7 October, p 15.
16. Remer, R and Ferguson, RA (1995) 'Becoming a secondary survivor of sexual assault', *Journal of Counselling and Development*, 73(4): 407-413.
17. Burgess, AW and Hazelwood, RR (1999) 'The victim's perspective', in AW Burgess and RR Hazelwood (eds) *Practical Aspects of Rape Investigation: A Multidisciplinary Approach.* CRC Press: Boca Raton.
18. Brownmiller, S (1975) *Against Our Will: Men, Women, and Rape.* Penguin: Harmondsworth.
19. Easteal, P (ed) (1998) *Balancing the Scales: Rape, Law Reform and Australian Culture.* The Federation Press: Sydney.
20. Jordan, J (2004) 'Beyond belief? Police, rape and women's credibility', *Criminal Justice*, 4(1): 29-59.

Chapter 6

1. Koss, MP (1990) 'The women's mental health research agenda: Violence against women', *American Psychologist*, 45(3): 374-380.
2. Ahrens, CE and Campbell, R (2000) 'Assisting rape victims as they recover from rape: The impact on friends', *Journal of Interpersonal Violence*, 15: 959-986.
3. Goodman, LA, Koss, MP and Russo, NF (1993) 'Violence against women: Physical and mental health effects. Part 1: Research findings', *Applied and Preventive Psychology*, 2: 79-89.

4. Gore-Felton, C, Gill, M, Koopman, C and Spiegel, D (1999) 'A review of acute stress reactions among victims of violence: Implications for early interventions', *Aggression and Violent Behavior*, 4(3): 292-306.

5. Gutner, CA, Rizvi, SL, Monson, CM and Resick, PA (2006) 'Changes in coping strategies, relationship to the perpetrator, and posttraumatic distress in female crime victims', *Journal of Traumatic Stress*, 19(6): 813-823.

6. Kilpatrick, DG, Saunders, BE, Veronen, LJ, Best, CL and Von, JM (1987) 'Criminal victimization: Lifetime prevalence, reporting to police, and psychological impact', *Crime and Delinquency*, 33: 479-489.

7. Littleton, HL, Axsom, D, Breitkopf, CR and Berenson, A(2006) 'Rape acknowledgment and postassault experiences: How acknowledgment status relates to disclosure, coping, worldview and reactions received from others', *Violence and Victims*, 21(6): 761-778.

8. Olle, L (2005) *Mapping Health Sector and Inter-Agency Protocols on Sexual Assault*. ACSSA Issues No 2. Australian Centre for the Study of Sexual Assault: Melbourne.

9. Resick, P (1993) 'The psychological impact of rape', *Journal of Interpersonal Violence*, 8(2): 223-255.

10. DeMaris, A and Kaukinen, C (2005) 'Violent victimization and women's mental and physical health: Evidence from a national sample', *Journal of Research in Crime and Delinquency*, 42(4): 384-411.

11. Foa, EB, Riggs, DS, Dancu, CV and Rothbaum, BO (1993) 'Reliability and validity of a brief instrument for assessing post-traumatic stress disorder', *Journal of Traumatic Stress*, 6: 459-473.

12. Frazier, P and Borgida, E (1999) 'Rape trauma syndrome: A review of case law and psychological research', in RR Hazelwood and AW Burgess (eds) *Practical Aspects of Rape Investigation: A Multidisciplinary Approach*. 1999, CRC Press: Boca Raton.

13. Ullman, SE, Filipas, HH, Townsend, SM and Starzynski, LL (2006) 'The role of victim-offender relationship in women's sexual assault experiences', *Journal of Interpersonal Violence*, 21(6): 798-819.

14. Sheffield, CJ (1995) 'Sexual Terrorism', in J Freeman (ed) *Women: A Feminist Perspective*, Mayfield: Mountain View, CA.

15. Ahrens, C, Campbell, R, Ternier-Thames, NK, Wasco, S and Sefl, T (2007) 'Deciding whom to tell: Expectations and outcomes of rape-survivors' first disclosures', *Psychology of Women Quarterly*, 31: 38-49.

16. Astbury, J (2006) *Services for Victim/Survivors of Sexual Assault: Identifying needs, interventions and provision of services in Australia*. ACSSA Issues No 6. Australian Centre for the Study of Sexual Assault: Melbourne.

17. Lievore, D (2005) *No Longer Silent: A study of women's help-seeking decisions and service responses to sexual assault*. A report prepared by the Australian Institute of Criminology. Australian Government's Office for Women: Canberra.

18. Brownmiller, S (1975) *Against Our Will: Men, Women, and Rape*. Penguin: Harmondsworth.

19. Kelly, L (1988) *Surviving Sexual Violence*. Polity Press: Cambridge.
20. Gavey, N (2005) *Just Sex? The Cultural Scaffolding of Rape*. Routledge: Hove.
21. Scully, D (1990) *Understanding Sexual Violence: A Study of Convicted Rapists*. Unwin Hyman: Boston.
22. Jordan, J (2004) *The Word of a Woman? Police, Rape and Belief*. Palgrave Macmillan: Houndmills, Basingstoke.
23. Williams, L (1984) 'The classic rape: When do victims report?' *Social Problems*, 31: 459-467.
24. Winkel, FW and Koppelaar, L (1991) 'Rape victims' style of self-presentation and secondary victimization by the environment: An experiment', *Journal of Interpersonal Violence*, 6(1): 29-40.
25. Brison, S (1998) 'Brison, S (2002) *Aftermath: Violence and the Remaking of a Self*. Princeton, New Jersey: Princeton University Press.
26. Easteal, P (1994) *Voices of the Survivors*. Spinifex Press: Melbourne.
27. Raine, NV (1998) *After Silence: Rape and My Journey Back*. Three Rivers Press: New York.
28. Sebold, A (2002) *Lucky. A Memoir*. Back Bay Books: New York.
29. Fitzgerald J (2006) 'The attrition of sexual offences from the New South Wales criminal justice system', *Contemporary Issues in Justice and Crime* No 92, Crime and Justice Bulletin: NSW Bureau of Crime Statistics and Research.
30. Kelly, L, Lovett, J and Regan, L (2005) *A Gap or a Chasm? Attrition in Reported Rape Cases*. Home Office Research Study No 293, Home Office: London.
31. Lea, S, Lanvers, U and Shaw, S (2003) 'Attrition in rape cases: Developing a profile and identifying relevant factors', *British Journal of Criminology*, 43(3): 583-599.

Appendix 1

1. Blakely, K (2007) 'Reflections on the role of emotion in feminist research'. *International Journal of Qualitative Methods*, 6(2): Article 4. <www.ualberta. ca/~iiqm/backissues/6_2/blakely.htm> accessed 6 December 2007.
2. Campbell, R (2002) *Emotionally Involved: The Impact of Researching Rape*. Routledge: New York.
3. Kelly, L (1988) *Surviving Sexual Violence*. Polity Press: Cambridge.
4. Liebling, A and Stanko, B (2001) 'Allegiance and ambivalence: Some dilemmas in researching disorder and violence', *British Journal of Criminology*, 41: 421-430.
5. van de Zandt, P (1998) 'Heroines of fortitude', in P Easteal (ed) *Balancing the Scales: Rape, Law Reform and Australian Culture*. The Federation Press: Sydney.
6. Campbell, R and Wasco, S (2000) 'Feminist approaches to social science: Epistemological and methodological tenets', *American Journal of Community Psychology*, 28(6): 773-791.

7. Jordan, J (1998) *Reporting Rape: Women's Experiences with the Police, Doctors and Support Agencies.* Institute of Criminology: Wellington.
8. Jordan, J (2001) 'Worlds Apart? Women, rape and the police reporting process', *British Journal of Criminology*, 41(4): 679-706.
9. Jordan, J (2004) *The Word of a Woman? Police, Rape and Belief.* Palgrave Macmillan: Houndmills, Basingstoke.
10. Hengehold, M (1994) 'An immodest proposal: Foucault, hysterisation and the "second rape"', *Hypatia*, 9(3): 88-108.
11. Madigan, L and Gamble, NC (1991) *The Second Rape: Society's Continued Betrayal of the Victim.* Lexington Books: New York.
12. Taslitz, AE (1999) *Rape and the Culture of the Courtroom.* New York University Press: New York.
13. Culbertson, R (1995) 'Embodied memory, transcendence, and telling: Recounting trauma, re-establishing the self', *New Literary History*, 26(1): 169-196.
14. Ford, L and Crabtree, R (2002) 'Telling, re-telling and talking about telling: Discourse and/as surviving incest', *Women's Studies in Communication*, 25(1): 53-87.

Appendix 2

1. Williams, T (1998) *The Bad, the Very Bad and the Ugly: Who's Who of New Zealand Crime.* Hodder Moa Beckett: Auckland.
2. Taylor, P (1998) '"Lone Wolf": The Malcolm Rewa Story', *Sunday Star Times*, 31 May, p A5.
3. Corbett, J (1998) 'Lone Wolf: Career of a Rapist', *New Zealand Herald*, 1 June, p A11.
4. Taylor P (1998) 'Rapist weds in jail', *Sunday Star Times*, 31 May, p 1.
5. Corbett, J and Larkin, N (1998) 'Rewa's gripe gave vital leads', *New Zealand Herald*, 1 June, p A1.
6. Belgrave, K (1998) 'For better, for worse ...' *Weekend Herald*, 13-14 June, p H3.
7. *New Zealand Herald* (1998) 'Rewa plans to write memoir: Daughter', *New Zealand Herald*, 1 June, p A3.
8. Taylor, P (1998) 'Angel dust helped victim through Court ordeal', *Sunday Star Times*, 31 May, p 1.
9. Henger, K (1998) 'Rewa was no stranger to early victim', *The Dominion*, 3 June, p 9.
10. *The Press* (1998) 'Horror at rapist's TV statement', *The Press*, 2 June, p 3.
11. *The Dominion* (1998) 'Rewa's false apology', *The Dominion*, 3 June, p 10.
12. *The Dominion* (1998) 'Rewa jailed for minimum 22 years', *The Dominion*, 4 July, pp 1, 3.
13. *The Evening Post* (1998) 'Victims celebrate as Rewa jailed', *The Evening Post*, 4 July, p 3.

Index